"Rich, riveting, and right on target for today's cultural conversation. Fregia's vivid storytelling pours our feet into the pieced-together shoes of Johnnie Roy Houston, to walk with him the streets of poverty, prejudice, and unjust imprisonment. I couldn't put it down."

– Kelli Sallman,
Lead Editor and Writing Mentor,
Kelli Sallman—Writing & Editing

"Olin Fregia uncorks the life and times of Mr. Johnnie Roy Houston and invites us to imbibe, slowly. This isn't a book to guzzle. This book is a Cabernet. I read A Forgiving Fire *at a leisurely pace, flipping back a page or two along the way to sip the words, those passages that satisfy the thirst for goodness and beauty and truth born of suffering and celebration.* A Forgiving Fire *is a book to savor."*

– Dr. Reg Grant,
Department Chair and Senior
Professor of Media Arts and
Worship, Dallas Theological Seminary

I0809517

A FORGIVING FIRE

An essential story for anyone who has faced injustice.

A memoir of Johnnie Roy Houston
as told to Olin Fregia

STONE TOWER PRESS

A Forgiving Fire:
An essential story for anyone who has faced injustice.

Stone Tower Press
7 Ellen Rd.
Middletown, RI 02842
stonetowerpress.com

Paperback ISBN: 979-8-9919831-3-6

Cover: Created with the assistance of Adobe Firefly
Text: Designed and formatted by Amy Cole, JPL Design Solutions

Printed in the United States of America

In loving memory,
to Johnnie Roy Houston—my friend and cowriter.
I miss our long sessions and Juneteenth front-yard pit barbecues.

♦ ♦ ♦

And to family and friends—
thank you for your inspiration.

♦ ♦ ♦

A portion of the sales of *A Forgiving Fire* will go to groups supporting criminal justice reform.

CONTENTS

PREFACE

A *Forgiving Fire* is an as-told-to memoir—a commissioned work. I recall the commissioning this way: I witnessed a contrite Johnnie Roy Houston share his testimony before one of the oldest African American churches in Dallas, Texas. Inspired by the preached message that day, "God has Got a Blessing for You," a down-on-his luck Houston rose with his family and made his way to the front to recommit his life to God, a promise he made many years before because of all God had done for him.

"I spent twenty-six years in prison for a crime my twin brother committed, but God never failed me." With pricked ears, the collective church body leaned forward in a moment of silence, drawn in for more story, more explanation. But Houston, too full to go on, broke through a lingering pause with an explosive, "Thank you! Thank you! Thank you, Lord!" The stained-glass windows shook with every shout.

After the service, I made my way to him and extended my hand. "I would like to interview you for the church newsletter." Five minutes into that first interview, I realized his story of fate, faith, and forgiveness belonged to the world.

As I thanked him at the end of the session, he grabbed my hand and drew me close and said, "No, thank you, son. God told me you gonna write me my book."

I said yes because who am I to argue against God? From that day, we had an enriching, enduring friendship forged from hours of interviews, Sunday suppers, weddings, funerals, hurts revisited, and prayers.

Johnnie painted his story with colorful strokes, but having only finished the tenth grade, he would sometimes struggle to describe what he was seeing with his mind's eye. He entrusted my ears to translate onto paper what he was reliving and feeling. Our exchanges often morphed into its own "call and response," a collaboration some might call an "as-told-to commissioned work." I call it "his story, *our* words."

The Houston twins—(L-R) Johnnie Ray and Johnnie Roy, age 11—take a break from the Bastrop summer heat, 1939.

one

TWIN DON'T MEAN SAME

HAVE YOU EVER HELD FIRE IN YOUR HANDS—fire that didn't burn you? Deep in the heart of the heart of Texas—Bastrop, Texas—on the backside of the bottoms, that low land of the Colorado River's bend southeast, a land no sensible man would claim as good, a strange fire, June fire, burned. Once a year, I came to this place and held this fire in my dirt-brown hands and flung it as high as I could and watched it twirl back to the ground like falling stars, leaving a trail of orange-red flames against night-blue sky. If the fire was still burning when it hit the ground, I cupped it in my hands again, churned my legs as fast as I could, straightened my arms, then planted my feet, and launched it one more time.

Every Juneteenth Eve, the Negro people of Bastrop made the stuff of strange fire out of old cloth that was cut into rags, wound into balls the size of baseballs, then soaked in coal oil all day so they'd be ready for the next night. They filled ten-gallon wash-tubs full of those cloth balls and hid them from us kids until it was time—when the pink evening sky faded into night blue, when only the moon and car headlights lit a patch of the bottoms. Then all the children old enough scrambled to those tubs full of coal-oil balls, grabbed as many they could carry, and hunkered down at their favorite spot, ready to throw fire. At the signal, they'd light and toss those flaming rag balls as high as they could, lighting up the June night sky with fire that didn't burn.

Once a year, colored people came to the bottoms, where no good thing happened, and they made for themselves a good time. Juneteenth had no script except where the spirits led. And on this night, there was all kinds of spirits hovering over the bottoms: Lone Star and Pearl beer spirits, Jack Daniels, and home-brewed chock—a strange concoction men made out of fruit peelings and time. And the people said, "It was good." We danced to whatever played on the Victrola my Uncle John Washington rigged up on the back of his truck: "Every Day I Have the Blues" and "See, See Rider (See What You Done)." Spirits moved the people. Some of the old folks would say, "It's too good to be good."

Juneteenth was more than a holiday. It was like a family reunion for the people who lived around there. We may have gotten the news of the Emancipation Proclamation late, but we was making up for lost time.

When I was a boy, the bottomland was my special place. That fire was my fireworks one special night a year, June nineteenth—Juneteenth. But the summer of 1944, when I was sixteen, my Juneteenth changed. A different kind of fire began slowly eating at me from the inside out.

On this Juneteenth night, my momma Ella Houston, my sister Mozell, me and my twin brother Ray, and every other browned face near Bastrop congregated at this turn of the Colorado River where wicked currents and March to April floods had long since carried off the good topsoil, leaving sand and clay that grew little more than green chinaberry trees, tall pines, and polk salad weeds. Juneteenth was my Christmas and Fourth of July all rolled into one, so I ate like there was no tomorrow: turkey drumsticks and fried chicken, slow-smoked barbecue, big wooden barrels of lemonade and red Kool-Aid, and desserts of every kind—apple pies, strawberry cakes, lemon cookies, and peach cobblers. If heaven had a dessert table, this was it.

Somewhere between the eating, drinking, and dancing, somebody hollered, "Get the fire!" I raced to a number ten tub to get the biggest fireballs, but here came my twin brother Ray with his buddies Red Winston, C. P. Johnson, and Raymond Riles. People called me and Ray identical, but my momma could tell the difference. Ray was shorter and stockier, and had these hard-to-describe eyes. My momma called them "trouble eyes." At certain times, he'd get that look. It meant trouble wasn't too far off—mostly for me.

Ray grabbed my tub with that look in his eyes and said, "Roy, let me give you a hand."

"Y'all can't take the whole tub, now, Ray. Gimme some," I begged. But he didn't say a word. He laughed along with his buddies, yapping like angry hounds. When I reached for the tub, he gave me the eye, dumped the whole load in a mud puddle, then ran off with his pack into the night. I knew where they was headed—they was headed to Rufus Jackson's place where all the action was. It was really called The Yellowstone Grill, but I called it "Rufus Jackson's" because he owned and ran the juke joint. He was a good man—a good *business* man—who didn't mind catering to whatever your heart desired. For Ray and his gang, their heart was always set on three things: gambling, drinking, and girls.

"Goddamn it, Ray," I mumbled, not wanting my momma and them to hear me. I was hot enough to set off one of those coal-oil balls. He had done it to me again. Ray loved to agitate me, especially when he was with his posse. I couldn't understand how we could be twins but be so different. My momma would say, "Roy, baby, twin don't mean same."

With bucket in hand, I managed to rescue a few of the fireballs before they got wet. At the signal, I lit one and threw it as high as I could. Whatever anger I felt left me for a moment as that fireball and then another and another left my hands. It was a strange fire that did not burn you. I couldn't explain it. No one could. All I knew was you had time to grab one in your hands and chuck it. Their orange tails twisted and twirled like they was writing cursive on a blackboard. They was my fireworks—my rockets' red glare. We couldn't afford what other folks bought on the side of the highway outside of town, but to me, the fireworks we had was better than those store-bought bottle rockets. They was my own private shooting stars.

Sometimes my star collided with somebody else's, spraying cinders everywhere like Roman candle sparklers. And when those flaming rags hit the ground, sometimes they exploded then burned out. If you got to them before they faded out, you could give them one more glory ride. It was enough to make me almost forget about Bastrop and Ray—almost.

My momma yelled at me, "Where is your brother? It's getting late."

I shrugged my shoulders so as not to tell her an outright lie. If I told her the truth, she'd send me after him right then and there. I was forever going after him, trying to get him before he got into trouble with the law. Ray was the oldest by twenty minutes, and it felt like I had been serving him from our first breaths.

"Johnnie Roy, I said where is your brother?" When Ella Houston spoke, it was louder than a whisper, but not much more. Her voice had thinned like her cotton-colored hair. She was a large woman with hands like hollowed-out valleys, worn down by six children, one husband gone bad, and twenty loads of wash a day for as far back as I could remember. I loved to hear her call my name, even if it meant trouble.

"I think him and Red Winston hitched a ride home with Uncle John and them," I said with my head down, focused on the bucket of balls, not wanting her to see my eyes. She could always tell if I was lying by my eyes.

"He'd better be there when we get home or you're gonna go find him," Momma said.

"Yes, ma'am," I said back. Well, I knew what that meant. My favorite night of the year was over. I was gonna have to go find Ray.

I loaded up our stuff: two folding chairs, Momma's frying skillets, some leftover pit meat my uncle called "good eating pork" (but I knew it was some possum he had killed in the woods behind the house), blankets, and one fireball I stashed in an empty gallon syrup tin that I used for a lunch bucket. I hopped in the back of Clarence McIntosh's daddy's wagon. Momma and my sister Mozell rode up front. It took about an hour for that old mule team to wind up the wagon path and then down the east side of the levee that ran along the backside of the bottoms. Lying on my back, I had time to count the stars. The air was thick with the sweet smell of coal oil and the sound of my mother's honey voice humming away. I had an hour before I had to go and get Ray.

When we got home, Momma gently grabbed me by the collar. She could tell I was none too happy about going to fetch Ray. She said, "Look here, baby"—that's what she called me most times when Ray wasn't around—"Ray ain't gonna do right, right now, so you gonna have to keep him. He is your blood, no matter what he does." Momma rubbed my nappy head, hugged me and whispered my name, then said, "Go get your brother."

I had before me a mile-and-a-half walk to Rufus Jackson's place way down the east end of Pine Street. With every step, I thought about how I could already be cleaned up and in bed. But no, here I was again, going to get Ray before Deputy Norman Owens and some of those other deputies got ahold of him. Owens had warned my mother that he was gonna get tough on Ray if he kept breaking the law.

Whenever I had to fetch Ray, I always started out down that street simmering mad and ended up boiling hot because my mind would dig up all the times Ray got me in trouble. Tonight was no different. As my feet were churning, my mind was too. I got to thinking about the time he stole meat off my plate. We didn't have meat in the house a lot—I mean real meat, not something wild and strange that Uncle John or me and Ray killed in the woods and brought home for Momma to cook. But that week, we ate high on the hog because one of the families she did clothes for gave us part of a slaughter they didn't want. It was feet, brains, tail, and jowls, but we thought it was something special, something you could put in navy beans to give them flavor.

Momma was at work that day, so Mozell, who was four years older, fixed our plate for lunch. "And don't forget to say your blessing, and Momma wants y'all go and get a twenty-five-pound block of ice when y'all get through eating," she ordered. Mozell loved to act like she was our momma when Momma wasn't around.

No sooner had she turned her back and I closed my eyes to pray than Ray snatched the meat off my plate. I guess he thought my piece was bigger. So I hauled off and hit him with my plate and wailed on him hard.

Mozell hollered, "Get off your brother. Wait till I get me a switch." She strutted toward the door to get a switch—a holly berry tree limb—to whip me, but that day, I wasn't studden no whipping.

I screamed back at her—"Y'all need to leave me alone. It wasn't none of me. It was Ray who started it. He took my meat"—but she didn't break stride. I told her, "You ain't whipping me today." Before she got to the door, I grabbed the big old jar of Vaseline that sits on the dresser and hauled off and hit her right in her ribs.

You'd have thought I broke one of her ribs, the way she hollered. "You wait till Momma gets home. You gonna get it then," she screamed, grabbing her side.

"Oooh, you gonna get it now, Roy," Ray said. He was right. Momma didn't stand for us to fight each other—ever—no matter the reason. I was in for it. So I left the house and stayed out all day sitting under the big old oak tree that was my thinking place.

I waited under that oak tree all day till I finally got the courage to go home and get it over with because I knew, by then, Mozell had told Momma what had happened and Momma had picked out the tree limb she was going to use. But when I walked inside, she didn't say a word. Neither did Mozell. Ray sat there grinning, as usual. We ate dinner, same meat as lunch—not a word. We washed the dishes—not a word. Then me and Ray went to bed—still nothing. I thought maybe they didn't tell Momma. Maybe I was home free. That's when the bedroom door swung open. Mozell hit the lights, Momma hit the bed covers, and I hit floor, trying to crawl under the bed. So did Ray.

"I told you boys there ain't gonna be no fighting each other," Momma yelled at me. Mozell grabbed my foot, pulling me from under the bed.

"Momma, it wasn't none of me. Ray started it, taking my meat," I said.

"And I'm gonna finish it," Momma said, out of breath, swinging and missing me. By that time, Mozell had cornered Ray.

He hollered as he tried to wiggle free, "Momma, it wasn't none of me. Roy hauled off and hit me. Then he threw that jar at Mozell."

Momma popped Ray a good one. Then she stopped before she could tag me one more time. She sat on the bed crying, her head in her hands. "Y'all stop it." Deep sobbing breaths chopped up every word, "Y'all … is … blood. Don't … you … ever … raise … a hand … at … each … other … for nothing ever. Y'all got enough against you to have y'all against each other."

It was over as quick as it started. Momma and Mozell walked out without saying another word. I lay in bed sorry I had made my momma cry. Ray lay there laughing.

I will never forget the night Ray made me make Momma cry.

By the time I had rehashed them memories of Ray's ways, anger had gotten me to running—more like a stomp—and I covered those last few blocks to Rufus Jackson's in no time. Bent over, hands on knees, heart trying to jump out of my chest, I looked up at the neon sign: The Yellowstone Grill. Mr. Jackson was what they called that fancy word for a businessman—an *entrepreneur*. Not all the carry-ons at his place was good, but most Bastrop coloreds looked up to him because he owned something while most brown people barely owned the shoes they wore. He had a restaurant and pool hall up front, a barbershop next door, and an unofficial gambling shack in back. It was the only place where a colored man could go and turn a hard day's dollar into some fun. Money changed hands brown hand to brown hand. It didn't involve bowing and scraping. You could have a decent time, trouble free. You could get Elgin red-hot link sausages and a beer and listen to some blues. Even the Chitlin' Circuit—Peg Leg Bates, Muddy Waters, and them—came through every now and then. If you was looking for some *trouble*-fun—like gambling—Mr. Rufus could serve that, too, but you had to go out back.

I knew where Ray was.

I ran through the spring-loaded screen door that led out back, and there was Ray with Red Winston, C. P. Johnson, and Raymond Riles—the Get Over Gang. I used to call them that because they was always trying to get over on somebody. Ray was always the center of the action. Surrounded by his posse, he knelt on the ground, a longneck beer in his left hand, a pair of dice in his right hand held high, ready to throw down.

"Ray," I called out, but he didn't pay me no mind. Red Winston did. Red always had something to say first when I ran up on Ray to bring him home.

Red said, "Well, there he is, Ray, your baby brother—no, your babysitter. What do you say, Roy? Want to get in the game? Oh, I forgot. Your game is playing with coal-oil balls." With a gold front tooth that he was proud to show off every chance he got, Red was all mouth and no fight. I was in no mood for his lip. One more word from him, and he was liable to get a *fat* lip. But I wasn't studden Red. I came for my brother.

I hollered again, "Ray, Momma say come home."

Ray shouted back, never looking up, "Now, you might as well go on home, Roy, 'cause I ain't going, not till I get my money back from Red and then some. With his dice hand raised and ready, he turned toward Red and said, "Those shoes is mine."

I came right back at him. "Ray, now, I ain't got time for none of your stuff tonight. Come on, now." I knew I was wasting my breath because he wasn't coming without a fight. I could hear it in his laugh. Some nights he'd come home without a fuss, and we'd walk home clowning around, talking about what we was going to do when we left Bastrop, what we'd do with a million dollars, what we'd do if we had fifty cents, who was better, Patterson or Liston—we carried on like brothers. But tonight, he was in one of those moods. You could tell by his trouble eyes. There was going to be a fight. I grabbed his dice hand. "Ray, I said—"

Before I could finish, Ray swung around with his left hand and smashed that beer bottle upside my head. I held onto his arm and swung him off his feet and rolled on top of him till we was face-to-face. Blood ran down my forehead. Quick as a cat, he grabbed my right arm, turned his hips, and before I knew it, he was on top of me. I managed to get to my feet with him on my back, fight his arms till we was face-to-face again, only to have him lower his head into my chest and bulldoze the both of us into a bunch of rusty trash cans.

"Come on, now. Get him, Ray," the Get Over Gang shouted as he rolled on top of me with his free hand cocked, ready to throw a punch.

Red Winston called in the bets. "I got a quarter say Roy going down for the count." The onlookers had circled around us like we was a pair of dice in the last game of the night with a week's pay riding on every throw. Red egged us on. "Kick his ass. Seven come eleven!" Ray's fist landed flush on my mouth. "Oh, that's a good one! Baby need a new pair of shoes. Roll them babies again, Ray!" The Get Over Gang hollered and whooped. *Bam!* They roared as Ray backhanded me, cutting me over my left eye.

It was his last lick. I grabbed his neck with my free hand, nearly crushing his Adam's apple with my thumb. The force sent him falling back. I pounced on him—my eyes partly blinded by the blood pouring out of the cut on my forehead. Letting go of his dice hand, I grabbed a rusted garbage can top that was inches away and raised it over my twin brother's head. At that moment, it seemed like all the sound in the air was sucked out of the night. Red Winton and time stood still and watched. In my mind, I could see my mother standing on the porch watching, waiting for us to round the corner, but I couldn't hear her. I couldn't hear nothing. I held a rusted, jagged, garbage can top over my twin.

All of a sudden, a size twelve cowboy boot broke a hole in the air, and the sound rushed back in. "Y'all niggers stop right here, now," barked Deputy Owens as he kicked that rusted, jagged trash can lid right out of my hand. The place was surrounded by his other deputies, all two of them—Dave Eskew and Joe "Dude" Milton. Someone had called in that there was trouble at Rufus Jackson's. "Looks like you boys can finish off y'all's Juneteenth at my place," Owens said. He turned to Eskew, the one we called "Wyatt Earp" because he always walked with a flicked hand to his side like he was ready to draw and shoot somebody. He ordered Eskew and Milton, "Load them up, all of them, but keep these two separated, pointing to me and Ray. They're liable to kill each other before we get to the jailhouse."

Owens had recognized my brother Ray, but it took him a moment to figure out it was me underneath the towel someone had handed me to stop the blood from my busted forehead. "Roy, that ain't you," he said. "Well, Miss Ella is gonna have to come on down in the morning and get y'all."

As it turned out, they loaded me and Ray in the back of the same deputy's personal car. The county couldn't afford to have but one real police car. I was off to jail. I had never been to jail except to get my brother out. Owens had warned my mother that if he had to lock Ray up many more times, he wouldn't be responsible for Bastrop doing what Bastrop do to get rid of troublemakers. My mother knew what that meant. That's why she was always after me to bring Ray home before the law got ahold of him and did something bad.

The whole trip downtown, I never took my eyes off Ray, who sat next to me, grinning with his buddies. Red Winston was leading the bunch. "Say, Ray, you think your brother gonna like the accommodations? At least there, y'all won't have to sleep in the same bed."

When we got to the county jail that sat right next to the courthouse, they lined us up and led us up the back stairs. I was scared. People have been known to go up those stairs and never come out. But I knew nothing like that would happen, seeing there was so many of us there. And the place was full of "us." It was a busy night for the sheriff with the overflow of Juneteenth good-timers who had spilled out from the bottoms into the streets.

We all was put in the same cellblock. I went to a corner as far as I could from my brother and his posse. I found a spot that had a view of a piece of the night sky through a high window that let in a slit of moonlight between the two-inch bars. I stood looking up to the light, trying to close down my mind, but I couldn't.

The smell of the cell was in my head and wouldn't let go. The open commode was full and couldn't be flushed. Soured barbecue and bourbon vomit soaked the mattress next to me. Urine had stained the concrete floor yellow.

I couldn't shake the sounds either: steel doors slamming, keys jingling against leather belts, leather boot heels clopping down against concrete floor. Sitting in a jail full of brown faces was not how I figured to spend my Juneteenth. I stared out that tiny window at the moonlit sky—all that was left of my favorite day of the year. In my mind, I could see my mother standing on the porch looking for her boys, but I couldn't hear her. I could see the orange trails of those burning coal-oil balls twirling across the sky. I closed my eyes, and I made a promise to this strange fire, falling star: "I ain't never going to jail again."

two

THE TRACKS

IT FELT LIKE I HADN'T CLOSED MY EYES at all when I heard the rattling of keys and the voice of Deputy Milton. "You Houston boys, get up on out of here. I didn't call your Momma this time. But you tell her that the next time I catch y'all gambling, y'all will wind up here for longer than a night. Now get on home."

We was the last ones let go. I didn't say one word to Ray as we walked home. He had that shit-eating grin on his face I had seen a hundred times—that look that said, "It ain't no trouble as long it got *you* in trouble."

I didn't pay him no mind. All that was on my mind was what Momma must be thinking: her boys—both boys—didn't come home. I could see her standing on the porch with her large, lye-bleached hands tucked under her arms, hands worn down like teeth on a cotton gin, worn down from separating the little good in her life from all the sticks, stones, and trouble Ray and me brought on her, the load of trying to keep a roof over our heads and food on the table and our tails out of jail. I have seen her before, standing on the porch she called her prayer closet, arms folded, gently rocking from side to side, so much so that the boards under her feet creaked with every rock as small prayers seeped past her barely opened lips: "Lord help. Lord help. Lord help." Her sad eyes would be closed, but her head would be tilted toward the wind as if she was looking with her ears for something. I asked her once what she was listening for. She told me, "I be listening for voices I know because I never know what's coming down the road—good news or bad—whether you or Ray or your daddy is coming home, or somebody coming to tell me the worst." She always worried whether we'd make it across those tracks.

You see, Bastrop was two worlds—twin worlds, the "haves" and the "have-nots"—divided by the M-K-T (Missouri, Kansas, Texas) tracks, sometimes called the Katy Line. It was later named the Union Pacific track, but we just called it "the tracks." It was the blast of that train horn that always let me know where I was and what time it was. On the northwest side of town, north of Chestnut and west of the tracks, there was roast beef on Sundays and people who walked upright and head high. On the southeast of town, there was possum for Sunday dinner, and browned people bent over from the weight of sacks loaded with pounds of wet cotton, and tons of *Yes sirs* and *No ma'ams*. If you was a Negro and was caught on the northwest side on the wrong day, you was asking for trouble. Bastrop was twins, and like my momma would say, "Twin don't mean same."

So my momma would stand on the porch that was her prayer closet listening for voices she knew because there was no guarantee we'd come home. She'd be listening and praying, "Lord help. Lord help. Lord help."

I didn't much believe in the Lord's help. Every time I had to bring Ray home from Rufus Jackson's, we had to pass through one side of town to the other and be reminded there was two Bastrops. We was born on March 1, 1928, but it might as well have been 1828. Texas got the Emancipation Proclamation news late, and sometimes it seemed like Bastrop didn't get it at all. As far as I was concerned, the Lord lived on the northwest side with the white people in big houses who had good jobs and could shop in the fancy downtown stores. God lived, I believed, with the people who got to go through the front door to do business, the people who lived in homes like mansions, like the one Dr. H. B. Combs lived in.

While Momma, Ray, Mozell, and me lived on Dr. H. B. Combs's farm by the time I was sixteen—north of downtown off Church and Wilson Street—how we lived was like our color and kin on the southeast side of the "have-nots": Negroes in sharpshooter shacks, doing bowing and scraping work, and shamed at backdoor service windows on Colored Saturday. We rented a house from Combs for next to nothing because we worked for him and other white folks there.

Combs was a doctor, banker, and co-owner of the post office. His two-story yellow house was something to behold: a balcony in front, two tall columns, even a pole like there is in a fire house to slide down and a yard full of pecan and fruit trees. And his house wasn't even the biggest on that side of town. There were streets on the northwest side lined with houses that I imagined were like the mansions God promised us when we all get to heaven. Northside folks got theirs first.

Southside folks—my color and kin—had to wait for ours. Until our homegoing, we had to make do with homes that were sharpshooter shacks where you could shoot a gun in the front door and the bullet would go out the back door without hitting a thing. When we did business on the north side, we had to go around back. If Negroes wanted to buy a hamburger on Colored Saturday, we had to go to the back window where the café had their trash cans. If we wanted to buy groceries, we had to wait in the colored's line. Northside folks could cut right ahead anytime they wanted to. They even had the right of way on the sidewalk.

Life on the south side was a hand-me-down life. Our schoolbooks at the one all-colored school—Emile High—were hand-me-down books from the Northside schools. Their students took much delight in letting us know how much they wanted us to have their books. Notes were written in the back like, "This is how you spell nigger, nigger." They colored over the people in those books, too, to make them Sambos. Coloreds' jobs were hand-me-down jobs. Whatever was beneath them "haves" to do was loaded on our backs: cleaning their toilets, washing their clothes, picking their cotton. And when we had the miracle of free time, we could go to our hand-me-down colored park—Kerr Park—and swing on rusted swings.

By the time I was sixteen, Momma, Ray, Mozell, and me lived in the shadow of Dr. Combs's big mansion in a hand-me-down house on his twenty-acre farm that ran south toward the Colorado. Before then, we lived on the south side in nothing more than a shack. And I had an older half sister, Leola, who also lived on the south side off South Main, but I seldom saw her, seeing as how she was twenty-six years older than me and Ray. She was busy with raising eleven children.

But Momma met Dr. Combs's sister, Laura, from one of the white ladies she did work for. Miss Laura Francis liked my momma and talked her brother into renting to us to get Momma to work for him. Some say we was better off living where we was, but in my mind living in the shadow of the "haves" was worse. We was reminded every time we crossed the tracks to go to school, to Mount Rose Baptist Church, or to Kerr Park—God lived northwest.

To get from the jailhouse to home that morning, we headed west on Pine Street. It was the quicker and safer way some days. You see, it was an unwritten rule that if a Negro was caught downtown any time other than Saturday, trouble—bad trouble—could find you.

There was an underside, other side to Bastrop. Some people wore cowboy hats and stiff-collared white shirts or pleated gingham dresses to town, but in their closets hung Klan robes. I know. My momma and other colored women who worked in white folks' homes would find those robes. When the time was right, the Klan would rear its head and have a parade—like the time they marched down Chestnut Street to send a message. There was this colored man who was seeing this white woman. Me and Ray watched that parade from behind a fence, wondering if some of them men under those hoods was the people our momma worked for. I heard that the colored man left town. It scared a lot of colored folks, so they behaved, especially on Saturdays—trading days—the only day it was OK to be downtown.

But not everybody was scared.

My grandma, Emma Atkins, would tell a tale of this colored man who went to town in the days when they tied mules and wagons to hitching posts on the streets. He got off his mule-drawn wagon on Main Street, his boots all shiny and black, his hat cocked to one side. These white people saw him all dressed up and got out their guns and started shooting at his feet for fun. They said, "Dance, nigger, dance." And he danced until they ran out of bullets. Then he went and got the handle of his axe. He came at them swinging it and said, "Dance, white man, dance. And after y'all through dancing, y'all can kiss my mule." Except he didn't say mule. That's the tale she told.

"Nigger Saturday" was the unofficial official name for the only day of the week that Negroes was allowed to be seen downtown. I don't like the word *nigger*, so I called it "Colored Saturday." All the rest of the week you was expected to be out working for the man—tending to his crops, cooking his meals, and cleaning his yards. But they gave you a pass on Colored Saturday to clean up, dress up, and handle whatever business you might have, giving your money right back to the white man. If they caught you downtown Monday through Friday, that would be your ass.

No way Bastrop northwest of the tracks was going to let Negroes off from work to celebrate Emancipation neither. Colored Bastrop always celebrated Juneteenth the third weekend of June. If the nineteenth fell on a workday, there would also be a special night that night starting at sundown. The morning after Juneteenth 1944 was a Tuesday—the morning when we walked that long walk home from jail—so I couldn't get back home fast enough, especially from underneath the shadow of that jailhouse. It gave me chill bumps every time I passed it by because them old folks would tell stories of the ghost of a colored man who haunted it. "C'mon, Ray, let's go!" He was dragging his feet as usual, to agitate me.

"You c'mon, Roy. Let's get something to eat. I'm hungry." He had some money left over from his gambling the night before. "Let's get a hamburger."

"I ain't studden you, Ray. We ain't got time." I wasn't thinking about getting any food from downtown because that meant we'd have to go to the back door of the hamburger place and get cussed at. That hamburger lady would say, "What y'all want, niggers? That'll be twenty-five cents. Now get on." No, my mind was on my mother. What would normally take us ten minutes to walk took us a good hour. And there she was waiting on the porch. I could hear that distant Katy train blow her horn.

"Where y'all been? Lord have mercy!" Momma hollered like she was mad, but I could tell by the way she stomped her foot like she did in church—that full of the Holy Ghost stomp—she was happy. But no sooner had we hit that porch, than she started to wail on us. With one hand, she grabbed me by the head, and with the other open hand, she popped me, like an agitated momma cat tired of her kittens playing when she was in no mood. Then she grabbed Ray and did the same. It didn't hurt none, except to know she was broken by what we had done, by not being home where she knew we'd be safe. Every time I came home without Ray (sometimes I couldn't find him) it was like she'd been thrown by a horse, knocked down so hard that she didn't get up the same. A little of her was buried. She got up less than she was before. I wondered how much of my momma was left each time something like this happened—her children caught on the other side of the tracks.

We was big enough now that me and Ray could pull away when Momma tried to whip us, but I never did. I knew some of those licks was her licks of joy because she had something to hit on. Her boys was home.

"I said where y'all been?" Momma yelled again.

I said, "It wasn't none of me. Ray was down at Rufus Jackson's, and him and Red Winston and C. P. Johnson, Raymond Riles, and them was gambling, and I tried to get him to come home, and I kept saying 'Come on, Ray. Momma say come home,' and we got in a fight, and Red and them egged us on, and Owens and Dude Milton broke it up and hauled us to jail and wouldn't let us go till this morning because he said we might not get home 'the way people was stirred up being Juneteenth, coloreds getting beside themselves,' and they let us go this morning." I said all that in one breath.

"What did I say about getting home, about gambling, about fighting each other?" Momma said.

"Momma, it wasn't none of me." Before I knew it, she slung me against that screen door, my cheek catching the edge where the screen had come loose. It drew blood. Then she slung Ray into me, and we both rolled into the front room. Ray was laughing under his breath the whole time.

Momma yelled, "What I say about fighting each other instead of looking after one another? Get in there and take off them clothes. Where's my switch?"

"Momma, it wasn't none of me. This ain't fair." Why did I go and say that? She grabbed my neck and lifted me off the floor—the floor!—then dropped me just as fast, pitched her voice way high, and looked past me as if she was talking to another person in the room I could not see. It was as if she was in another world.

"Where'd you get the notion that life's 'pose to be fair? You mean the 'fair' like the days your daddy comes home drunk because he can't stand what this town has done to him? Is this the fair you looking for?" She clasped her hands like she was praying, holding them up to her teary face. "I'm gone from sunup to sundown with these hands in folks' bleach water, in their toilets and in their pots and pans so I can bring home some scraps off their plates so y'all don't have to eat meat out of them goddamn woods all the time. Is that the fair you looking for?"

The only time my momma would cuss was when she was

speaking to that otherworld person we couldn't see. By now, Momma had sat down with her head in her hands, blood running out her nose because she had worked herself up so. She continued to speak to that otherworld. "I done seen *Fair* come on the colored side of town and take colored women away in his wagon and do whatever Fair pleased to do, then drop her off right in front of her own children the next morning." When Momma would get in that "otherworld talk," it was her time to unload a fed-up spirit. Sometimes she'd get that spirit overflowing when she remembered the child she had lost who was now in that otherworld—safe, maybe. I don't know. She'd talk so hard, she'd collapsed in the chair, tired, naked in a way no child should see his momma—not bare, but broken—like a screen door broken. Nothing can stay in and nothing can stay out.

With a voice barely above a whisper, she slowly came back to this world and said to me, "Roy, baby, life may be fair for some, but Fair don't live everywhere." By now, she forgot about whipping us. Me and Ray stayed in our room all day. She didn't go to work that day. From our bedroom door, barely open, I saw my momma sitting at the kitchen table where the sooty flame from the near-empty kerosene lamp kept back the dark. She was still there at sunrise.

Every morning before Momma would go off to work, she would lay her heavy hands on our nappy heads and slowly rub each like she was crowning us as her kings, and she would call out our names long and low. "Roy … Ray …" It was pure honey. But today, she met us at the kitchen table with the family Bible pressed to her chest. Given to her by her mother, Grandma Emma, this book—leather-brown and spine-broken—was stuffed with papers between pages yellowed and torn. She opened it, took out a large sheet folded several times that looked like it come out of a newspaper, and then she spoke real even.

"Boys, Momma loves you. Lord know I do. Do anything for you, but y'all keep it up and you'll wind up in that courthouse jail like that Cook boy. And God have mercy on your souls because there won't be a thing in the world I can do to help either of you then. Tobe's momma couldn't help him. Babies, they hung that boy up in that jailhouse for little more than wearing the wrong pair of shoes."

I looked at Ray. He looked at me. Then I said to Momma, "What you mean 'the wrong pair of shoes'? Who is Tobe?"

She raised her voice as she raised her head, looking right at me, then past me to that otherworld person. "You know that jailhouse y'all spent the night in? Something bad happened there before y'all was born. Tobe Cook was a colored man, young enough to still be called a child in my eyes. He got on the wrong side with the law. He was arrested, tried, and convicted for a crime he claimed he didn't do. All they had for evidence was little more than a shoe print in the sand that anybody could have made. As his momma watched, they put a noose around his neck and hung him from a ring up on the second floor of that jailhouse." Her voice pitched low when she tripped over that dark place in the story. Even though she turned her head to hide the tears, I saw her eyes fill up as she pushed that folded paper toward us. "The last words she said to her boy was, 'If'n you done it, own it. Tell the truth and if guilty, own it like a man. You can then better meet your God.'"

As my momma was telling me and Ray that part, she pulled us close, her eyes full and hands wet. She said, squeezing us tight, "Stay out the way of them laws. I ain't gonna be around always to help you. Keep your hands in God's hands. Always tell the truth. You can better meet God that way, you hear me?" Then she slowly rose from the chair like somebody had relieved her of the last full sack of cotton picked for the day. Each bone of her back took its own good time finding its proper place. "I'm going to work, now. Stay around here and help your sister, and stay out of trouble."

Me and Ray said together, "Yes, ma'am." I don't know what Ray felt about what Momma had just laid at our feet, but I felt heavy, like whatever was in her sack was now my load. I never thought of Momma not being with us. I never thought about the hanging side of Bastrop.

When Momma was gone, I knew Ray would soon be gone too, to hook up with the Get Over Gang. They weren't called the Get Over Gang for nothing. Red Winston, C. P. Johnson, Raymond Riles and them, with Ray in the lead—they took every opportunity to get over on anybody they could. It didn't matter none to Ray to pull a fast one on Momma even though she said stay at home. With him gone, I saw this as an opportunity too. I unfolded that piece of paper Momma had pulled from that Bible.

It was a page from the *Bastrop Advertiser* newspaper, June 10, 1892. The headline read, "Tobe Cook Hangs for the Murder and Rape of Miss Ida Belle Moore." They called Tobe (his real name was Henderson) a "fiend incarnate." It told how he grabbed this sixteen-year-old girl, dragged her under a one-strand barbed wire fence, carried her through the woods to a secluded spot where he murdered her—choked her to death—and then left her cold.

Just like Momma said, the law's main evidence was foot tracks made by a pair of moccasins Cook had on made from old boot tops. We all have worn shoes like that, I thought, made from somebody's leftover shoes. Boots became shoes, shoes became slippers, slippers turned into whatever—otherwise coloreds would be walking around barefoot.

The paper said that Tobe was "a rather good-looking specimen of the Negro race, and would be considered rather bright and intelligent." It said that he was known as a womanizer, messing around on his wife, fooling around with a couple of girls in the field where that girl was killed. On that day, Tobe was wearing the wrong shoes and the wrong reputation.

I could read all right, having made it through the ninth grade and headed to the tenth, but not without the help of my finger guiding my eyes. They raced across the page together faster than I had ever read anything before. The trial lasted a day. Tobe told them he was working in another man's field from sunup to sundown. He even called out that white man's name and the name of his daughter, who he worked for that day. But it didn't matter. The jurors was in that decision room less than an hour before they came out with a verdict. The first vote was unanimous: "Guilty of murder in the first degree, punishable by death." The judge overruled a second trial.

My finger couldn't keep up with my eyes. That Friday morning, his momma came to see her boy. She sang and prayed. Then she hugged him real close and said to him, "If you ain't done it, stick to it. But if'n you did, tell the truth and own it. Tell the truth and if guilty, own it like a man. You can then better meet your God." It was the way Momma had said it to me and Ray.

The words on that newspaper page got ahold of me so that I started reading out loud. Mozell was outside doing laundry. Ray was nowhere to be found. It was me and the story of Tobe Cook. I didn't care if she heard me as I read on. "It was about 10:30 a.m. Rev. W. Wootton, Elder S. W. Wormley and Deacon Theodore Tilmore were there to help Tobe meet God." They walked him to a washtub filled with water. Tobe was led to the water to be baptized, clapping his hands to an unknown rhythm. Reverend Wootton leaned his head toward heaven to open his throat and toned out as he placed his hand over Tobe's face: "I baptize you, Henderson Cook, in the name of the Father and the Son and the Holy Ghost." Then he put Tobe under that water, and Tobe came out as he went in, clapping that same rhythm. He changed into a suit of clothing that a colored man would hardly have worn in life: gray wool sack jacket and high-topped, brown patent-leather shoes with stripes. He was dressed, ready to meet God.

As they escorted Tobe past a wooden structure with a trap door, a rope hanging from a large steel ring fastened in the ceiling was waiting for him. Tobe said, "Here is an innocent man dressed up for the gallows." As he ascended the stairs "sure-footed," he looked up and muttered, "Here we go."

I lost all track of time as the newspaper told the last minutes of Tobe's life. "At 1:45 p.m., they read his charge using his nickname 'Tobe.' He interrupted, 'My name is Henderson Cook. That is the name I was given when I was born and it is what I'm gonna die with." At 2:00 p.m., he spoke his last words, "Will I tell you the truth or a lie with the rope in my hand ready to die? What is better to meet God with?" Then he turned toward the window and held out the rope where all could see, and repeated his last words, "What is better to meet God with—a lie or the truth?"

At 2:12 p.m., they tied up his legs "like a bird readied for roasting." At 2:16 p.m., they tied his hands behind his back. At 2:17 p.m., they placed the rope around his neck and slid the black cap over his head. "It could be heard in a muffled tone from under the cap: 'Innocent blood. Innocent blood.'" They sprung the trap door at 2:18 p.m., and "the spirit of Henderson Cook had his meeting with God." He was buried in clothes a brown man hardly wore in life and shoes not cut from the tops of old boots.

I slowly closed the paper and tried my best to fold it the way Momma had left it. I put it back in the leather-brown, spine-broken Bible. I walked out the front door, past Mo who was peeling something for dinner. She yelled at me, "Where you going? Momma said for y'all to stay put. What's wrong with you?" I paid her no mind.

I walked out the yard to the trail that led into the woods that led to the bottoms to that old oak tree that was my thinking place. There, I sat and thought about a time when my mother would not be around to help me. I thought about what might have become of Tobe and what might become of me. I cried. As the orange-yellow sun came to rest behind a thicket of pines, a long horn blast from the distant Katy train interrupted the cicadas—for a moment—then they started up again. Then I started my way home before dark.

three

THE COLORADO

MORNING CAME WITH NO MENTION OF WHERE I had run off to the day before. The Bible with the newspaper story of Tobe was where Momma left it. The house was full of the smell of Bright and Early coffee—her favorite—black and strong. Two cups was waiting for me and Ray the way we liked it—creamy and sweet. Momma seemed different—lighter. A smile spread across her face as she peeped over her cup at us as we all sipped and slurped together. No one said a word.

She broke the silence. "I got to get on to some washings. Y'all try to get some yard work. OK?" Then she, as always, slowly rubbed our heads as she called out our names long and low. "Roy ... Ray ..." It was, to me, sweeter than the sweet cream you put in coffee.

No sooner had she closed the door, than me and Ray looked at each other with one thought—the Colorado. *She* was our salvation from the long, hot summer ahead. Having her about a half a mile away was like having our own almost-private swimming pool. And since the cotton-picking season hadn't started yet, we had a handful of free days to be lazy and crazy.

My uncle John got us calling the Colorado "she" because he called her a two-faced-woman. He said, "She can be mean as a witch or a lady. She a gamble. You get what you get." (Except he didn't say "witch.") That was part of the fun of having the river in our backyard. She was a gamble. I said to Ray, "Let's go swimming."

The usual gang—Red Winston, C. P. Johnson, Raymond Riles, and Precious McMarion—met at our special spot, the big tree across from the sand island that sat in the middle of the river. We was all there shooting hooky from something we was supposed to be doing at our houses. We egged each other on about who was the best swimmer. Precious McMarion was my best friend, but the weakest swimmer. I liked him because he didn't like trouble like Ray and his posse. But he was on his own today if he decided to jump in and race with the rest of us. My brother led the pack counting us down, "One, two, three," and we took a running jump. Precious was the tail. Me and my brother was neck and neck. When you hit the middle of the river, it was as if someone jumped on your back, as if someone grabbed your arms, as though a sack of potatoes was strapped to your legs. But you had to keep moving your arms as hard as you could, no matter what. Before you knew it, you was in clear, quiet water. All you had to do then was float till you could reach out and grabbed a low limb or long grass. That day, I got to the other side first, then Ray, C. P., Red, and then Raymond.

But there was no Precious. He was past halfway, but that dark side of the Colorado was on his back, that "witch" got ahold of his arms, that sack of potatoes weighed down his legs. He was caught in a suck hole—a mysterious, untamed undertow that could pop up anytime, anywhere on the river. We hollered, "C'mon, Precious, swim," but the current keep pushing him under and downstream. We ran along the bank trying to keep up, hollering, "Swim, swim!" With each stroke, Precious's arms flapped like a broken wing until all of him went limp. All we could see was his forearms, then hands, then the top of his head. He disappeared, then bobbed back up. The time between his head going under and bobbing up was longer and longer until only the back of his shoulders was poking through, his body now in the quiet water near bank. We stopped running and hollering. I prayed the only prayer I knew—the one I heard my mother pray all the time—"Lord, help."

The next thing we knew, Precious's hand punched through the water. He grabbed a bunch of long grass. We screamed, "Precious, c'mon, pull," but the grass didn't hold. One by one, the weeds broke away until there was only one. Precious held onto it, and it held in return. Finally, his head popped up. He started coughing and spitting. Red hollered, "Precious, you sissy!" Ray jumped in, pulled him through the muddy edge until he was safe on dry ground. We all ran to where they was, turned him over and pounded on his back and screamed, "C'mon, spit it out!"

He did, coughing up more water and mud with each slap, then he erupted, "I made it across. Y'all didn't think I could do it. I did it!"

We dove the rest of the day teasing him, "Thank the grass for Precious's ass." That was the Colorado—her nasty side.

We dried off, dressed, and went our separate ways home, each responsible for his own lies about the day. Momma met us at the porch. She gave me a pat on the butt. With an uppity voice she said, "Well, how was y'all's day today? I don't remember it rained." Our undershorts had not dried all the way, but she didn't say nothing more. That was Momma. She picked her fights. We was home—safe. She left it at that.

A week later, me, my brother, and Mozell was off to the cotton fields. I hated picking cotton. The way picking season was set up, it was near close to the slavery I read about in the history book from Mrs. Ruth Manuel's class at Emile High School—the school where all grades of coloreds was made to go. The farmers owned the land, the equipment, the seeds, and the gins. You might as well say they owned us in the field too. We got pennies for the pounds we picked. But like it or not, fair or not, we did what we had to do. We needed the money because Momma's washing work had been cut back because of her hands. By now, they was so raw because of the scrub board and lye soap, they'd bleed. The white, sudsy water would turn rusty red from her blood. We had to pick for her sake.

But life wasn't all thistles and thorns and cotton burrs. We got a break each time we moved from one nearby town's fields to the next—from Taylor to Smithville, Elgin to Copeland. By now the summer days was already so hot you could fry an egg on a rock. So I headed straight to the river when I could. I'd float for hours in inner tubes in those quiet parts. Every care, for the moment, would sink to the bottom like they was limbs and leaves caught in a suck hole.

Normally my mind would be a thousand miles away from school, but for some reason that summer, school was more on my mind. No—not *some* reason. *The* reason was Juanita McMarion, my best friend's sister. I liked her, but I didn't outright let her know it. She was two grades ahead of me. I would unintentionally bump into her on purpose. All she said was what she always said, "I ain't studden you, Johnnie Roy Houston." *Studden* was her favorite word. It meant, "I ain't paying you no mind." Truth is, I was paying her a lot of mind and hoped I was on her mind a little too. This day, I was drifting and dreaming of Juanita: she had smooth skin, paper-bag light; lips and hips full beyond her age; and quiet, puppy-dog eyes but a bulldog spirit—feisty and fun. I drifted for hours, my hands steering my tube in lazy circles.

I tried not to think of school. Except for seeing Juanita, I didn't like school much. I was ready to quit. I had learned that Fair didn't go to Emile, either. When me and my brother would walk to school, the white kids on their buses called us names. Then me and Ray was teased at our school because of the lunch we carried in buckets: a big square of cornbread covered with syrup and a piece of hog jowls on the side, if Momma had it. She would put a spoon in it. We rattled as we walked. The other kids with the good lunches could hear us coming. Calling us the "Syrup Slurpers," they had a song waiting for us: "Roy and Ray, what y'all say? What y'all got for lunch today? Cornbread and syrup, like yesterday." Me and Ray fought them every day.

Except one day. That one day, the teacher fought for us instead. Before our first lesson, Miss Birdie Lee walked over to my desk and reached under it, pulled out my lunch bucket, and opened it. "Class, y'all always talking about these Houston brothers, about what they eat. There is nothing wrong with syrup, hog jowls, and cornbread. I'd eat it." She turned to me and asked, "Johnnie Roy, can I have some of your lunch?"

The class giggled when I said, "Help yourself." She reached down in there and got my spoon. Every eye was on her. Every mouth was wide open, including mine. It took forever for her hand to come out of that bucket with a heaping helping of cornbread and hog fat covered in thick sorghum syrup. She slowly brought the spoon to her mouth.

I could tell she didn't want to do it. The veins in her neck was popping out. Sweat was running down from underneath her wig. A girl in the back hollered out, "Don't do it, Miss Lee." Somebody on the other side in front—a boy, I think—hollered out, "I bet a nickel she don't do it." Miss Lee opened her mouth wide, closed her eyes, and into her mouth the spoon went. She didn't swallow right away. Her jaws ballooned out like a bullfrog." Somebody in the front of the class hollered, "She's gonna blow." Miss Lee made a grunt sound from the back of her throat like the sound you make when you been punched in the gut. Then a hoot like a hoot owl's hoot spilled out the side of her puckered lips. Ray, who sat next to me, just about lost it then hollered, "Go 'head, Miss Lee. Do it!"

She chewed two or three times. Each time that grunt grew to a growl. Then she swallowed. The veins in her neck popped out blue. I swear I saw a tear roll down her cheek. She swallowed hard again, and that spoonful went down—and stayed down. The class whooped, hollered, and clapped like the circus was in town. Then it went quiet when Miss Lee rocked back against my chair enough to move it and me. With some cornbread, jowls, and syrup still in her mouth, she took the longest minute and spoke with a catch in her voice, "Now you see there, how good that is." We went on with class with Miss Lee touching her stomach every now and then. They didn't tease us none that day. We came home feeling like we left—like kings.

Momma met us at the porch like she normally did, with one hand out to give us a hug and the other to get a note—looked like we had one nearly every day. When we walked on in the house with nothing to give her but our empty lunch pails, she asked with that uppity voice, "Well, how was y'all's day?"

Grinning from ear to ear, I said without looking back, "It was all right, but you gonna have to start putting a little more in my lunch bucket 'cause Miss Lee sure did enjoy my lunch today. Didn't she Ray?"

Ray busted out laughing, "She sure did, Momma—loved it."

Clang. Momma dropped our buckets. "What you say, now?"

Clang, clang. Startled, I snapped back into the real world, nearly overturning the inner tube. I had drifted right into a trot-line rigged with small cow bells to let the owner know some-thing was on the line or someone was trying to make off with their catch. So I headed home, rolling that inner tube a few feet in front of my steps. My mind stayed on Juanita and school, unsure of both.

Once it got past the Fourth of July, me, Ray, and the usuals—Red, C. P., and Raymond Riles—tried to cram as much fun out of the Colorado as we could. But there were others who would come and go, who would take advantage of the cooling waters, boys like us—boys just trying to get relief from the heat and the heavi-ness of Bastrop. School would be right on us before we knew it, and summer had melted away like the twenty-pound blocks of ice me and Ray would have to tote home from the Red & White store to keep our ice box from being just a box. "God must have built Bastrop right over hell, 'cause it sure is hot like it," my Grandma Atkins, my mother's mother, used to say. I think she was talking about any day in July and August. We always wished we had more summer. It was gone—almost. Me and Ray did work around Dr. Combs's farm and cut yards to make money between cotton harvests. We got fifty cents a yard and a hot drink of water from garden hoses that had been sitting in the hot sun all day. But no matter how hot the sun or mean the people, me and Ray always had the Colorado.

On one of those egg-frying days, we headed to our favorite swimming hole—a shady spot under that big old elm tree where Precious learned, the hard way, to swim.

This day, Ray upped the ante. "I bet y'all a dollar each, I can get across and back before any of y'all."

We jumped in. Again, I beat Ray, there and back. Then this boy A. J. Williams, who hung out with us every now and then, kept mouthing off that it wasn't nothing to swim across and back. So he jumped in too. About halfway he started to struggle. You could tell by the sound his arms made, slapping the water hard like the sound of Momma slapping wet clothes against a washtub. But somehow, he made it to the other side.

"Go ahead and walk over the bridge," we yelled at him because we knew there was no way he could swim back. He was spent.

I yelled, "C'mon, man. We ain't got all day. Take the bridge 'cause you ain't swimming back." Why did I go and say that?—because he got mad and cussed me and my momma like we had cussed him or called him a sissy or something.

Bent over and breathing hard, he hollered back, "It ain't nothing. Give me a minute." He took about ten minutes, and then he jumped in and slapped his way past halfway. Then he hit a suck hole. It got to spinning him around—one time, two times—then on the third time, under he went, and he didn't come back up. We was too tired to jump in to try to get him, so my brother ran to the police station to get help. All the while, we was watching and praying, and praying and watching the spot where he sunk. When those deputies came with a boat and divers with masks, tanks, and fins, it had already been thirty minutes since we saw A. J. go under. His folks was on the banks with half of colored Bastrop. You could hear his momma crying clear across the bottoms, filling the place like flood waters, like thunder trapped in the trees. "Lord, Jesus, help, Lord, Jesus. A. J.!"

Ten minutes after the divers jumped in, they pulled out A. J. feet first with a rope tied around his ankles like a rodeo calf. The funeral was a week later. Mount Rose Baptist Church was packed. I sat outside on the steps, but I could hear everything: his momma crying and that preacher preaching, "Pride goes before a fall. Let this be a lesson—pride goes before a fall." That's all I remember of his sermon. I couldn't get past the thought that somehow I had a hand in A. J.'s drowning because we—I—egged him on, knowing how he was—not to be outdone. He gambled with the Colorado witch and lost. His momma's crying lived in my head a long time. It haunted that shady spot under that big old elm tree where we hung out. We didn't go swimming there ever again.

four

GAMBLING

By summer's end, picking season for the most part done, we had money in our pockets and time on our hands before the start of school. It was a good time to go fishing—me, Ray, and my daddy, Johnnie "Tude" Houston. He never told us why they called him "Tude." Momma said it was short for *attitude* because he could be a mean cuss one moment, all liquored up, and the next time you saw him, when all was right with the world and with him, he was like a shade tree—good to be under. With Labor Day around the corner, we didn't know when we'd see Daddy next because some holidays he'd disappear into a bottle for days. So this morning was as good a time as any to fish. We had a fresh can of worms we had dug, Daddy's homemade boat in tow, and a special guest: Momma. She never went fishing with us. She hated the water, but she said OK because we hardly spent time together—her and the men in her life she liked to call "her kings." She figured she could turn it into a picnic.

Daddy launched himself in his little boat onto the water, just off the bank where the rest of us stood baiting up our hooks. He liked to fish from a boat because he said, "You got to be where the fish be." He pointed over a ways and said, "Ella, go on and drop your line right near that log over there," winking at us because it was funny to see her cast that cane pole. "A big old mud cat is sitting right there waiting for your frying pan."

A blind man trying to thread a needle had a better chance of succeeding than Momma did trying to hit the water, let alone that spot near that log. But it wasn't a minute before her stopper disappeared. She didn't pay it no mind till we hollered, "Momma, you got something. Pull, Momma, pull."

"Lord, help," she cried and then gave a real hard yank. She sure did bring it in. On her line was an eel. She thought it was a water moccasin, so she jumped in the water trying to get away from it. They passed each other—Momma headed in the water, the eel to dry land. She landed face first in knee-deep water, flapping and slapping, trying to swim. That poor eel hit the ground crawling like he had legs. Daddy jumped in after my momma, not that he needed to. She could have stood up and walked out.

So here we was—my momma in the water, the eel hightailing it toward the bushes, and all the fish we had hoped to catch scared off by all the commotion. Me and my brother was on the ground whooping and a hollering till our sides hurt. "Momma, why you jump in the water? I guess you had to be where the eels be," we joked.

That evening at supper we had fried chicken. I turned to Ray and said, "I sure had me a taste for some eel. You, Ray?" Momma popped me upside my head. Then under her breath, she tried to hide a giggle that finally seeped out to a full laugh. We all laughed—Momma and her kings.

A week before school, a mixed crowd met at a new meeting place—a different shade tree that was now our official headquarters since A. J. had drowned. Some of us was there to swim, mostly to race each other, while some was with Ray and his posse—and some wannabes—to shoot dice.

Ray was king of that tree. A nearby fallen log was his throne. After us swimmers climbed out, we'd find a piece of sun to dry off and a patch of shade to catch our breaths and watch King Ray rule. "Seven come eleven," Ray shouted with a voice that was intentionally as irritating as the sound of Mrs. Manuel accidentally running her nails along the blackboard. He would pitch his voice real high and trap the sound in his nose like the sound a trumpet makes with a mute—that thing you stick on the end of it to make the notes thin. His voice irritated everybody, and he knew it. He tossed the dice and called out to Red Winston with that irritating voice, "I'da been your daddy, Red, if the line hadn't been so long. Seven come eleven."

What Ray said and how he said it would piss you off, to get you off your game. The voice and the trash talk was all a part of his hustle. You see, when you was agitated over what Ray was saying, you took your eyes off what Ray was really doing with his hands—a straight drop. He jiggled the dice in his hands till he had the faces of the dice in the combination he wanted. Then he dropped them over his finger real weak-like so they'd roll two times and hit the ground with the same sides he had in his hands to start. He didn't throw dice. He dropped dice. While you'd be paying attention to his mouth, he'd be hustling you with his hands.

He said to Red, "Got you. Pay up."

Red paid up, but it was a setup for the next man up with deeper pockets. That would be Tuffy, whose eyes were always on Ray. He hung out mostly with Ray's clan of the Colorado River summer crowd. He was a wannabe tough guy when he could break away from his strict grandmother's apron strings, but he wanted to be with Ray—better yet, be Ray. If you could do something, he would always say he could do it better. His mouth would run and run and run. He would ask anybody who'd listen, "Wanna shoot some craps? I'm gonna lighten your pockets today. Anybody want to fight? I'm a gonna whip you like a stepchild. Anybody want to race across the river? Tarzan is my middle name."

Truth be told, he always lost in craps. He always got the shit beat out of him. He was always last out of the water. But Ray and them let him hang around because of the way he looked and sounded. He was a live cartoon—a sixty-pounds-soaking-wet-with-rocks-in-his-pocket cartoon with glasses thick as Coke bottles. They wasn't even his glasses. They was his grandma's. He was always losing his. He was the same blind as she. Then, there was Tuffy's voice. He stuttered—I mean, real bad—every three words bad. So Ray let him hang around because he was a walking, talking, live cartoon good for a laugh, and he was good for Ray's hustle because Ray practiced that limp-finger dice rolling on Tuffy. Ray's target was always on bigger fish. Tuffy was just Ray's way of sharpening his hook. And taking Tuffy's money in the process was just Ray doing what Ray do—get over at every chance.

This day, like always, Tuffy was an easy, eager patsy. He, as usual, had been watching Ray take Red, unaware of the setup. He figured whatever Ray could do, he could do one better. He wanted to challenge Ray. "Wuh-wuh-wuh-wait up. I'm going to li-li-li-lighten up somebody's puh-puh-puh-pockets today."

Before he could get out the final "puh," a voice came out of the bushes. "Everybody, freeze!" It was Deputy M. A. Justice, another law who had warned my mother, "Mrs. Houston, gambling gonna land your boys in jail or worse." He and the other deputies came down on us with their guns drawn. He shifted to one side the cigar he was giving a work to and mumbled, "Didn't y'all hear me? I said everybody freeze."

One of them flunky deputies, Dave Eskew, hollered, "You heard him. Freeze now! Put them dice down and your hands up, goddamn it! Your little gambling session is done." Eskew was a cartoon himself. He was tall, thin like a rail, and snaggletoothed. His arms was always stiff at his side, his right—his flicked hand—turned in like he was about to draw. He always walked like that, like he was right out of a Wild West movie ready for a gunfight at the OK Corral. People laughed at him because he acted like he was the long arm of the law. Not too long before, he went down to Rufus Jackson's to arrest this colored woman who was wanted for something. He came in there walking like Wyatt Earp. He pulled his gun and she, half drunk and every bit of three hundred pounds, wrestled him to the ground and snatched that gun from him, and she wouldn't give it back. For the longest time, he tried to pay us to go get the gun back. It took everything I had in me now not to bust out and say, "I see you got your gun back," but I kept my mouth shut seeing as we was already in knee-deep trouble.

The laws picked up all the money and dice and started marching everybody down through the woods to their cars. A small voice piped up on my right. It was Tuffy. "Muh-muh-muh-Mr. Justice, you right about the rest of them gambling. But it wasn't none of me. I wasn't gambling." Justice and them laws kept marching us. Tuffy spoke louder. "Mr. Juh-Juh-Justice, I said you sure right about the rest of them, but I wasn't gambling, they was."

Justice pulled out his blackjack and swung around and popped Tuffy upside his head and said, "What you said, nigger?"

Tuffy stammered out, "Yessah. Yessah. Yessah, I was ga-ga-gambling."

Justice popped him a couple times more, and each time, Tuffy stammered, "Yessah, I was ga-ga-gambling," and Justice answered back, "I thought you was."

We laughed all the way to the cars—the laws too. Justice tried to hide it, but he had a tear running down his face as he chewed on his cigar, almost choking on it he laughed so hard. Even though we was all laughing, I thought, This is it. I'm going back to that jail I swore I wasn't ever going back to. I could hear my momma warning me the other morning, "Please don't gamble. You watch your brother. I ain't going back down to that jail 'cause of y'all."

Bam! Bam! As Justice reached for the car door to start loading us up, a shot or shots, or what we thought were shots, rang out. We all ducked. *Bam!* We kids hit the ground, mostly face first, kicking up a cloud of dust. With my cheek to the dirt, I saw that Eskew, bringing up the rear, out of our sight, had fired his pistol in the air. Then Justice had slammed the door extra hard. The laws burst out laughing louder. Justice could hardly speak. "I'm gonna let y'all go this time. But if I catch y'all gambling down here again, it won't be no laughing. Don't be caught on the river gambling no more. Ya hear?" Still cracking up, they sped off in their own cloud of exhaust smoke.

Wiping off our dirt-dusted faces that looked like we had seen a ghost, we all looked at each other to say, "Time to get home." Then here came Tuffy. "I wasn't stuh-stuh-studden them lah-lah-lah-laws. I wasn't going to no-no-no jail. I was gonna hand out some ah-ah-ass whippings."

"Yeah, Tuffy, you the mah-mah-man." We all took turns making fun of him nearly all the way home, copying his stutter. "It wasn't none of me gah-gah-gambling." As it turned out, Tuffy was king of the gambling that day. We would have gone down to the jailhouse if it wasn't for him. He got them laws' minds off arresting us that day.

My uncle was right. You never knew which Colorado you'd get—the witch or the lady. That day, we got "Lady Luck." We rolled a seven and nobody went to jail. But Lady Luck is a tease. Before we made it to Church Street, Ray had fingered some dice again and slipped off down a cut-off to Pine Street, headed east past the tracks to Rufus Jackson's place.

And he wasn't the only one itchin' for some luck. There are different ways a man can bet on his future. It was the end of the summer I was sixteen. And I decided to make the biggest gamble of my life. As Ray went his way, I decided to roll a seven the hard way.

five

JUANITA

GAMBLING WAS IN RAY. HE'D NEVER CHANGE, but I had to make some changes. I was getting mean. Nobody could tell me nothing because I hated what Bastrop told me: "You can work in the fields, boy. You can stay in your place on Saturdays, boy. You can drink scalding water from somebody's lawn hose, boy." If I stayed in Bastrop any longer, I'd wind up working all my life as somebody's boy or turn out like Ray—running with the wrong crowd, scheming to get over on everyone. We was back at school—the tenth grade. But my mind was someplace else—Corpus Christi, Texas. My brother Immer, older by twenty years, had a motor company there. He didn't exactly own it, but he might as well have. He was in charge of fixing up all the used cars, enough to get them salable, and then he'd get a cut. He could show me how the car game worked. He could be my foothold out.

I called him Christmas 1944. I snuck off to the Red & White grocery store. Mrs. Rosanky, the owner—real nice German lady—never closed the store. She let me use her phone for a minute. "Merry Christmas, big brother. Y'all need any help down there at Osage Motor Company? You show me, I can do anything y'all need, painting, simonizing—"

"Hang on, little brother. How is Momma? She get my present? Now, what about school?"

"She fine. I think she got something from you. Everybody's

fine. I'd be coming after I finish school. Look, I can't talk for long. So what do you say? Can I come?"

"Well, you just c'mon when you ready. Love you, boy."

"Love you too." I wanted to tell him I was ready now.

◆ ◆ ◆

Winter lasted only a minute. March 1, 1945—my birthday—came and almost went like it was just another day.

But toward evening, Momma called me to the kitchen. "Happy Birthday, baby. You thought I forgot, but you know I couldn't, not my kings. How it feel to be seventeen?" She placed on the table a two-layer chocolate cake with vanilla icing and a carton of strawberry ice cream—my favorite. "Where's Ray?"

"He gone somewhere—him and Red." I dove right into that cake. "Thank you, Momma."

"Now leave some for your brother. Lord, I don't know what I'm gonna do with him," she said, her chin dropped near down to her chest. Then she turned toward the kitchen sink, her back to me. Something was wrong. She mumbled, "*Bad* is a street you just don't want to go down."

"Ma'am?" I asked. I didn't know what she was saying, but I knew something was wrong. "Momma, you OK?"

"Yeah, I'm fine." She paused a long time, then said, "Johnnie Roy, you promise me that you'll keep yourself out of jail. You promise me, ya hear?"

"Yes, ma'am."

She shifted to one side then the other to find a position where her feet didn't hurt. They had started to give out on her. Sometimes she'd stand with her back to me at the kitchen sink, cleaning collard greens or cutting up onions, shifting from side to side. There at the sink, she'd cut and talk and cry. She tried not to let me see her cry, but I could tell it in her voice when she was in pain. Our kitchen sink talks wasn't so much about her hurting hands and feet. She talked about her life—the brothers she hardly ever saw. I remember seeing only Uncle John out of McDade. She never talked about her father, Masters Washington. The rest of her family was scattered, maybe some of them was in jail—I don't know. Maybe that's why she hated to see Ray go down that road. Maybe she had heard from one of her brothers that day.

Her voice caught on a swallow. "And see after your brother. He's your twin no matter what. I don't care how different he acts. Twin don't mean y'all the same, but brothers does means y'all blood—will always have the same blood. Ain't no place you can go, or nothing he can do that's gonna change that." By now, I could see her try to wipe her eyes. "Them onions," she said, but it wasn't no onions. It was about all the weight on her: her twins always at each other since the day we came out of her, Daddy's drinking, her lost brothers, those bleeding hands and bad feet. It was like a cloud came over her—a cloud like one of them twister clouds that sometimes came in March to April storms, when cool air mixed with warm clouds full of rain and wind. Her tears was just rain that comes with the storm.

I wanted to leave Bastrop—no, had to leave—before Bastrop sucked me under like a Colorado River suck hole, but I couldn't leave Momma, not after what she just placed on me when she stood at the sink spilling herself out. So I didn't tell her I had been talking to Immer about going to work for him. I had no choice but to stay as long as I could.

Juneteenth, like Christmas, took forever to get here, but when it did, we wasted little time getting to the celebrating. School was out. It was time for fireballs, all the food you could eat, and any and everything you wanted to drink—including that homemade chock. Friday night, the bottoms was thick with "happy" people. Somebody tried to hand me a cup full of chock, but I said, "Thanks, but no thank you." I had had a taste at home. I hated it. My daddy loved it. I never did take a liking to hard liquor. Maybe it was because I seen what it had done to my daddy.

I saw him that Friday night at Juneteenth. He gave me a big bear hug. "Johnnie Roy, my boy." He grabbed me tight to keep from falling. He was torn-down drunk. "Where Ray? Let's go fishing, without your mommy. Hey, you remember that time …" He didn't finish his thought, laughed, and slipped me a dollar. "Shush. Don't tell nobody where you got this." He stumbled off into the night.

John "Tude" Houston was a good man, but like many good men, "They got thorns," my momma would say, "things that trouble them all their lives." I didn't know exactly what his thorn was. All I know was he worked hard all week trying to provide for us, doing odd jobs, picking up work where he could—plowing, picking up trash, and hauling for people who paid him next to nothing. Along the way, I guess he picked up drinking. Maybe, he drank to live with himself. I once overheard him talking to a white man who he had done some work for—hauling away brush, I think—and the man underpaid him. My father spoke to him in a quiet voice: "Sir, I know my place, and I don't mean no disrespectful, but I think we talked about five dollars, sir."

"I think you take what I gives you," the man sneered back.

My daddy didn't say a word on the way home. He looked straight ahead, his face drawn, his jaws clinched so tight his neck twitched like something was fighting to get out. A piece of him was back there where he and that man transacted business: a man's place traded for a man's duty to feed his family. I made a promise to myself that day that I would never let a man place me in a place where I had to say to him, "I know my place." A man should never assign another man "a place." I didn't think less of my daddy that day. I understood more about why him, and men like him, could drink themselves to death. They was trying to drown what was killing them inside. Maybe that's why some Fridays he disappeared into a bottle. He mostly drank chock that he made himself from orange peels, apple peels—whatever fruit peels he got his hands on. He mixed in some yeast, then let it ferment, sitting in a still for a day and a half, maybe two. He'd check on it for another two days to a week. My daddy knew it was ready when the bottles he transferred the mash to popped their corks. A whiff of it would almost knock you down. A sip would definitely put you on the ground. It knocked my daddy down many a day, but he'd get back up and drink again.

When my daddy had some money, especially on a holiday, he wouldn't fool around with the homemade stuff. He'd head to Rufus Jackson's to drink all the beer and good whiskey he could afford. That July 4, in 1945, he left at noon and didn't come home. His horse, Old Blackie, showed up right at dusk at our porch without him. She strolled up huffing and snorting like she was trying to talk—like she was trying to tell us where Daddy was.

"Go tie up Blackie around back, unsaddle her. Your daddy ain't coming home tonight," Momma said, like she knew Daddy would be all right. The next morning a couple drove up with Daddy in the back seat. They had spotted him in a ditch. "Just his hat was visible on the side of road," they said. They knew who he was, so they brought him home still drunk. He passed out on the living room floor. Momma let him lie there until he came to. When he did an hour later, Daddy jumped up screaming, "Who hit me? Who hit me?" He went to swinging at thin air. "Who hit me?" he hollered again, then collapsed, almost hitting his head on the table. Me and Ray watched as Momma cleaned Daddy up, all the while she was crying so we couldn't hear her, but we did. When he came home like that—and he did a lot—it meant one thing: a fight. He tried to fight my momma. He never hit her, but he made out like he would, so me and Ray would fight him, but not really. We tried to keep him off her until he sobered up. We'd circle him like a pack of hunting dogs, lunging at him with baseball bats, but never hitting him. He'd try to swing on us, but, as drunk as he was, he always missed. Soon he would burn out and fall on the floor, out like a light. Momma would run a bath for him, clean him up, and put him to bed.

We heard her crying and talking to him like he could hear her, "John 'Tude' Houston," Momma said, "you a good man."

This July 5 morning that he came home without Blackie was the last time for my momma. She couldn't take it anymore. They separated but didn't divorce. She told me later that the John Houston she married, she was still married to. But the John 'Tude' Houston that he had become couldn't stay in her house for the good of the home. She loved him nonetheless.

With my daddy gone, and Momma's work slacked off because of her hands, things definitely had to change. Come fall, me and Ray would not go back to Emile. Deciding not to go back to school meant taking every cotton-picking work we could find that summer. We went where the work was in and around Bastrop: Taylor, Smithville, Elgin.

In my mind, picking cotton was the hardest way to make a living. You got up before daybreak. They strapped you with a sack, and that was the last time you stood up straight till sundown. All day, your back was bent so your eyes was level with the cotton bolls. You had to pick the white, leave the green bolls that hadn't opened yet, and move as fast as you could till dusk. Your back would take on a bow shape like the bend of a barrel, forced into an unnatural shape, curved by stressing wet wood with metal bands. You was a broken thing—bones out of joint. By the end of the day, to stand up straight took forever. It hurt so bad, it was almost better to stay hunched.

The cotton field was a hard life, but we found time to make us some fun. Me and Ray decided one day to get back at that scale boss for cheating us out of our right cotton weight. So we picked as many sticks and stones, green bolls, and whatever else we could get in as many sacks as we could, along with some cotton. We laid them out for the morning weigh-in like they was from last night's pickings. From way out in the field, we watched, waited, and listened. Then it started. That cotton gin coughed, strained, and whined as those teeth, trying to separate the cotton, hit all those sticks and stones, rocks, and green bolls. All of a sudden, we heard those gears seize up. Then smoke poured out of the guts of the gin. Before you knew it, the place was on fire. Here came the fire trucks, but they was too late. We didn't laugh out loud then, because they'd have known it was us. But on the way home, we could hardly walk for laughing. That smoke was a beautiful thing to see. I made up my mind that day that the only way I would pick cotton again would be if somebody held a gun on me. I hated picking cotton.

Most of that summer, I was mad at the world. The only thing that softened me up was Juanita. I saw her through her brother—Precious. It was a strange name for a boy, but he was named after his daddy. Me and Precious, Jr., hung together with the McIntosh twins. We hung out at the river spot with Ray's gang, but we was different. We wasn't looking for trouble, so we started calling ourselves the "Get Along Gang." Our idea of fun was going downtown on Saturdays to the picture show, eating popcorn, and watching a Western. Of course, hanging out with Precious meant seeing Juanita.

Every time I'd go to Precious's house, Juanita would be there looking at us like she was invited to come along. Her hair was coal-oil black and wavy. Her skin was the color of sweet potatoes, eyes the shape of almonds and the color of creamed coffee. Though she wore cut-off overalls mostly, you could tell she would have her momma's soda-water-bottle shape someday soon. She'd ask, "Where y'all going? Can I come?" Every time, I frowned and snapped back at her, "We ain't going no place, and no, you can't come." Precious would say, "Yeah, that's right. You can't come." I don't know why I did that—play like I didn't care. I guess I was scared. The mean part of me didn't want anybody to get close. I wouldn't look at her when I said, "You can't come" because she took the frown right off my face, and I was OK with that frown for now.

She'd snap back at me, "Oh, you're so mean, Johnnie Roy Houston. I ain't studden you. I can go anywhere I want to, and you can't stop me." She'd put her hands on her hips and imitate my frown and say again, trying to get me to look at her, "I ain't studden you." Whenever I went by Precious's house, me and Juanita generally had the same "I ain't studden you" conversation, but each time we locked horns, I looked at her longer and longer.

One Saturday after a good day of yardwork, extra money jingling in my pocket, I came to their house looking to go to the movies. I knocked at the door and hollered, "Hey Precious, Precious Mac." No one answered, so I hollered out again, "Hey man, let's go."

The door sprung full open. It was Juanita, of course. She snapped at me right off, "I ain't studden you, Johnnie Roy Houston. I'm coming. You hear me with your mean self?" She brushed past me with that coal-oil black hair greased back into a single ponytail with a red barrette holding it tight. She was wearing a dress with tiny flowers—no overalls this time to hide her figure. She said, "You better come on. We're going downtown. Precious and them are already there. I ain't gonna be late. Don't just stand there. Come on. I ain't studden you, Johnnie Roy."

When she got those legs moving, I could barely keep up, not that I wanted to. I loved to see her stride. I followed her all the way to town with a smile on my face. "Hold up, now! Slow down!" I hollered at her, catching my breath with every step. I finally caught up with her two blocks from the Palladium movie house.

"I ain't studden you, Johnnie Roy Houston," she came back, still using my full name—except it came out different this time, sweeter. She grabbed my hand, and at some point, along the way to the Palladium, without saying a word, she became my girlfriend—my first. I said to myself, *I'm gonna marry Precious McMarion's sister.*

As often as I could scrape up extra money, we'd go to the movies on Saturdays and have a good time. I didn't mind sitting through the war news reels that came before the feature. The Japanese had thrown the first punch but the US was kicking butt. But it didn't take long for our movie time to hit a sour note, thanks to Ray. He always liked to copy me, to do what I was doing, but to do me one better. If I'd go swimming, he'd try to race and beat me. If I'd cut a yard, he'd jump at the last minute to get a slice of my pay. When I started dating Juanita, well, Ray tried to date her sister, Wilma. She was younger than Juanita, but in every way just like her, like twins. She had them eyes, hips, and legs too. So the Saturday before Labor Day 1945, we called ourselves "double dating" at the movies. It wasn't my idea. It was mostly Ray's so he could freeload. Me and Juanita sat in our normal seats, near the projectionist up in the balcony, the only area where coloreds was allowed. I loved watching him load the reels. He even let me help. Ray and Wilma sat in the corner, far away from the light of the projection room. No sooner had they dimmed the lights and started the movie, than Ray had a notion to put his hand under Wilma's dress. I heard a slap. First, people thought it was part of the movie, the slap was so loud. But it wasn't the movie. Wilma had hauled off and slapped Ray as hard as she could like she was trying to slap the black off him. It sounded like lightning had struck a tin roof—*ka-pie-yauoo!* Then she cussed him out—I mean she cussed him out: "You goddam son of a bitch." Then she stood up and hollered out to Juanita, "C'mon! I'm going home. And you know Daddy don't want me walking home alone late at night. So come on, Juanita."

Juanita said back, "C'mon, Wilma. Sit back down next to us."

I put my two cents in too. "Yeah, Wilma, sit back down next to us, please." But she wasn't studden us. So there marched the McMarion girls, storming out the movie like freight train locomotives tied together, steam everywhere. Wilma was mad at Ray. Juanita was mad at Wilma, and I was mad at Ray, Wilma, and Juanita because that was the end of my Saturday night. And there was Ray, sitting and grinning like nothing had happened. He was the only one not mad at nobody because he was with the somebody he loved to be with—*Trouble.*

♦ ♦ ♦

Come September, school started without me and Ray. To keep enough courting-money in my pocket and help Momma out, I took every job I could get: cutting yards, throwing papers, and picking cotton, but they wasn't going to cut it. I needed a real job and I found one: ward steward at Camp Swift Army Base, about seven miles north of Bastrop off Highway 95. Overseas, World War II was just about over, but it managed to lap at the Colorado's muddy banks. Thousands of troops—even German prisoners—came through Swift. My job was cleaning up the hospital ward and loading and delivering food steam carts to feed the wounded. My ward was B-13—and was as long as half a football field. I saw some sickening stuff there. One soldier had a hole in his stomach as big as a softball. I watched them dress his wounds by putting their fists inside that hole (they had on gloves), and pull out all kinds of rotten tissue. Then they would stuff it with cotton and bandage it up, only to do it again a few days later.

The work was hard, but the money was good—forty dollars a week good, plus I made money on the side buying liquor for the soldiers. They'd give me big bills. I'd run down to Rufus Jackson's and buy what they wanted, then sneak it past the front gate (I think the guard knew what was going on), and I'd keep the change. I even got Ray and Juanita jobs there. She was a maid on the same ward with me. Sometimes we'd have the same shift, so we'd spend time on our breaks like it was a date.

Like clockwork, we had a standing date night on Saturdays—sometimes the movies, sometimes shopping, going to Champ White Barbecue on Main for hickory-smoked ribs, then ice cream. Sometimes we'd sit at her house and do nothing but talk or listen to the radio. Things was good. I had money in my pocket and a girlfriend who got past my meanest. She would talk to me and I'd listen. So one Saturday, when we was sitting in her living room listening to the radio, I turned to her. "Now, we been going together for a while now. Now, if you want to be with somebody else you need to let me know."

With her head laid on my shoulder, she smiled back at me. "Now, I ain't studden you, Johnnie Roy. You know I don't want to be seeing nobody else." She grinned a wide grin, so wide it showed her gold tooth.

So I asked her, "Juanita McMarion, will you be my wife? I ain't got enough money for a ring, but I got a big check coming in two weeks, and we could get married in your mother's house or mine—it don't matter—and we can barbecue, and we can do the same double shift so we can save up money, and I can borrow a car from my brother Immer—" I rattled all that in one breath before she cut me off.

"Will you slow down and let me answer you, or do you think you already know the answer? I ain't studden you, Johnnie Roy Houston. Yes, I will marry you."

Five months before my eighteenth birthday—on Saturday, November 17, 1945—we was married in Juanita's mother's house. It was packed full of people. Momma had on her favorite blue-flowered dress she would wear to church on Choir Anniversary. Being the church musician, she had to have on her best that day. Daddy was there—sober. Mo helped with the cooking. Ray was there, but he didn't stay long 'cause there wasn't no liquor. My momma didn't want no trouble. Trust me, there would have been trouble if there had been the hard stuff, with Ray, Red Winston, and that bunch around.

This day was my day—mine and Juanita's. I felt free. Meanness didn't have an invitation at the table to spoil things. The only cloud in the sky was the thought that, eight days later, I was going to Corpus Christi, not just for a honeymoon but a new life. My momma hugged me close and hard after Reverend Ollie Powell was done with the vows. She whispered, "Now Johnnie, you get out of here with your new wife. Y'all go and make a life, a whole life. Don't you worry none about me."

So on a partly sunny Sunday, eight days later, we loaded as much stuff as we could into an Olds 66 Immer lent me. The world was ahead of us. As we crossed the tracks, the jolt of the tires rolling over the railroad ties rocked Juanita, who had dozed off. I pulled her close, kissed her head and asked, "You all right?"

"We're fine." She smiled a smile bigger than the question. Then she said as she stroked my cheek, "What about you?" She must have seen the tear welling up in the corner of my eye because she whispered, "We'll be back for Juneteenth."

A sudden thunderstorm popped up. So strong was the rain, the windshield wipers could barely keep up. But as fast as the shower came, the rain stopped like someone had cut it off from a faucet. I rolled down the window to catch the cool, clean, rain-washed air. The sun didn't wait long to peek back out. Then there appeared to the east, rainbows—not one but two. It took me back to the first time I had seen a double rainbow. Me, Momma, and Ray was walking back from picking cotton. A rain came up, quick and hard, like today, so we ran under a tree. We couldn't have been there five minutes when the rain stopped. Just like today, the sun wasted little time in poking its head out again before getting ready to set down for the night. And there they was, not one, but two rainbows.

"Momma, where do rainbows come from?" I asked her, before Ray did (because we both wanted to know). We had gotten into an argument the week before about where rainbows came from. He said little men with funny hats. I said rainbows came from rain. "Why you think they called them rainbows?" I told him.

"Rainbows come from God," she said. "It means God has made a promise to someone, and he has placed a pot of gold at the end for the person who believes in that promise."

"Wow! Gold. Why did he make two of them?" I asked.

"Because there is two of you," she said, and smiled back. That settled it. If Momma said it, it was true. With that news, we took off running like we was shot out of a cannon, in search of our pot of gold. We followed those rainbows that sank behind a grove of trees. The more we ran, the further those rainbows drifted, until we was so deep in those woods, we lost sight of Momma. We got worried, and she got worried too.

"Roy, Ray! Y'all get back here." The more she called, the more we moved toward her voice, until we popped out a mile from where we started. There was Momma, with a frown on her face, trying to hide a big old grin. "Where y'all gold?" she asked.

Now, every time I saw a rainbow, I smiled. I knew Momma was pulling our legs, but part of me wanted to believe her, that there was a pot of gold out there, that something good out there was waiting on me, waiting for me to go and find it.

As our Olds moved onto Highway 49, south toward Corpus, I hoped rainbows was true. The rain-washed air felt good against my face. I turned to Juanita and squeezed her hand as she drifted off to sleep. I whispered into the wind, "It's going to be OK. We'll be back for Juneteenth."

six

JUNETEENTH

Thursday, June 13,1946. Eight months had passed since coming to Corpus Christi, Texas. Work was nonstop at the Osage Motor Company, and Immer had started his own company on the side—The Houston Motor Company, 1219 Sam Rankin Road—fixing and turning over used cars Osage didn't want to bother with. Juneteenth couldn't get here fast enough for me. I needed a break.

I sent Juanita on ahead to help with the cooking, not that she was in any condition to help much. Juanita was eight months pregnant—big and napping all the time—carrying in her belly my pot of gold at the end of the rainbow.

I planned to come up on the bus from Corpus Christi the following Tuesday because, with a baby on the way and all, I wanted a bigger payday. Immer wanted me to stay over the weekend to finish up some bodywork that needed to be done. As I "Bondo-ed," buffed, and beat out dents, all I could think about was barbecue brisket, pink lemonade, and fireballs. There would be plenty of celebrating when I got home. Best of all, I'd see Momma.

Tuesday, I took the last bus out headed north. The hum of the tires against the road and the whirr of the diesel bus engine lulled me into a half-sleep. I call it a "half-sleep" because I drifted in and out of sleep so much that sometimes it was hard to tell when I was awake or dreaming. I swear I could smell, taste, and touch things in my sleep.

I guess you could call them dreams "half-dreams" too. What was real and what was conjured up swirled together like the Colorado River's swift and quiet waters. All I know is that it didn't take me long to drift back to Juneteenth. I could see the strange fire of them coal-oil balls of rags—how they lit up the sky with orange-yellow tails when you tossed them as high as you could, and how they would crash to the ground, cinders flying everywhere. I could hear my mother holler out, "Go get you another, baby." I could smell the sweet smoke. I always wondered about this strange fire that gave you enough time to throw without burning you, like the fire of those fire eaters you see in the circus. They spit fire and nothing happens to them.

In this half-dream, I was already at the bottoms. There was tables and tables of food: ribs, sausage, corn on the cob, pies, pies, and more pies—peach, pecan, and lemon meringue—all lined up in a pretty row. In big old barrels full of chunks of ice was fire-engine red Kool-Aid and pink lemonade so sour it would lock your jaws up. All the same spirits was moving on the waters of the Colorado too: homemade chock and Johnny Walker Red. The Holy Spirit, thank God, was there to keep things in order because, as one of the old-timer domino players would say as he slammed big six down, "It's too good to be good."

Joy hovered over the face of deep, swirling the waters of the Colorado and stirring up the hearts of browned faces and feet. I could hear the clang of horseshoes crack like lightning and the thunder of dominoes slammed down by old men with hearty laughs. I could hear those same old men spin tall tales made taller with every drink. I could hear the cries of babies spooked by all the noise. The thick, wet night air mixed with the sweat of browned bodies running, dancing, laughing, and lying. There wasn't two sides to Bastrop there—the "haves" and the "have-nots"—divided by the M-K-T tracks. Everybody there had little but wanted for nothing. It felt good.

I dreamed all this in a half-dream as the hum of that old diesel engine and the rhythm of State Highway 304 rocked me like my momma. In half-sleep, I could see her round face, lit by my uncle's truck headlights, and I could smell the smoke of Juneteenth fire.

"Smoke. Smoke! Hey, son, wake up. Wake up! You smell that?" Choking and coughing, the elderly woman in the seat next to me shook my shoulders. Smoke had filled up the back of the bus. It smelled like burning leather.

"Hey, stop the bus! Something's burning back here," I hollered at the bus driver. I ran up there and grabbed him by the shoulders and yelled, "Hey man, something is burning back here." He pulled the bus off the road and slammed the doors open.

"Everybody out! Up front! Up front!" he shouted. All the passengers—it was about thirty of us—spilled out onto the side of the road, eyes watering, mouths spitting up soot, lungs burning. Smoke poured out of the luggage compartment from underneath, near the rear wheels. The driver ran back and got one of the fire extinguishers, but it was too small. By then, the smoke had grown thicker and blacker and had drifted over to the other side of the road, making it hard for cars on both sides to see. I thought as I helped that old lady find a place to sit to catch her breath that there's gonna be a wreck if they don't get this fire out. The driver got on his radio and called somebody to call the fire department.

Finally, two fire engines pulled up and put out the blaze, but that bus wasn't going nowhere. I overheard the driver and the firemen talking, saying it looked like somebody had forgot to close the lower compartment that separated the luggage from the engine batteries. Some of that baggage had shifted and shorted out a battery—that's what they figured.

We sat there for about an hour till another bus showed up to take us the rest of the way. I couldn't sleep. That fire rattled my spirit. I had a bad feeling after that. I told myself that ain't nothing but the devil trying to steal my joy. We finally rolled into the Bastrop bus station around midnight. Then it didn't matter. I was home.

I slept in late but not too late. The rattling of pots and pans woke me. Today was Juneteenth. I was at Juanita's folks' place, and they had already started cooking for the night. You know how they start cooking early for those big days—the cakes and pies first, the meats on pits later. Juanita cut me a big piece of buttermilk pound cake for breakfast and gave me a big old buttery kiss on the lips and asked, "You want to go to the store and pick up some things?"

"Yeah. What you want?"

She came back with a list and the keys to her daddy's '39 Ford. I gave her a big buttery kiss back and a pat on her baby belly. The Red & White grocery, here I come. But first, I stopped by my momma's house to see if she needed anything. I was banking on the winds of grace blowing with whoever she was working for this week, that she was allowed to work from home, knowing good and well Momma would be getting things ready for tonight. She gave me her list, then I was on my way. I took my time. With the windows down and a song on my lips—not sure what I was singing, but it was happy because I was happy, happier than I had been in a while—I eased on down Main Street to Mrs. Rosanky's place. That's what I called the Red & White because she was the owner and clerk.

The grocery market sat off Main Street, right in front of the bank. It hadn't changed in all them years we'd been trading there. It was a combination grocery store, feed store, and luncheonette. There was long aisles of canned goods, cereals, breads, candies, sugar, flour, and beans stacked from floor to ceiling. In back, there was a long meat counter. We traded there because, of all the grocery stores in Bastrop, she treated brown people like they was people. She didn't holler at you to hurry up or make you go to the back of the line. Maybe she was fairer because she was German. I figured her people was glad to be here—being strangers and all—and she might have understood the strangeness of how coloreds was treated—worse than strangers. Her people was all over Bastrop,

Elgin, Smithville, and Taylor. They had a hand in everything too: corn mills, cotton gins, blacksmith shops, and grocery stores. With her thick German accent and smile full of teeth, she'd speak to you liked she knew you—really knew you. Everybody had credit. That was good business as far as we was concerned. The Houstons didn't have much, but we did have a good name. If we said we'd pay, we paid. It might take a while, but we was good for it.

But today, it wasn't going to be credit. I had money in my pocket from working at the Osage Motor Company. It would feel good to walk through the aisles and fill up my basket and order what I wanted at the meat counter without having to suck up my pride and squeeze out those words, "Could you please put it on our account? Momma will be in as soon as she gets paid." No. Today it was going to be cash.

That bell above the door clanged as I pushed it open. She was busy at the checkout counter and didn't even look up as she greeted me, asking "Kann ich dir helfen?" in her usual broken German—or sometimes it was Czech—to see if I needed any help. Czechs were the other set of foreigners who was everywhere and in every business in Bastrop in search of a better life. Both had found what I was looking for: *dobrý život*—a better life for my pot of gold on the way.

I said, "Jak se máš, Mrs. Rosanky?" asking back how she was. I always spoke a little Czech to her because she liked to hear it. Maybe it reminded her of her "old country." Often, she referred to home, over there, wherever there was. "I'm good," I said. "You can help me with not one list, but two!"

She looked up when she heard my voice. "Well, I'll be, if it ain't Mr. Johnnie Roy. Jak se máš?" She always said my name with my first and middle name and a "mister" in front of it. I guess it helped her keep me straight from my brother. Whatever the reason, I liked how she called me.

"We're getting ready for Juneteenth, so I got a lot," I said.

She smiled, "Well, I tell you what, Mr. Johnnie Roy, you give me what you want from the meat counter, and I'll get it while you get the rest on your list." So she went on back, and I went down every aisle. It felt good—free—to not have to put something back on the shelf because it cost too much. I was a-humming and a-picking, a-picking and a-humming, even reaching for a Hershey chocolate bar, telling myself, "I bet Juanita would like this," knowing good and well it was really me wanting my favorite candy. Today was going to be that kind of day—a Hershey bar day.

With everything on my list in the basket, me and Mrs. Rosanky met back up at the front counter about the same time. She added it all up and gave me that big German smile. "Das will be twenty dollars even, Mr. Johnnie Roy."

With a grin that felt like it went from Smithville, east, to Taylor, west, I handed her a crisp twenty-dollar bill. I thanked her and strutted out the door with an arm full of groceries and a chest poking out with pride.

This was going to be a good—no, a great—day. It was Juneteenth.

When I got back in the car, I looked at the gas gauge and saw it was almost on empty, so I stopped at the filling station a block from the store and got some gas. Four dollars was enough. I filled her up with ethyl and drove to the house. With the car window down, my arm hanging out, and my hand tapping on the side of the door to the sound of Louis Armstrong's "Blues for Yesterday" on the radio, I cruised down Main Street. I wasn't much for singing, but I wasn't studden who heard me. I felt like singing, with that not-as-hot-as-it-could-be June air blowing my singing right back in my face. "I've got the blues for yesterday, it keeps on hauntin' me. I got the Blues deep down, the days that used to be." It didn't take long before I drove up to Juanita's folks' house, radio blasting, ready for some dominoes.

Before I could even get out of the car good, Juanita—with her mother, Lenora, right behind her—ran out crying, "The law looking for you!"

"Looking for me?" I asked. "What they looking for me for? I ain't did nothing."

Juanita was in tears. "I don't know."

I asked, "Who? Who come up here looking for me?"

She stammered, barely getting the words out, she was so upset. "Sh-sheriff Cartwright, Norman Owens, Dude Milton, Deputy Justice. All of 'em!"

I got out of the car hollering. "What they said they wanted?" I didn't mean to yell, but it didn't take much to set off my temper.

"They asked if you was here. They was looking for you, and they said they was looking for Ray too."

I asked, "For what?"

She said, "Beating up and taking some money off somebody. I told them you had gone down to Mrs. Rosanky's. You didn't see none of them downtown?"

I said, "Naw. I ain't seen none of those laws. Well, I'm gonna go back down there and see what they want."

I got back in the car and burned rubber to City Hall and went inside. There wasn't nobody in there. I went on down to the courthouse, a few blocks down, and drove around back to the jailhouse parking lot, and knocked on the rear door where the jailer stayed. There wasn't nobody there. One of them prisoners hollered down from the third-floor window, "They all gone. They out looking for somebody."

I walked around to the courthouse, all the while my heart was trying to throw a piston. My mind was racing ninety-to-nothing. I knew that if Owens and Dude Milton and them was looking for me, it wasn't good. They was the same laws that ran up on us at the swimming hole, messing with us, threatening to take us to jail for nothing. It was their way of putting fear in us so that when we got older, we'd know our place. And it worked, because I was scared. But I had no reason to be. I ain't done nothing.

There wasn't nobody in the courthouse, either, so I got back in the car and took off to my daddy's house. He lived about three miles out of town. When I drove up, he came out of the barn and walked to the car. I asked, "Daddy, you hear anything about Ray or somebody robbing somebody, beating somebody up?"

He said, "Naw, I ain't heard a thing."

I told him I was looking for the laws because they was looking for me and Ray. My daddy said, "Well, son, I don't blame you. You doing the right thing. You know you ain't did nothing. You ain't got nothing to be running for. Just stick around down at the jailhouse. You'll run into some of them soon enough." My daddy had his own run-ins with the law for no reason, except for too much drinking, so I knew he could tell me what all this meant, but "just stick around" didn't set right with me. "Just stick around" was what I saw old Black men do around here who had given up, who let Bastrop get the best of them. I wasn't sticking around waiting for something bad to happen, but something still tugged at me saying, "Don't run. Don't run." So I went back to the car waiting for whatever.

I didn't have to wait long.

Down the road came a big old cloud of dust like one of them August dust devils that pop up when the cotton fields are bare and bone dry. It was a car—not a police car but a civilian car—moving like there was no tomorrow. It had those little red emergency lights in the front grill, flashing. There was another car—this one a police car—High Sheriff Ed Cartwright's car—running close behind. It didn't look like they was going to stop in time before they hit me or the barn. The front car fishtailed one way, and the rear car, the other way—barely missing one another, kicking up rocks and dirt as they came to a stop. Out of that cloud jumped Norman Owens, eyes fixed on me like a bloodhound on a rabbit, his straw cowboy hat pressed half-cocked up his forehead. Before he said a thing, I walked up to him and asked, "You looking for me?"

"What's your name?" he shouted back.

I shouted back at him, "Y'all know my name. My name is Johnnie Houston, Johnnie Roy Houston."

"You doggone right we looking for you, nigger. Where you been?"

I said, "I been running all over town trying to find out why y'all looking for me. I ain't done nothing."

"Well, I don't know about that. Turn around and let me handcuff you," Owens said out the side of a mouth dripping with tobacco juice. "Turn around here now. Don't give me no trouble."

"You don't need no handcuffs on me, man. I ain't did nothing." My voice went high in my nose like it always did when I got agitated. I was a firecracker ready to pop. "If I had done something and wanted to get away, I could have been to Mexico by now."

"Well, we gonna play it safe. Now turn around," Owens barked. Sheriff Cartwright didn't say a word. He watched as Owens handcuffed me, put me in the car, and raced to the jailhouse raising up a bigger cloud of dust. I wasn't believing what was happening: one minute I was toting arms full of bags of groceries to celebrate Juneteenth, and the next minute I'm riding in the back of a police car, hog-tied. That fire on the bus had been a sign. Something bad was going down.

Those other flunky deputies, Dude Milton and M. A. Justice, sat in the back with me like I was gonna jump out and take off running in handcuffs. No one said a word except for Deputy Owens, who kept talking like he was in charge. It was the longest three miles of my life. All I could think of was that I ain't done nothing wrong. This will be over as soon as I tell them where I been all day—with my in-laws and at the Red & White store. They carried me back downtown to the courthouse, up the long stairs to a little room the sheriff used as an office, and sat me down there. Sheriff Cartwright looked me square in my eyes with his face an inch from mine. I could smell the tobacco and bourbon on his breath. "Well, you want to tell us about it?"

"Tell you about what?"

"About that man you beat up and robbed out there in the country early this morning."

I said, "Man, I ain't beat up nobody and robbed nobody this morning. I was at my father-in-law's house in bed with my wife. I didn't get up till round about seven o'clock. Then I went down to the Red & White store to get meat and stuff for my wife to get ready for the Juneteenth. When I got back to my father-in-law's house, I met them standing at the door crying, talking about the law had been there looking for me. I knew I ain't done nothing, so I told them I was going on downtown to find some of y'all to see what y'all was looking for me for."

"Well, you might as well come on out and tell us because we know you did it," Owens snapped back.

One of the other deputies, Dude Milton, got up and opened the door and said, "Why don't you run? Why don't you get up and run? Run on out the door—the door is open."

I said, "Man, what's the best I get for jumping up and running? Y'all will shoot me in the back saying I was trying to escape. If you going to shoot me, you might as well shoot me right here where I'm sitting."

Deputy Eskew joined them. I was a coon up a tree, surrounded by bloodhounds. Eskew said, "Well, we're going to carry you over to the jail and lock you up. And you better be ready to make a confession when we get you up there, or we're going to kill you."

They carried me to the third floor where all the cells was. "All right everybody. Rack up," Eskew shouted. Everybody up there who was in the "run-around" where inmates was allowed to congregate freely had to get back in their own cells. They locked them all up. Then Eskew opened up a cell at the far end and said, "All right, nigger, come on out of there." And there he was—Ray. He walked out that cell—my brother—not saying a word. He looked long and hard at me with those trouble eyes. On his face was that grin I had seen a million times, but this time, it felt different. I knew his look. When he took the meat off my plate when we was boys, he had that look. But I knew he was mostly playing back then. When he would run off to Rufus Jackson's to gamble and I had to go get him, he had that grin. It meant he was aiming to get his way. But today, that look was mixed with something I had never seen before—it was mixed with sorrow.

I looked at him just as hard. As we met each other at that cell door, we was no more than a foot apart, so close I could reach out and grab him and ask him, "Ray, what have you done?" But I didn't. He walked right by me, and we traded places. I was led into that cell; Ray walked out to freedom. As the guard slammed my door, they opened up all those other cell doors, and let those other guys back out in the runaround area.

That was the beginnings of my Juneteenth. About two hours later, I heard keys rattling at my cell door. My favorite day was about to go from bad to a hell I wouldn't wish on my worst enemy.

seven

CONFESSION

NORMAN OWENS BARGED THROUGH THE CELL DOOR with the other flunkies following so close that if he'd tripped, they'd have fallen like dominoes: Dude Milton, David Eskew (the Gun Slinger) and M. A. Justice. They was all called constables or deputies or marshals at some point. It didn't matter what they called themselves. To me, they was all flunkies of one man, the High Sheriff Ed Cartwright. He controlled them all. They had taken off their guns. But they strutted into the cell with shit-eating smiles and surrounded me with blackjacks in their hands.

"Now, Johnnie, we know you did this. We're gonna go downstairs to the district attorney, and he's gonna have some papers for you to sign saying what you did. Now go on and sign them so we can get this over with and go home," Owens ordered, spitting tobacco juice in a coffee cup.

I snapped back at him, "I ain't signing nothing 'cause I ain't done nothing." No sooner had I got that second *nothing* out of my mouth than a blackjack club came down hard on the back of my head. It nearly knocked me off that cot. A fist from the other direction knocked me nearly right side up.

"Now, Houston, I told you we ain't got time for this. You're gonna sign this confession, and we'll be through for the night, or we can put another knot on your head." No sooner had Owens got out *knot* than another whop came down from the other direction.

This one was harder than the first. I could barely see straight. Their faces went blurry. My ears was ringing, and I could barely make out what they was saying. *Whop!* There came another hit with a blackjack, this time across the side of my face, knocking the sound right back into me.

"Oh, you're gonna sign it, nigger. We ain't got all night," Deputy Justice said. All of a sudden, I couldn't keep my head up. The next thing I knew I was on the floor. I must have passed out. Like tuning a radio, my hearing came in and out, until finally I could make out what they was saying. "Get him up. He's ready to sign." They grabbed me by my arms and led me downstairs.

We went into an office. An old man in a suit, sitting in one of those big, swiveling office chairs, peeped over his glasses at me. They called him "DA Williams." This man gave me a pen and some papers. "Here you go, boy. Sign it on the second page."

It took a minute for me to make out the words: "I, Johnnie Roy Houston, on the 19th of June, 1946, sometime between 4 and 6 a.m. did by force, rob a Dr. H. B. Combs, inflicting bodily harm—"

"I didn't tell you to read it. I said sign it," one of those deputies said, and then, *whop*—a blackjack nearly took my head off. Owens got right in my face after they picked me up. "He didn't say read it. He said sign it."

I fired back, "I ain't signing nothing without a lawyer."

They all laughed. Then Cartwright, watching from the corner of the room, said, "You don't have a lawyer, and if any lawyer shows up here, he's gonna get what you're getting. The best thing you can do is sign these here papers."

"I don't know nothing about robbing Dr. Combs. I got into town last night. You can ask my wife—"

Before I could get out *my wife* good, Owens whacked me right on top of my head. Then he reached out, opened a drawer and grabbed his gun, drew back the hammer. "Oh yeah, you're gonna sign it. Now tell me you ain't signing it. We didn't ask you nothing about your wife, now did we? We got the witness who says you done it. We got the victim who says you done it. Now sign this here confession, or we're gonna kill you."

By now my left eye had swelled up almost closed. Blood ran down my neck. I told them again, "I ain't signing no confession." This time I was knocked to the floor. I could feel the tip of a cowboy boot pressed into my cheek.

Owens said, "Now Johnnie, you can walk out of here, or we can drag you out feet first and you'll never see that sweet momma of yours again. It don't matter to me none."

Part of me was thinking about bolting for that door, swinging as I went, but I was nothing but about 190 pounds, and them two deputies was big, twice my size. They would have wrestled me to the ground and shot me, claiming I resisted arrest. If I didn't sign that confession, they was gonna beat me till I was as good as dead.

Owens shoved that pistol close to my face. "Now tell me again you ain't gonna sign." Milton and Justice got me up off that floor, then put that pen in my hand. "Sign it here and date it 'June 19, 1946,'" Owens instructed.

I scribbled on the line.

As those two flunkies dragged me back up to the cell, I could hear Owens tell them, "We might ought to call Doc Bryson to look at that cut on his head. Hurry up and clean him up. It'll take an hour for the doc to get here from Elgin." Fading in and out, I didn't even hear that cell door slam. But what did stick in my head as I sunk into unconsciousness was the date they told me to put on that confession—June 19, 1946 … June 19 … June …

◆ ◆ ◆

"Johnnie Roy, Johnnie Roy, wake up, baby."

"Momma, Momma," I mumbled through a jaw swollen as a bullfrog's. None of this could be real, just a bad dream. I always used to call out for my momma when I had bad dreams. But it was strange how close she sounded.

The voice grew louder. "Johnnie Roy, it's your momma. Wake up, baby." Then there was the familiar smell of lye-soap hands, Royal Crown hair pomade, and the starch of fresh-pressed clothes—the scents of my momma. It wasn't no dream. I turned my head, and there she was.

"Oh, my God!" She lost her breath when she saw my face. "Oh, my God! What they done done to you?" Tears rolled down her face.

"Momma, they beat me, them laws. They say I robbed and beat up Dr. Combs. I ain't done no such thing. You know that."

She brushed aside the tears with her balled-up fist and told me, "I know you didn't. When you didn't come back from Mrs. Rosanky's by noon, I got worried. So I walked to Juanita's to see if they seen you. They was crying, talking about how the laws had been looking for you about some robbery. I know you couldn't have done it." She caught her breath like she 'bout to cry. "I need to tell you something about your brother."

I had a feeling that Ray had something to do with all this. I told her, "Momma, when they locked me in here, Ray came out of this cell."

She said, "I went looking for Ray, so I went on down to Mr. Rufus's. If he was going to be anywhere, he'd be there. When I got down there, there was talk about him and Red Winston having been there. Mr. Rufus told me they was gambling with blood money, bragging about what they had done, how they knocked Mr. Big Shot Bastrop in the head and took what was due them. Johnnie Roy, I don't know where they at now, but I'm gonna get to the bottom of this and get you out."

No sooner had she said that, than one of them deputies opened up the outer door. "Time's up. I told you, Mrs. Houston, you only had a few minutes. Y'all need to finish up, you hear?"

Momma put her arms around me and hugged me hard, but was careful not to press against my broken face. She drew me near to her mouth and whispered, "I'm gonna get you out of here if it's the last thing I do. Don't do nothing crazy. Momma is coming back." As the guard grabbed her hand to loosen her from me, she broke down. Her chest rose then fell. Out came a moan like the moan of a slaughtered animal when they gut it—air and blood and bowels rushing out. That was the sound she made when that deputy pried her last fingers clamped hard around my arm. "No, God, no! Let me loose. Let my boy out of here," she screamed.

I told her, "Wait till I get my hands on Ray. I'm gonna kill him. I'm gonna kill him."

She hung onto the cell bars, her weight fighting against them deputies who was pulling her by the arm, ripping her sleeve. She yelled at the top of her voice, "Y'all let me go." They finally hauled her out with her last words ringing down the hallway. "I'm gonna get you out, Johnnie Roy."

"Goddamn Ray," I said as I fell on my cot. "Goddamn Ray."

The next morning, that doctor from Elgin—Dr. Bryson—dressed up my wounds. He said I'd live, but the look on his face said, "By the grace of God." Deputy Eskew banged on the cell bars an hour later. "Get up, Houston. Time for a little trip."

"Where we going?" The way they beat up on me, a "little trip" could have meant anything, but nothing good. He handcuffed me and led me downstairs to Deputy Owens's car. "Where y'all taking me?"

Eskew snapped back, "You know where we're going—where you did what you did." He turned east on Pine and headed out to the country. We went about three miles to a spot where the pine trees thinned to a clearing hidden from the road. "Get out, nigger. We here."

"Where?"

There was an old barbed wire fence that surrounded a house a nail or two away from being a pile of wood. Eskew yanked me by the arm, not caring if I hit the side of my swollen head against the door. Owens and Eskew led me down the path to that house. "Put your foot down here. This here is your print," Owens said.

Right there was a footprint in the clay soil. I said, "That ain't none of my footprints. Look here. My foot's too big." I put my foot alongside the print, but he tried to force my foot on top of it. I knew what he was trying to do. If I would have put my foot down on it, it would have wiped it out, leaving my print. Then he would have claimed that there was a fit. "I ain't doing no such thing. That ain't my footprint," I snapped back at him.

"The hell it ain't." Justice whopped me upside the head, then grabbed my foot as Owens held me. He jammed it right over that footprint.

Eskew chirped all the way to the car, "I told you it was gonna be a fit."

I didn't want to get into it with him because I knew what he was made of, what he did to a soldier from Camp Swift, the Army base just outside of town. I heard with my own ears when I was working as a busboy at a café right before I went to work at Swift. A bunch of them soldiers was at the café raising Cain, messing with the customers. It got out of hand, and the owner called the law. Eskew showed up, and one thing led to another. He shot a soldier, shot him dead. I was in the kitchen, but I heard it all. In my mind now was this: if Eskew would shoot a man—a soldier—in broad daylight in front of everybody and God, then it weren't no telling what he'd do to me down here in these backwoods. It would be his word against mine, except I wouldn't have no word because I'd be dead.

We made it back to the jailhouse. As Eskew led me upstairs, he promised me that I'd be lucky to ever see a judge. "You wait till it gets out that your footprint matched the one at the scene of the offense. The men of this town is gonna hand out their own justice. Y'all niggers get all liquored up for that damn Juneteenth bullshit and can't keep your hands off one of our prized citizens—hell, our doctor and banker. Yes, sir. People are pretty stirred up, stirred up enough to take the opportunity to pull your ass out of that cell—the cell that might be accidentally left unlocked one night. And then wait and see if you ain't fitted for a good old-fashion rope necktie."

"Now, you cut out all that talk about putting anything around anybody's neck," Deputy Owens cracked back at Eskew. "Old Johnnie here is gonna have his day in court." They both laughed under their breath, but it wasn't no joke. If Sheriff Cartwright couldn't keep his deputies from shooting a soldier in broad daylight, it wasn't nothing for the jailhouse doors to be accidentally left open.

I didn't sleep none that night or much of any the nights of those three months and fourteen days it took them to bring me to trial. Until then I lived in fear, not knowing if I was even gonna make it to trial. I'd lie in my cot late at night, jumping at every door slam, every car honk, every headlight flicker catching the corner of my cell window from the traffic below, every footstep down the hall when everybody was supposed to be gone. I'd lie there thinking about the story my momma told me about what they did to Tobe Cook back before I was born. Seemed, too, like every old person had a recollection of what they called the "Pecan Tree Lynching." It was part of the soul-story of Bastrop. Oh, they hang whoever they please in Bastrop. I might be next.

A day or two after Eskew's threat, I got my first visit from Juanita. "Oh my God, Johnnie, what happened to your face?" They had to bring her a chair—her so full with the baby and all. The sight of me hit her hard. "Who did this to you?"

"Who you think?" That's all I said. I was ashamed my wife had to see me this way. The look on her face looking at my face was almost too much to handle. But I wasn't going to break down and upset her even more. "Don't you worry none about me. How's the baby?"

Juanita's voice was shaking like she was about to cry. She took a deep breath and got under control and said, "She fine. Kicks like crazy." She put my hand on her belly, and the baby kicked. "Don't you worry about us. We got to get you out of here. They say Ray know something too, but he says he don't." She took a long pause, then the dam broke. Tears poured down. "What we gonna do?"

It started me to tear up, but I held back as best I could. I told her, "You let Momma and them take care of this. I don't want you up here again. You hear me? I don't want you to see me like this. It ain't good for the baby, you getting all upset." I hugged her but not too hard then yelled, "Guard, we through here."

She wiped the tears from my swollen face and said, "I love you."

"I love you too," I told her. "You don't need to be up here again." The guard took her away. Then I broke down for the first time since I been up there.

Four days after my arrest—June 24—they had a grand jury hearing to officially indict me. It was really a trial before the trial. The High Sheriff, Ed Cartwright, and all his deputies were witnesses along with a Dr. Joe Flemings out of Elgin. I don't know why him. It was Dr. Bryson who tended to me. But the main witness to identify me was Dr. H. B. Combs. It didn't matter that his mind wasn't right—fresh from a beating.

Judge John Tate asked all the questions. "Now, Dr. Combs, we know you can't walk up here with your injuries, so you can stay there in your wheelchair."

The bailiff swore him in, "Do you swear to tell the truth, the whole truth, nothing but the truth, so help you God?"

"I do," Dr. Combs said, in a whisper like he just got up from sleep. I hardly recognized him. He had a bandage around his head, nearly covering his forehead to his eyebrows. His arm was in a sling. He was already a skinny man, but he looked even skinnier than before. I thought, seeing him like that, that whoever did that was low as a dog. Dr. Combs was a good man—sometimes. One time he refused to pay me and Ray for some work we did for him. Me and Ray confronted him. And he finally paid us. That was the only time I was sideways with him. We got our money and that was it. At least it was with me. I couldn't speak for Ray. I didn't say a word about this. Nobody would believe Dr. Combs wasn't a saint.

The judge sat up. "Dr. Combs, can you tell me what happened to you on the morning of June nineteenth?"

He didn't say nothing for almost two minutes, like he was trying to wake up from a nap, trying to focus. You could see he wasn't right, his head resting heavy in his hands.

The judge spoke to him again, "Dr. Combs, did you hear the question? I know this is difficult for you. We need you to speak up so the jury can hear you. What happened to you on June nineteenth?"

He started slow. "Well, I got a call that someone needed a doctor somewhere outside of town. I didn't know where it was, so I met the caller—he called himself Henry—at the bus station, and we drove out to an abandoned farm. Then …" He stopped in the middle of his sentence and put his hands up to his head again to hold it up like it was too heavy, like a watermelon too heavy for the vine.

The judge jumped in like he was agitated, like he had some place to go. "Go on, Dr. Combs. And we need you to speak up."

Dr. Combs continued. "When I started to walk to the house, somebody jumped me, hit me in the head, and knocked me to the ground. He took my wallet. I had about thirty dollars."

The judge asked, "Now, Doctor, I need you to take your time, all the time you need, and tell the court who hit you and took your money? Did the suspect, Johnnie Roy Houston, assault you?"

"Umm—I don't know," he mumbled.

The judge sat up in his chair, his face beet red. His voice got tight like a rubber band. "Dr. Combs, I need to ask you again. Did Johnnie Roy Houston assault you that morning?"

Three times the doctor mumbled, "I don't know." Each time his voice got lower. Each time the judge got more frustrated and asked him again. Finally, Dr. Combs took a long pause, rubbed his forehead, and lowered his head. The judge, the grand jury, and the district attorney—Leslie Williams, the same man that had handed me the pen to sign that confession—leaned in. It was so quiet, you could hear the second hand of that clock that hung above the judge's bench go tick, tick, tick. "Um, yes, he's the one."

With that said, the judge dismissed the grand jury. They came back an hour later with something called a "true bill." It meant to me that everything they heard, they thought was true. I thought, If this is what "true" looks like, a lie has a twin, and I'm in deep shit.

◆ ◆ ◆

One night not long after the pretrial, my worst fears came true. It was about ten o'clock. Eskew was gone, probably to the colored side of town, messing with people like he liked to do, arresting anybody for looking at him the wrong way or drinking too much or settling gambling debts with his fists. It didn't matter to him. He liked messing with colored people. It made him feel good about his worthless self. Deputy Owens, who lived in the basement of the jailhouse because they couldn't pay him—his car was gone too. There wasn't nobody in the other cells that night. All of a sudden, I heard a bunch of trucks pull up in the parking lot outside my window. By the full moon, I could see twenty, maybe thirty, men piling out carrying ropes and bats. Some of them had shotguns. They was talking loud enough for me to hear: "Leave them running. It ain't gonna take long." I heard footsteps up the back stairs. Late at night, you could hear a mouse fart, it was so quiet in that jail. So I nearly messed my pants when I heard them footsteps. I knew it. Eskew done left that back door open.

I heard the doorknob to the cell common area *click, clank, click,* but it didn't open. They tried turning it again. Nothing.

"Goddamn it," one of them said. "Eskew was supposed to leave it unlocked."

Another of them cussed, "Now where the hell is shit-for-brains Eskew?"

Then one of them hollered out for me to hear, "We coming back, nigger. You sit tight, you hear?"

I heard them run down the front stairs, no doubt headed to the basement looking for Owens. The next thing I heard was them getting back in their trucks. "If he's any place, he's at Grandy's." They burned rubber, cussing and a fussing. Every tick of that clock that hung in the commons area felt like it took a day as I waited for them to come back. If they found Eskew or Owens, I was a dead man.

They didn't come back. I don't know what happened. Maybe they couldn't find him. Maybe he was out drunk somewhere. Maybe it was too late to come back when they found him. All I knew was, they didn't come back.

I started to think maybe God got in the way. Momma used to say, "Just because you don't see God move, don't mean he ain't moving." I wasn't much on God. I went to church, but church wasn't in me. It was something I did for Momma. And I did like to see her play that piano and hear that preacher at the Mount Rose Baptist Church say, "Whup on it, Sister Houston, whup on it! Knock the ivory off it!" Other than that, I didn't have much to do with church or God. But that night when them men with ropes didn't get to me, I began to see what my momma was saying.

That posse never did try again.

I didn't go to trial right away because they had to wait till Dr. Combs recovered from his beating. Being seventy-five years old, it took every bit of that three months for him to get right. But they finally set my trial for September 13, 1946. I circled it on a calendar Momma brought me to mark the days until I got out. During those long days of waiting, I thought about the what-ifs: What if I'd decided to stayed in Corpus, skip Juneteenth, and make some money? What if they couldn't find a replacement bus for that bus that caught fire, the one I was on when I came back to Bastrop? I would not have been where they claimed I was. What if that midwife never wrote on my birth certificate, "Two boys"?

Another day I circled on that calendar was Sunday, August 18, 1946, because I got a special visitor. Juanita pushed past the guard with a bundle in her arms. "Well, what do you think? She looks like you." Juanita pulled back the blanket, and there she was—all seven pounds, twenty-one inches of her. "Look at that nose. I want to call her Arlene. I don't know why. I just like the name, and I ain't studden you if you want to call her something else."

I didn't say a word for a minute. I just looked at her. I didn't want to hold her at first—didn't want to drop her—my pot of gold named Arlene. "She does look like me a little. Arlene is fine. Whatever you want to call her is OK by me." I stuck my finger out, and she took told of it like it was the last weed on the bank.

Juanita smiled. "Go ahead and hold her. She ain't gonna break. She was born on Friday, and they didn't want me to take her out till me and her got stronger. But I told them I wasn't studden them. So here we are."

I cradled her, not knowing what I was doing, but when she opened her almond-shaped eyes—eyes like her momma's—and smiled, I knew nothing in the world was ever gonna be as good as this. I forgot I was in jail. I put my face to her face and whispered, "Rainbow." She cooed. I held her for a good hour.

"Visiting time over in there," the guard shouted.

As I handed Arlene back, Juanita started to tear up. "Johnnie, your momma and them getting up some money to get you a lawyer. I think he's out of Waco." The guard grabbed her by the arm. "I love you, Johnnie Roy."

"I love y'all too. Don't bring her up here again," I said and turned away as quick as I could. "I'm getting out of here soon enough."

The day after Labor Day, ten days before the trial, Momma visited me again. "Johnnie Roy, how you doing, baby?" I didn't have the heart to tell how I really was—how they tried to lynch me, how I wasn't sleeping or eating. I could see on her face this whole thing was hard on her. Her normally round face was drawn in and full of lines. She hugged me and said, "We got you a lawyer. He's out of Waco. His name is Harold Walden." She was looking at a piece of paper, struggling to read. "Harold Weta Walden," she said.

"Momma, y'all can't afford no lawyer, let alone someone out of town," I said. I learned later from Mozell that my Grandma Atkins sold her home to get me that lawyer. She had one of the biggest homes in Bastrop for a Negro. It had three bedrooms and plenty of fruit trees in the yard: peaches, plums, pears, and blackberry vines. Me and my brother used to go down to her house and pick berries till our hands was as blue as a bluebird. Then we'd come in, and she'd bake us a cobbler. She was part Indian: her hair, jet-black and straight; her nose, narrow with a crook; her skin, cinnamon colored. She frowned all the time like the Indian carving in front of those drug stores. Me and my brother wouldn't give up till we got her to crack a smile. We'd trick her into calling me, "Ray," and calling Ray, "Roy." We'd change clothes to confuse her. "Ray, get in here," she would holler. I'd holler back, "I'm Roy." She'd finally crack a little smile. "Y'all got me." I loved going to her house. It was a good day whenever we'd go to Grandma Atkins's. Now, that house—the house where I was born—belonged to somebody else so we could pay for some lawyer out of Waco. It made me sick to my stomach that all this had to be done for me when I knew I ain't done nothing they claimed.

"Now, Johnnie," my momma said, holding my hand as she was leaving, pulling me close so Deputy Justice couldn't hear, "Your brother done took off to West Texas somewhere to pick cotton, he and Red Winston. He might not be at your trial. I'm gonna get to the bottom of this. You tell that lawyer what you know. Let God do the rest."

The next time I'd see her would be the morning of the trial.

eight

THE TRIAL

FINALLY, TRIAL DAY WAS HERE—September 13, 1946—Friday the thirteenth. Now, I wasn't superstitious, but I had an uneasy feeling and upset stomach on that morning. Maybe it was because I was going to trial in an hour, and I hadn't yet seen nothing looking like a lawyer. Maybe this Mr. Harold Weta Walden believed in unlucky days, so he had decided not to show up.

The trial was set to start at nine o'clock. Finally, a few minutes after eight, in walked Mr. Walden. He stuck his hands between the bars and introduced himself. "Mr. Houston, I am Harold Weta Walden." He was an old man—maybe fifty—but if he was fifty, it was a hard fifty. His calloused hand had the shakes. He said, "Now, I have looked at their evidence and your confession. The best thing here is we plead guilty and maybe they'll go easy on you. You know how it is around here."

"Man, I ain't pleading guilty to a damn thing!" The veins in my temples was about to burst out of my head. "What kind of lawyer is you? You ain't asked me what happen. You ain't asked me what kind of evidence I got. You ain't asked me how they got that confession!"

I had got so loud, I bet they could hear me all over that jailhouse. The guard cracked open the cell door and asked, "You all right in here, Mr. Walden?"

"Yeah, yeah. Give us a minute," he told the guard. Turning

back to me without even much looking me in the eye, he said, "All right, you tell me what happened."

"Well, I came up here from Corpus Christi to celebrate Juneteenth. I just got paid from working for my brother at the Osage Motor Company. I didn't need no money. I went to the Red & White grocery store to get what we needed to cook. I had money to pay for the food. My wife and mother-in-law knew I was at the store. Mrs. Rosanky waited on me. I talked to her. She'll tell you I was at the store." The words came flying out my mouth so fast I could hardly keep up with my thoughts. I got louder and faster. "I went looking for the police when I found out they was looking for me. Now if I had beat up someone and stole their money, why would I go looking for the police?" By now, Walden was looking me in my eyes. He could see I wasn't lying. "And when they caught up with me and brought me down here, I saw my twin brother walking out the cell they put me in."

Walden asked, "What about that confession they have and the footprint they have?"

"They ain't got shit. They beat that out of me. I had to say what they wanted me to say to save my life. And that footprint ain't none of mine. My foot's too big." By now, I was boiling over.

Walden tried to calm me down. "Now look here, son, you can plead not guilty if you want. I can't guarantee you'll get justice. There are twelve people out there in that courtroom who live in this community. They go to Dr. Combs when they need a doctor—hell, when they need money, they go to his bank. Hell, they can't mail a letter without him. Do you really think they're going to let this go without some blood? They're going to get some blood. The only choice you have is how much they're going to get. You plead guilty, they may not give you the chair. You go in there fighting, and I tell you they're going to get their pound of flesh. You know what I'm trying to say to you, Mr. Houston?"

"I know one thing. I ain't guilty, and I ain't done nothing. Now you my lawyer or ain't you? Not guilty—that's my plea." No sooner had I said that, than Owens and Justice came in my cell with ankle chains. I told them, "Now y'all don't have to do that. I don't want my momma to see me in chains. I ain't running nowhere."

"We ain't got a choice," Owens said as he jangled them in my face. "Now don't give us any trouble." He led me down the stairs—*jingle, jangle, jingle, jangle* with every shuffle of my feet. Because all I could do was shuffle like an old man, it took forever to get down the stairs. Walden tried to tell me something, but I didn't hear him. All I could hear was my shuffling, sliding feet and that jangle, like the jangle of a chain you put on a junkyard dog. Sounds like that are the sounds that get in your head and never get out. I bowed my head the whole time. When we got down to the second floor, we took a right down the hall that led to a walkway that took us to the courthouse.

The hallway led us to a heavy wood door with a sign above it: Twenty-First District Court, Bastrop County, Texas, Judge John H. Tate—the same judge who had sat at the grand jury hearing. As I stepped in the room, that jangle was the only sound I could hear—no people talking, no chairs squeaking, no papers shuffling. As I looked up, all eyes was on those chains. When I turned to the left and looked out, my eyes caught my mother's eyes. I could see her doubled over like somebody had punched her. Mozell was holding her up. Ray was next to Mo. I was surprised he showed up after Momma had said he and Red had run off to West Texas. I glanced at him, but he wasn't about to look me in the eyes.

The few Negroes they let in the courtroom was in the back and on the left side. The whites sat on the right. Somebody in the rear cried out, "Oh, God. Jesus help," when they saw me chained up. Right then, all the other sounds rushed back into the room: the whispering people, the shuffling papers, squeaking chairs, and the jingle, jangle of my chains.

They led me to a seat next to my lawyer, who was at one desk in front of the judge. On the other side was the district attorney,

Leslie D. Williams, the man who gave me the pen to sign that confession. I bet a dime on a dollar he wrote it too. He looked the same—not in how I remembered him from that night—but in how he looked like all the other old white men in crisp white shirts and khaki-colored suits, wearing business-as-usual smiles, the ones who controlled the affairs of this town and kept their heels on the necks of brown folks in Bastrop County. My lawyer, the DA, the judge—they looked the same too. Like the cotton gin man who cheated us at the scales, like the movie theater manager who made us sit upstairs, like the man at the hamburger stand who called us "niggers" and made us go in the back to get us our food—they all was one face to me. They say *we* all look alike. To me, they do. And all them faces in that court room told me one thing: nothing was going to change this morning.

As the judge, dressed in a black robe, walked in, a man in uniform like a deputy's shouted, "All rise! The honorable Judge John Tate, Twenty-First District Court of Texas, presiding." The judge sat behind his big desk. Then that deputy man turned and shouted, "The State of Texas versus Johnnie Roy Houston, case number 3834. You may be seated."

The judge said, "Mr. Williams, is the State ready to proceed?"

The DA replied, "Yes, Your Honor. We are."

The judge spoke again. "Mr. Walden, is the defense ready?"

Walden said in a shaky voice, "We are, Your Honor. If it please the court, the defense would like present a motion to dismiss due to the forced confession."

The judge banged his desk with a big hammer. "Seeing that your motion to strike said confession was presented to the court before the court's main charges have been read to the jury, your motion is denied."

I snapped in the ear of Walden, "Man, how can they do that? They beat that confession out of me, and we can't claim that?"

Walden said, "Shush, keep it low. I told you how they're going to be. I'll re-present the motion later if they let me."

"If they let you?" I said to him. He didn't react. *Shit, I'm sure enough in trouble.*

Walden shushed me again. Then turning to the judge, he said, "Your Honor, the defense has filed application for the benefits of the suspended sentence provision, asking that my client—having never been convicted of a felony in this state or any other state and since his general reputation is good—that if convicted, he be placed on probation instead of jail."

"Probation!" I fired back in Walden's ear, but I knew the whole court could hear me. "Man, I ain't been convicted of nothing to be put on probation for."

"Shush. This is procedure," he whispered to me, never looking me in the eye.

The judge said, "Is there a problem here, Mr. Walden? If not, let's get this going."

"No problem, Your Honor," Walden mumbled back.

The clock on the wall read 9:05 a.m.

"Bailiff, read the charges," ordered the judge.

The deputy man who had first said "All rise"—now I knew he was the bailiff—he faced the court, all prim and proper, and read the charges like he was reading a truth already settled in heaven:

> The defendant, Johnnie Roy Houston, on or about the nineteenth of June, AD one thousand and nine hundred and forty-six and before the presentment of this indictment in the County of Bastrop and State of Texas, in and upon H. B. Combs did make an assault, and then and there, by the said assault, and by violence to the said H. B. Combs, and by putting said H. B. Combs in fear of his life, the defendant did rob H. B. Combs of thirty dollars.

The judge looked directly at me and asked, "How do you plea?" I looked him square in the eyes and said, "I ain't guilty."

That DA started things off. "Your Honor, we call to the stand Sheriff Ed Cartwright." The sheriff was a tall man who wore boots with spurs that jingled and jangled when he walked too. But his walk was a strut, not a shuffle. When he strutted like a rooster into a room or a store, or strolled down the street, everybody knew who was in charge. He wore a big tan cowboy hat that covered his face. It was almost like he was looking through the hat. He was in charge of this moment. I heard people say about justice around here, "Whatever the sheriff says, goes." I was about to find out.

The bailiff said to him, "Do you swear to tell the truth, the whole truth, and nothing but the truth?"

He mumbled, "I sure do."

The DA asked him, "On the day of June nineteenth, can you tell me how you encountered Dr. H. B. Combs?"

"I—we—got a call from Dr. H. B. Combs that he had been beat up and robbed. So, I went out to his office. From the evidence we gathered, this is what happened: About eleven p.m. on June eighteenth, someone, who gave his name as Henry, called Dr. Combs over the telephone and said that his wife was very sick and wanted him to come to see her. The doctor informed the party that he did not make any night calls. Sometime late during the night another telephone call came, but the doctor again declined to respond. Then about five-thirty a.m., on the nineteenth, the party called again and asked the doctor to come see his wife. At this time, he agreed."

The sheriff basically testified what Combs said at the indictment: Combs went out to this house after getting a call from someone named Henry, was hit in the head, and robbed of thirty dollars.

The DA asked, "And who did Dr. Combs say did this?"

Cartwright said in a tobacco-chewing slur, "He said one of the Houston boys, Johnnie Ray or Johnnie Roy."

The DA asked, "Did he say which one?"

Cartwright said, "Not at first. He was still kind of stunned from the attack. So we picked up both of them. Later at the grand jury hearing, he identified his assailant as Johnnie Roy Houston."

"I have no other questions, Your Honor." The DA smiled and walked back to his seat.

"Your witness, Mr. Walden," the judge said, not looking up from the newspaper he was reading.

"No questions, Your Honor," Walden mumbled as he shuffled some papers. He didn't even bother to look up either. I wanted to say, "Man, you ain't gonna ask him nothing like why they let my brother go or who was this Henry person? Dr. Combs knew me and my brother because we rented from him and worked for him since we were kids. He knew our voices. We couldn't have fooled him on the phone." But I kept it to myself.

Williams turned to the judge and said, "The State would like to call Deputy Norman Owens to the stand." Owens strolled up there like he was going to a Sunday picnic. Williams asked him, "How did you come about the footprints at the scene of the crime?"

Owens said, "We took the defendant out to the scene of the crime to see if his footprints matched the ones we found out there. He tried to walk over to them sideways to erase them, so I slapped him. Me and Deputy Justice finally got the defendant lined up right. His footprint was a perfect fit to that one in the clay."

Williams asked him, "Did you strike him to cause bodily harm, you know, bruises?"

Owen said with a grin, "No sir, I just slapped him."

Williams said to the judge, "Your Honor, we have no further questions for this witness. We would like to present to the court exhibit A, a signed confession of the defendant admitting his guilt. We also would like to present a deposition taken earlier from Dr. H. B. Combs, identifying the assailant as Johnnie Roy Houston. With that, we rest our case."

The judge spoke to my lawyer, "Mr. Walden, you may present your case."

Walden wiped his forehead with his handkerchief. The sweat had already wet through his suit, turning it from tan to brown around the arms pits. He peeped over his wire rim glasses at the judge. "We have no witnesses at this time. The defense rests its case. May I consult with my client?"

This time I lit into Walden. "You ain't gonna call no witnesses? My wife and my mother is here. They can tell them where I was, that I ain't did this. Mrs. Rosanky, she knew I was in her store. Call her up. You ain't gonna question that doctor? He never could tell me and my brother apart. Ain't you gonna question the sheriff about that footprint? That doctor knew me and Juanita didn't live outside of town. Man, what is the matter with you?"

"Shush," he said. He pulled me closer to him, his arm around my shoulder, "Shush, Johnnie. Settle down now."

"Man, don't you shush me." I wanted to slap his hand, but I couldn't with Owens standing right there. "Ain't you gonna call that Doctor Bryson? He saw me after they put that hole in the back of my head when they beat that confession out of me."

Dr. Combs didn't even have to take the stand because of that deposition. In fact, he wasn't even there! And because they presented that confession, which to me wasn't no confession at all because it had blood on it, they didn't have to call me to the stand neither. That trial was damn near decided before it ever got started.

Judge Tate had had about enough of our meeting. "Counselor, your pow-wow time is up."

Walden pushed away from me without saying a word and turned to the judge. "We rest our case, Your Honor." The best I could figure is that they must have threatened Walden like they promised when they said, "Call you a lawyer, and you can call him dead."

The judge read the charge to the jury. It amounted to a bunch of words that meant this: the evidence had to prove without a doubt that I was guilty. In my mind, there was plenty of doubt because they didn't hear any of my evidence. But as the jury left the room, I didn't believe that none of those jurors—none of them Black—cared if they did have all the evidence or not. They had their man—any colored man would do.

When they left the courtroom, it was 9:30 a.m. The laws didn't even take me back to my cell. I sat there thinking this was a bad sign. At 9:45, the jury was back.

Judge Tate slammed his hammer, bringing everybody to attention. "Ed, has the jury come to a verdict?" I couldn't believe my ears. He called the foreman by his first name.

"We have, Your Honor," Ed Nick said, smiling back. "We, the jury, find the defendant guilty as charged in the indictment and assess his punishment to the State Penitentiary for the term of fifty years."

The honorable John H. Tate slammed his hammer. "This court is adjourned." I mumbled the final words of Tobe Cook: "Innocent blood."

The clock on the wall read 9:50 a.m.

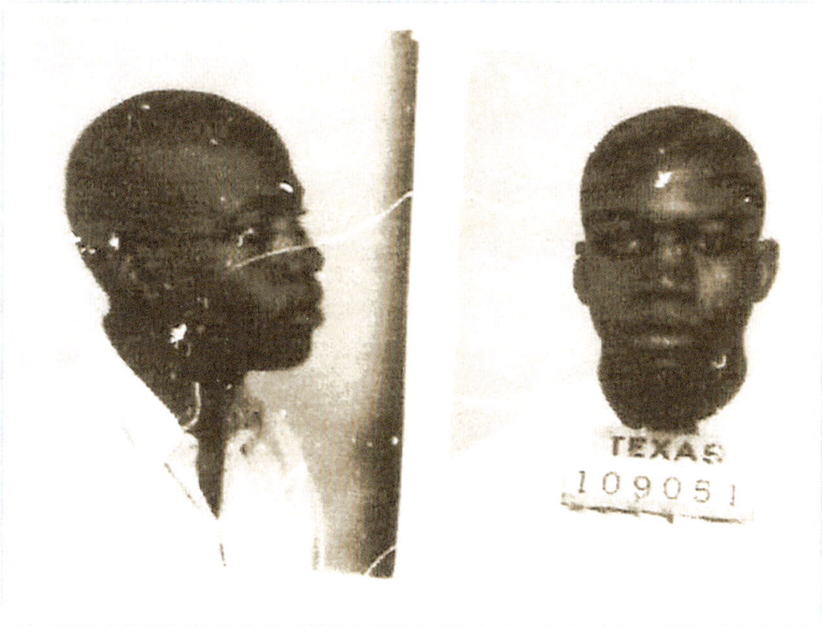

Johnnie receives new identity as Prisoner 109051, June 12, 1947.

nine

HOE SQUAD

WHEN I HEARD THOSE WORDS *GUILTY* AND *FIFTY YEARS*, I felt my spirit leave my body. I was there in the flesh, but what little life I had in me at eighteen went somewhere—a part of me died. I couldn't look at my momma. To see her see me die was like Tobe Cook watching his momma watch him hang. But the hangmen showed him grace that day. They put a hood over his eyes so that the last thing he saw in this life wasn't his momma's pain, so he wouldn't have to carry that picture in his soul into the afterlife. No man should meet God that way. So I took me some grace. I spared me that pain. I kept my head turned and down, watching only my shackled feet jingle, jangle out the courtroom.

When I had hunted in the woods as a boy, I wondered what happened to the life of the possum, squirrel, or rabbit when our .22 pellets hit it in midstride and kicked it in the air, tearing open a hole in it. Whatever was in them that had made them a possum, squirrel, or rabbit flew away somewhere. What was left, then, was no different from the rocks and tree stumps in the bottoms—lifeless, just there. That's how I felt the day the judge hammered a hole in me. Whatever I was before, it was now forever what I used to be. That was a dark place—the darkest place I had ever been—that "don't give a damn" place, that "don't ever talk to me about a God" place. God didn't show up for me. As far as I was concerned, God wasn't studden me, and I wasn't studden him. I was, now, no better than a dead possum, a dead squirrel, or a dead rabbit with a hole in him. Whatever I was before—a twin, an eighteen-year-old Negro in Bastrop, a son of John and Ella Houston—it all flew away. I was now number 109051, property of the Texas Department of Corrections, a rock with a number.

I didn't get my number right away. My shit-for-brains lawyer filed for a new trial—not that he cared anything about my hide. If he had, he would have called some witnesses at the first trial. No. He filed for a new trial to make it look like he gave a damn, to take more money from my mother. Ten days after the filing, the same judge—the honorable John W. Tate—hammered his hammer on me again. "Motion for a new trial denied." Then my honorable attorney, Harold Weta Walden, filed for an appeal. I didn't even testify in Austin. My lawyer didn't even go to Austin. He took more money from my folks to file that appeal, but that's all he did—file papers. Best I could figure, the Bastrop court sent their own version of the trial in a transcript. Who knows what they sent? All I knew was it was like somebody told me: "There ain't no such thing as justice in this town. It's whatever the sheriff says."

I spent six months waiting on the news of my appeal. Every day of that wait, I was reminded of Bastrop justice. On the second-floor wall hung the ring that held the rope that Tobe Cook had hung from. I couldn't take my eyes off it every time I walked down to get exercise.

I remembered how my mother made a point to tell us that Cook boy's story, to tell us, "You'd better straighten up and fly right because you don't want to be on the wrong side of the law in this town." I remembered bits and pieces of Tobe's story: how they found footprints that could have been anybody's, how he had a trial that didn't amount to nothing, just like mine. The only difference between the end of his trial and mine was that death came quick for him. They walked him up that flight of stairs to a sixty-eight-foot scaffold. On his feet was new, high-topped, brown patent-leather shoes with stripes—the first time he'd ever worn new shoes. He wore them for ten minutes. They put a rope around his neck and sprung that trap door.

My sentence was the same as his—death—except my death sentence was a fifty-year-long rope.

My momma and Juanita came to see me a few days after the trial, before any of those next hammers had fallen. Momma's hair was all done up. She was wearing her Sunday dress. You could tell she had been crying, her eyes pink like peaches. All she kept saying was, "Johnnie Roy, I'm gonna set this straight. I heard tell Ray and Red was popping off out about this. I believe Red was the leader. But we gonna get your lawyer file an appeal. Momma is working on getting you out of here. Baby, don't give up. Don't ever give up, you hear. God's gonna see you through."

I didn't want to crush her hopes, so I said, "Yes, ma'am." But I already had a made-up mind to do this time with no help from God, thank you.

I hugged Juanita as she handed me Arlene. "I thought I told you not to bring her here." But I was glad she did. Arlene cooed and grabbed my finger like the time before, only this time she acted like she remembered me. I held her as close as I could, making funny faces and silly noises for the longest time. I asked Juanita how she was holding up, and that was it. The right words was trapped in a suck hole. I told them, "I love y'all. Don't worry about me none. It's getting dark. Time for y'all to go."

I saw Momma one more time before Black Betty.

♦ ♦ ♦

June 12, 1947. It was a week shy of a year since I'd came back to Bastrop for Juneteenth and found myself in the middle of a nightmare. Today was one of my grandmother's "hot as hell days." She didn't know how right she was when she said, "God must have built Bastrop right on top of hell."

Owens and Eskew shackled my ankles and cuffed my hands. *Jingle, jangle,* I waddled downstairs to the rear door of the jailhouse. Waiting outside for me was Black Betty. I learned from the men taking the ride with me that that's what they called this big old black truck. It was like one of them laundry vans, only fitted with bars—cages—for hauling animals. And I was the animal that day.

As they swung open the van door, the smell of sweat hit me like a fist square on my nose. That van was full—maybe ten or twelve men. "Well, look-a-here. We got us some new meat," one of them said. Another said to Owens and Eskew, "Y'all put that sweet little thing next to me."

Owens shoved me up and yelled, "Now y'all behave and move on down." I slid down the metal bench, and was chained next to the caged man who thought he was running things.

"Welcome to Black Betty, New Meat," he said to me.

I didn't say nothing, didn't look at any of them straight in the eye. I was scared, but I didn't want them to know it, so I held my legs to stop the shaking and the rattling of them chains. I wasn't studden them. If they wanted to rumble with me, they'd have a fight on their hands. I wasn't going to let them punk me, so I didn't make a peep. I kept my eyes on my hands and listened.

The old timer who was the obvious leader of this group said to the man to his right, "What they got you for?"

The man said, "They say I kilt a man who was dipping in my honeypot, that I shot him six times. But I told that judge, 'Your Honor, as the good Lord is my witness'—he playing like he was in court—'I am innocent. I didn't shoot that man six times for messing with my wife. I am innocent, I tell you. I kilt him with just one shot. Those other five was target practice for the next "Jody" who feels like dipping where he ain't got no business.'" They all burst out laughing. I had to clinch my teeth so I didn't laugh too.

That leader then did a roll call: "What about you, Johnson, you guilty?"

Johnson said, "Naw."

The leader asked the next man, "What about you, Tiny, you guilty?"

Tiny stuttered, "No s-s-sir. It was mistaken i-i-i-dentity. They said the robber was fat and black. I'm fat and Injun." They all whooped and hollered.

"What about you, Gramps, you done what they say you done?"

This man—every hair on his head white as cotton—said without opening his eyes, "Naw. I was just borrowing that car."

The leader turned to the next man to his right. "What about you, Mercy Percy. You guilty?"

The one they called "Mercy Percy" was a punk—pressed jet-black hair and light eyes. "No sir. I just love y'all's company."

The leader went down the line. After each one answered, they burst out laughing like it wasn't no big thing to be riding in Black Betty, like they had done it a few times already. Come to find out, most of them had taken this ride before for killing, knifing, stealing. You name it, they done it. They probably was guilty—I don't know—but saying they's innocent seemed to help them take the ride.

Then the ringleader came to me. "What about you, New Meat? I bet you not guilty too?"

He slid his foot over as far as his chain would stretch and tapped my foot. I snapped at him and said, "Man, you better keep to yourself. Don't you ever touch me," I struck at him like a rattlesnake, but the chains held me back, cutting into my ankles and stomach. I didn't feel it at the time, but later I saw where they had left marks like I had been branded. I told him, "Man, you ever touch me again, I'll kill you."

He lunged at me like he was going to do something, but his chains stopped him inches from my face. Nose to nose, he smiled at me and said, "Oh we got a fighter here. You better learn, Li'l Nigga, you don't want none of this." He grinned at his buddies as he sat back.

The guard riding shotgun yelled back through a small, screened window, "Hey, hey, y'all better settle down back there before I come back there and bust some heads." We settled down, but I didn't take my eyes off that loudmouth. I had made up my mind that I wasn't going to let no one put their hands on me. I'd kill me somebody or die trying. He might as well be the first.

As Black Betty rolled up Main Street, I stared out the little window that let in a trickle of fresh air. We passed by Holt Dry Goods. People was doing business as usual: men in suits and hats, hands in pockets, leaning against the poles that held up the awning in front of O. P. Jones Grocery—men, no doubt, talking about the price of cotton at the Hanke Gin. We passed by a few coloreds who walked, head down, on the side of the sidewalk, running errands for the people they worked for, knowing their place on a day not Saturday. I thought, as we headed out of town on Highway 71, that the coloreds I was leaving behind was no different from me in this van. They was rocks and stumps just like me, except they didn't have a number.

Black Betty coughed a cloud of black smoke as the driver gunned her down the highway. I left Bastrop with a made-up mind that I wasn't ever coming back. I closed my eyes tight, playing like I was asleep, so they wouldn't see my eyes well up. I had three hours, 170 miles, and fifty years to go.

We made one stop in Brazoria County, past Houston, to pick up two more prisoners who, no doubt, would claim they been done wrong by justice like the rest of them.

They scooted down the bench on the other side and didn't say a word. An hour later, we was crossing Interstate 45. Next stop: the back gate of the Walls Unit, Texas Department of Corrections, Huntsville, Texas.

As we crossed the interstate, we passed by a big field surrounded by a fence with shiny barbed wire across the top. There was two large men wearing big cowboy hats, sitting on horses as wide as the men was. They cradled shotguns in their arms like they was rocking babies. One rider had tied to the hilt of his saddle several dogs on long leashes. Between the two horsemen was a low cloud of dirt and dust, long and straight, hugging the ground like a rolling dirt devil, churning like a train. Out of this cloud came music:

Twenty-two men all in a row.
Twenty-two men, twenty-two hoes.

Every now and then, when the wind shifted, the dust would settle to reveal men with hoes, moving in rhythm, the sun reflecting off their raised tools like the flashing of lightning, and the parched earth muffling the thunder of their hoes striking down. With every strike, dust kicked up and collected into that low rolling cloud. With those horsemen alongside it, that cloud moved out of sight as we drove through a white-picket gate. The voices faded as we turned inside the prison grounds, but I could still hear that cloud song in my head:

Raise 'um up, bring 'um down,
hoe squad, hoe squad moving down the line.
Twenty-two men doing their time.

The guard-driver hollered to the back, pointing at the disappearing ground cloud of men, "I hope y'all know the business end of a hoe because that there is your life—the hoe squad. Welcome to Huntsville, boys."

I would soon learn that the cloud of dirt moving like a dust devil was the daily work detail. Every swinging dick had to swing a hoe and "Twenty-two Men" was the work song to keep the men in rhythm. Johnnie, I thought, if you're going to survive in the belly of the beast, you'd better get with the heartbeat of the beast—the hoe squad. I figured I'd better get with the program—raising 'um up and bringing 'um down.

Black Betty's brakes squealed as she parked next to several concrete buildings. As we unloaded, everywhere I looked there was white—I mean … everywhere, white jumpsuits. I asked the guard, "Who's them in white?"

He came back, "Boy, you *are* new meat. Everybody in white is an inmate."

That guard led us to what they called the Diagnostic Center where they gave you an examination before they shipped you to a unit. But before I got shipped to my unit, I had to learn my first lesson. We was all in one room waiting for our names to be called. Then a guard called out mine: "Houston, Johnnie Roy Houston, go to exam room four." In there, this man in a white coat, chewing on a pen and holding a writing tablet, walked up to me. He looked at me straight in the eyes and asked, "Have you ever seen your mother naked?"

"Man, what did you say?" I sprung at him like he was a mouse and I was a rattlesnake. "What did you say?" In an instant, I was on him and the guards was all over me. I ain't been in prison an hour, and I was already fighting guards. They wrestled me to the ground.

"Put him on the table," that man in the white coat ordered. They slammed me hard on a metal table, strapped my hands and legs down. That man in the white coat put a piece of wood in my mouth, then he put some wires on my chest and hit a button on a machine. My chest knotted up like a hundred charley horses. My jaw locked down on that piece of wood with a death grip like a snapping turtle on a perch. My body would have flown off that table if I hadn't been tied down. My pants was wet. My heart kicked like a mule against my ribs. I later found out that button was part of a shock machine.

"Take him to the holding pen until he learns how to act," the man in the white coat ordered the guards. They dragged me down the hall. Inmates in that outer room was laughing; so was the guards. One of them said out loud so the whole hall could hear him, "You see this new nigger here. He ain't been here two minutes, and he's going bad on Dr. Shaw like he's gonna whip him."

They threw me in a padded room. Finally, my jaw loosed up enough for me to speak. I hollered out, "Dr. Shaw? He a doctor? I thought he was an inmate. They told me that everybody here in white was an inmate, and I wasn't letting no inmate talk to me like that: 'Have you seen your mother naked?'"

The guard slammed the door shut and said, "You dumb son-of-bitch, that was the chief psychiatrist and head doctor, Dr. Shaw."

"I need to see Dr. Shaw," I hollered through the slit in the door.

The guard said, "You damn sure do. You got to be crazy, jumping the Doc and you just got here."

I told that guard again, "I need to see Dr. Shaw."

They finally took me back to his office.

"What do you need, … let's see," he said, scanning his tablet, "Houston?"

"Dr. Shaw, I didn't know you was a doctor. I apologize. They told me that everybody here in white was inmates. So, when you asked me if I ever saw my mother naked, I wasn't about to have anybody here talk about my mother like that. I thought you was an inmate."

There was a long pause. Dr. Shaw looked at me, glaring over his glasses, first with a frown like he wasn't believing me, then with a slow-growing smile like he got what I was trying to say. Then he laughed and said, "Houston, I believe you're sincere. I guess now you know that everybody here in white is not an inmate. I am a psychiatrist—a mind doctor. We ask strange questions." He signed some papers, then turned to the guard. "Take him to Dr. Fredericks, then to intake." He turned to me, smiling. "Now, Houston, he's going to be wearing a white coat, but he's not an inmate. So don't jump him, all right?"

After they signed me in, took my clothes, and gave me *my* white overalls with my number on the back—109051—and my name on the front, they took me to that other doctor. He looked in my mouth, shined a light in my eyes, and said I was healthy as a horse. Next, they took me to a shower room, made me spread my butt cheeks, threw some powder on me, then made me dress.

That was my first day in prison.

I didn't even get settled in good before they shipped me off to my unit—Ramsey I Unit, Rosharon, Brazoria County, Texas, 102 miles south of Huntsville. Another hour and a half in Black Betty. Once I got there, they took me to a large room, like a gym. There wasn't any cells, just a large room they called a wing. Warden Leeford Gayther Bounds ran Ramsey. My wing was 104 cots lined up in rows as far as you could see one way, then the other, three feet apart on every side. Up against the walls was toilets and sinks. You did your business in front of everybody.

As I went to my cot, it felt like every eye was looking at me, and some of them eyes was men who had plans for me, men who made it their "get-by" work to turn out the weak, the new meat that came in every day. I didn't talk to nobody. I didn't look at nobody as I sank into that army cot that smelled of another man's sweat and piss. The place was full of the sounds of men cursing, laughing, fussing, flushing.

I laid my head down that first night when they called, "Lights out!" and that noise slowly died down. The room grew almost dark—dark enough to see outlines—and quiet enough to hear the shuffling of feet and the squeaking back and forth of cots rocking, the muffled sounds of grunts and whimpering. The only privacy you had was the thoughts you kept in your head. I had a made-up mind to keep my mind and my manhood, or die trying. I never closed my eyes that first night.

Before daybreak, they rang a bell, and a guard started to call out numbers: "Hoe Squad Number One, Number Two ..." They put me in Hoe Squad Number One. Work bosses with flashlights in hand led us out by horseback to the fields, mainly cotton. I knew the beat. I was born and raised on a farm, and I knew all about picking cotton, picking corn, and raising vegetables. I fell right in line. I picked more cotton than any man in the squad that day, so they made me the lead row—the one who set the pace.

I'd catch in on the first row and lead them out. It was back-breaking work in knee-crippling positions. If you had never picked cotton before, prison was a bad place to start. If you raised up for a rest, you faced a hoe handle cracked across your head. There was no breaks except the water breaks, ten minutes at most, three times a day.

The rhythm of the hoe squad was as regular as a heartbeat, everyday—Monday to Monday. Monday had no end, just *Hoe squad, hoe squad moving down the line. Twenty-two men doing their time.* My job was to keep that cloud of men moving. I would have them looking pretty too. Singing was the breathing of this moving cloud of men.

And they had more than one song:

Well Old Rattler, Old Rattler was the Sergeant's dog. Hey Rattler, Hey.
Well Old Rattler, Old Rattler, if he catches you, Old Rattler,
Tear the meat off your bones, Hey Rattler, Hey.

It didn't take you long to learn who Old Rattler was, especially if you decided to make a run for it. If you ran, those guards sicced five or six dogs on your tail. Old Rattler led the pack. He was Satan on four legs. Every time Old Rattler caught an escapee, they would put a gold cap on his teeth. He had a mouthful, so much so, that when he barked, his teeth rattled. Those dogs was everywhere. Every time the squad would go out, them guards would leash up two packs of them. They was bloodhounds, full blood with strong feet, large teeth, and big mouths. Once they got on your tail, especially Old Rattler, you'd better make it up a tree or over the fence, or you was dead.

One day, an inmate—a skinny, white boy—tried to escape. We was down there cutting sugar cane when he dropped his cane knife and made a run for it, zigzagging toward the fence. The dog-sergeant saw him and shot in the air five or six times. Then he turned loose the pack with Old Rattler leading the way. That boy tried to hop that fence, but the dogs circled him. Everybody quit working to watch. Rattler caught him first, jumped all on him, threw him down, and chewed on him. Rattler didn't kill him, just chewed him up for a good fifteen to twenty minutes, tore all the clothes off him.

I stood there with my mouth open as they drug off what was left of that boy, Old Rattler still snipping at his bloody heels. All of a sudden, something pushed me to the ground face first. I felt sharp metal pressed into my back—pressed hard like an elephant was sitting on me. Then I heard, "Nigger, who in the hell told you to take a break?"

The pressure let up and I rolled over. Above me stood a guard horse as big as an elephant, straddling me with his hooves pawing up a cloud of dust. I wiped the dirt from my face to look up the double barrels of a twelve-gauge shotgun pointed right between my eyes.

ten

BOSSES

ON THE OTHER END OF THOSE BARRELS and the slow cock of that shotgun's hammer was a boss I did not know. As slow as I could, I got up. I didn't want to scare him or that horse.

Those guard horses was special horses, bred in the prison for prison work, to carry those three-hundred-pound bosses for eight hours a day. They was wide as their bellies was deep, three parts quarter horse and one part draft horse. Their bloodlines went back to when Texas was a country. They was as mean as the bosses that rode them—maybe meaner. I soon learned Boss Wilson was the rider this day.

He saw the blood-look in my eyes, and sitting up there on that horse, he spat a long black stream of chew. Then out the corner of his mouth, he said, "Oh, we didn't upset you none did we? I eat niggers like you for breakfast. So jump!"

Boss Ellis, who was over my hoe squad that day, jumped right in. "Don't shoot 'em, Wilson. I got 'em. This here is Houston. He's my new lead row. I'll kick his ass. I'll take care of him."

"All right, Ellis, whatever you say. He's your nigger." Wilson yanked hard on his reins, grinned at me with the same blood-look, and said, "We'll be seeing you around, Mr. Lead Row."

That was my introduction to Boss Wilson. If Old Rattler was hell's watchdog, them work bosses was hell's watchmen. Cross them and they'd make your life—like I had just learned—a living hell. They wasn't all evil. Boss Ellis was all right as long as you was taking care of him in the field. But bosses like Wilson agitated up on you, like today, because they could, because it made them feel better about their sorry asses, I guess. I stayed out of Wilson's way. But believe it or not, he wasn't the worst boss.

After I heard what the boss they called "Hitler" did, I understood why they called him that. One day, while we worked in one field, Hitler carried out twenty Mexicans in his squad to a nearby field. He kept an automatic rifle in his saddle and two pistols at his side. That day, they was working in the woods, and one of those Mexicans jumped the fence and took off running. Hitler shot him before he got fifty feet. One thing led to another, and out of plain meanness he turned on the rest of those men and shot all of them—all but one.

Old Hitler marched that one survivor all the way back to the building. He left the others dead in the field, heads shot all to pieces. I heard he told the warden the reason he brought that one back was he had just one bullet left.

I didn't see them shootings, but our field had been close enough to hear it—and later that day, I saw what Hitler done. They picked up those shot-up Mexicans, covered them with sheets, and stacked them like firewood on top of each other on the water wagon. Kept in the field all day, those bodies on that water wagon gave up their blood. It ran down through the cracks like rain collected by storm gutters. Whenever that water wagon came by our squad, we stood in puddles of blood where we dipped. Yes, sir, we drank water with the dead.

After that, I knew them bosses were hell's watchmen, not because of what I heard, but because of the shooting I heard with my own ears and smelled with my own nose—blood and water mixed—and what I saw one foul day. We never knew on any given morning which boss we'd get. That day our boss, who I'd never seen before and never wanted to see again, was in a mean mood. He gave orders left and right, right and left—orders that didn't make no sense. "Pick up that pile of rocks over there and pile them up over here." No sooner we did that than he changed his mind. "Pick up these rocks here and move them over there." He wasn't the only one in one of those moods that day. There was an inmate who stayed in trouble. He kind of reminded me of Ray. Trouble was his best friend too. You could count on him pissing off a boss and taking the punishment that came with it. On this day, he said under his breath, "Fuck you. I ain't moving a damn thing."

That boss peeped from under his Stetson as he sat on his horse, his shotgun resting in his arms like a napping baby. "What did you say?" Then he took that Stetson and threw it as far as it could fly. "Now go get my hat."

That inmate didn't move at first, but then I think he saw what I thought I saw on the face of that boss—a face turned red as a beet, with veins the size of water hoses bulging out of his neck—the face of an explosion about to happen. Then that face emptied itself of color, turning as pale as a possum. Death was sitting on that horse.

That boss said again, but in a tone that was kind, almost sweet, "Sir, go and get my hat, if you please. That darn wind up and blew it out of my hand."

We all stopped working and watched as the troublemaker walked over to that hat, with every step his eyes switching from that hat to that boss and back to the hat again. His hands shook like a rattlesnake tail as he picked up the Stetson and slowly walked over to the boss. I swear it looked like that inmate wet his pants along the way. As he slowly brought that hat up to the horn of the saddle, that boss let his arm that was cradling his shotgun go limp. With the other hand holding the shotgun at the trigger, that barrel fell like a tree falls when it has been chopped just right, straight and slow. The muzzle landed inches from that inmate's nose. I heard a sudden, muffled crack like distant lightning, and with it, I saw a flash of light from the gun barrel. I felt the spray of something wet, like the spray of a peeled orange, across my face. With my sleeve, I wiped something that looked like scrambled eggs from my forehead—human brains. Some fell on my boots. The body of that inmate lay on the ground, spread eagle, blood gushing out of where his head used to be. What was left of that head was about twenty feet away, cracked open like a watermelon, the meat and juice staining the white sand with blood, leaving a circle of red that grew wider with every minute, fading from red to pink, from pink to pale white. The flies was there in no time.

Then that boss spoke calmly, "Now some of you fellas pick that head up and wrap it in this here napkin and put it with his body. Wrap him with this blanket and put him on the water wagon. Y'all all saw what happened: he reached for my shotgun, and it went off. Damn shame, he ruined one of my favorite hats. Y'all all saw it. Didn't y'all?"

No one said a word.

He yanked hard on the reigns of his guard horse, turning him toward the lead row. He spat, smiled to no one in particular, and said, "That's what I thought." He rode off in a cloud of dust, disappearing like a ghost. I never worked under him again.

I managed to stay clear of Old Hitler too. I never knew his real name, didn't care to. It was Wilson I had my mind on. Ever since we had that run-in when Ellis had to save my hide, I knew it wasn't the last time we'd square off. You know when somebody means to do you harm for no good reason—the way they look at you. Reason has nothing to do with it. "Just because" does. It wasn't long before I had a date with the devil on a horse.

No matter how hard I tried to keep to myself and stay clear of them bosses after I had looked up the end of that shotgun, it was unavoidable that me and Boss Wilson—the one who first put those double barrels to my face—would have our "come to Jesus" meeting. Hoe Squad One was picking cotton one day. I emptied my pickings on a big sheet and headed back to my lead row, dragging my sack behind me. Wilson rode right behind me, hitting his horse with his spurs, riding him so close on me that the horse's front hooves stepped on the end of my sack. Wilson—with his big old white Stetson cocked over his forehead, his mouth full of chew, and his big fat tomato-red neck rolled like baloney—had a habit of playing inmates that way. Today was my turn. Every time his horse planted himself on my sack, I yanked my sack as hard as I could to free it, only to have that horse charge it again, and with his full weight, pounce on the sack again and again. I couldn't go nowhere. I tried to pull away a couple more times, and each time, that guard horse—about fifteen hands high—clopped her hooves right on the end of my sack like a cat playing with a mouse.

Boss Wilson and that big old horse played with me like a toy for a while, till I thought, I've had a made-up mind to do my time and walk out of here a man—or be rolled out feet first. Well, I guess this is my day—the day I'm gonna get it. I was boiling. So when they rode up on me again, I timed myself, jumped up, turned, and screamed like Tarzan, beating my chest that whole time. I jumped straight up and hollered again, as loud as I could. That horse, snorting air through her flared nostrils, whinnied, reared up, and threw Boss Wilson. Then that horse galloped across the field, kicking up a cloud of dust. Wilson landed square on his ass, bouncing like a sack of meal, kicking up his own cloud.

He jumped up, pulled out his pistol and shot off a round in the ground. I thought he was gonna kill me for sure right then. "Here. Hold my gun," he ordered the dog-sergeant. "I'll take care of him."

Wilson ran toward me, grabbed my shoulder and swung at me, but missed. We locked up and hit that cotton field, rolling over two or three times, ripping up cotton with every roll. He managed to get on top of me hollering, "Nigger, I'm gonna kill you."

So I went to fighting for my life. I busted him in the jaw, sending his hat flying as I rolled in the opposite direction. He caught up to me, but I hooked him under his chin good. Oh, yeah, I was tearing him up, and the inmates was having a good time watching, laughing, and carrying on. I must have knocked him down two or three times. Each time, I dove on him and got off a punch before he could get to his knees.

An inmate tried to break us up. "Get out of the way! I'm gonna whip him," Wilson screamed. Then bullets whistled past my ear. A boss from Hoe Squad Number Two had made his way up to where we was with his pistol drawn, squeezing off a few rounds in the air to slow me down. Bosses didn't take too kindly to them getting their asses kicked by inmates. I rolled off Boss Wilson and raised my hands, my lungs full of dust.

"Naw, don't shoot him. I can handle him," Wilson said, spitting out a mouthful of chew, dirt, and blood. Then he backhanded me flush across my jaw. We went back at it again, tearing up another two or three rows of cotton. After he saw he couldn't whip me, Wilson ordered, "Come here, some of you niggers. Get his feet off the ground." So some of those Uncle Toms ran up and threw me down. "Turn him over. Handcuff him," Wilson hollered. They put me on a trailer load of cotton that was going up to the gin building. I was sent straight to the warden's office.

"Johnnie Roy, what happened to you?" Warden Bounds asked. That's what Warden Bounds called me—Johnnie Roy. He started calling me by my name the first time I met him after he found out that I outpicked and chopped everybody in Ramsey. I kept my nose clean and I did my work. He liked that. So he spoke to me like I was more than a number. He treated me like I was worth being called by name. He was a tall man with broad shoulders like he knew something about hard work, but I could tell by the pictures on his desk and wall that he came there from a side of the tracks different from me. On his office wall was a college diploma from some teacher college in Commerce, Texas. Next to that diploma was a picture of him on his 1937 college football team. He loved to tell me that he knew how to put a lick on a fella. "Johnnie Roy Houston, you play football?" he'd asked me every time I was in his office.

I'd tell him, "No sir, I quit school to help out my mother. But if I'd have had a chance to play, I would have put a whipping on somebody too."

"I bet you would have," he'd say to me. That's the way he talked to me, like I wasn't lower than him, like he knew that being white gave him an advantage, but it didn't make him better. I may have been wrong, but that's the feeling I got whenever we talked. I used to clean up his office when I came in from the field. He had a picture of a wife but no children. He had a sort of sadness in his voice sometimes, like not having children was a hole in him. He was a different white man from what I was used to. He would walk in the dining room every now and then and taste the food they was feeding us. "What is this mess?" he would ask. "That's not fit for a dog to eat. Change it!" He would pitch a fit if the food wasn't right. So when they dragged me into his office from that rumble with Boss Wilson, I felt that Warden Bounds would give me justice.

"Now Johnnie Roy Houston, what's wrong with you and Wilson?"

I told him, "It ain't nothing wrong with me. You know I don't play with none of those bosses out there." I told him the whole story about how I scared Wilson's horse after he rode it up on my sack.

The warden went to laughing. "What did Wilson do then?"

"He went to fighting me, and I went to fighting him like it was life or death."

"Well, did he whup you?" he asked like he already knew the answer but wanted to hear me say it.

I told him, "I don't know whether he whupped me or not, but I went to fighting for my life. I tore him up." The warden called in the tail-lead inmate they called Old Jones to see if I was telling the truth. Jones told him the same story.

He sent Old Jones and me out of his office. I could hear him on his walkie-talkie talking to the field captain. All of a sudden, Warden came flying out of his office, keys and hat in hand, eyes fixed straight ahead. "Houston, Jones, y'all come with me." We got in his car and flew down to that field, dust kicking up from underneath that big white Lincoln, air conditioner blowing full blast,

Hank Williams blasting out his radio. We was riding in style, Old Jones and me, and we was feeling good, knowing something was about to happen, that one of those bosses was gonna get his. We pulled up as close as we could to Wilson's squad. Warden Bounds slammed his car in park and jumped out running.

The field captain rode across two or three rows of cotton to meet the Warden, who barked, "Tell Wilson to get over here right now." Bounds made a beeline to Wilson. We was huffing and puffing right behind him. From a distance, you could tell Wilson didn't like what that field captain had to say, the way Wilson jerked the reins of his chestnut mare that had come back. You could barely make out what Wilson was saying—something about somebody's momma—as he rode hard toward Warden and us, head cocked up in the air like he was gonna try to whup up on somebody else.

All work stopped as inmates leaned on their hoes and sat down on their sacks to watch whatever was about to happen. The way me and Jones was smiling gave things away. Boss Wilson was about to get his.

A blast of August-hot Texas wind picked up every word they said and carried it to every square inch of that field. Warden Bounds said, "Boss Wilson, I thought I called down here to that field captain and told him to tell you to leave my horse in the field and bring your saddle and come on in and pick up your check?" Warden's voice was real calm at first, and then it jumped like a rabbit. "Well, did he tell you?"

Wilson said, "Well, Warden, uh, you see, uh, I told him to tell you if you wanted to see me, come out here and see me. I mean, I got some men out here I'm watching over." Wilson began to shrink before our eyes.

"Get off of there!" The warden, still cock-strong from his football days, reached up, dragged Wilson off his saddle, busted him upside his head, and then went to kicking him.

"Throw it on him, Warden! Put it on him, Warden!" All those inmates hollered like it was that boxer Joe Louis—the Brown

Bomber—fighting that German—Max Schmeling. "Put it on him!" The other bosses sat quietly on their horses. Any other time, they'd be hollering at us, "Y'all better shut up before y'all get your head thumped." Those inmates was so glad to see that boss get whupped, they could hardly control themselves, like it was Juneteenth or something. To see this side of justice was something none of them, including me, ever expected to see down here. So me and Jones was right in it, too, laughing and yelling, "Put it on him, Warden. Put it on him."

Finally, Warden Bounds let up. "Get your saddle and get."

Huffing and a-puffing, Wilson threw that heavy load across his shoulder and asked, "Hey, uh, Warden, can I put it in your trunk?"

The warden fired back, "What? No sir. You can't put it in my trunk. You hit that turn row, and I mean you hit it!" Wilson hit the turn row walking back to the administration building, the warden walking right behind him hollering, "Go 'head on. Get to that building." The warden came back to the car and told us to get in. He drove up right up behind Wilson just like Wilson had run up behind me with his horse. Warden backed off a bit and then ran up behind him again, blasting his horn. With each blow, Wilson jumped and we laughed. Wilson looked a mess. His khakis was wringing wet and dirty like he had been in a hell of a fight—matter of fact, two fights—me and then the warden. We finally reached the back gate where Wilson threw that saddle as hard as he could against the fence. "Old Jones, you and Houston get back to your wing," the warden said. We went to our wing, all right, but straight to the window that overlooked the guard dormitory yard where we and everybody else had a ringside seat to the end of Boss Wilson.

"Just hold up right there," Warden Bounds yelled at Wilson. "Now, you got thirty minutes to get your check and all your personal belongings and get out of my prison. I want you off the premises in thirty minutes. I don't want to see you anymore."

A couple of minutes later, Wilson stormed out of that dorm with all his stuff in three pillowcases. He crawled into his old Ford F-1 truck he was so proud of, and gunned it through the main gate, fishtailing it, throwing up gravel. By now, the whole unit knew what had gone down. You could hear cheering like some world war had ended. That was it—Boss Wilson riding off in a cloud of dust and shame.

Hoe Squad One was laid off for about two weeks while they hired another boss. But my layoff did not last that long. They moved me inside till things cooled down in the field. Warden Bounds knew that every field boss would be after me now because of what happened to Wilson. They wasn't going to let it rest there, an inmate getting the best of a boss. So, off I went to an inside job where all I did was mop floors, scrub toilets, and clean offices.

That was my first months of fifty years as number 109051. I survived the hoe squads, Old Rattler, and Boss Wilson. But surviving *missing* was another thing. Late at night, I slept in half-sleep, thinking about my momma, wife, and baby. I missed my momma stroking her hand over my head, calling my name low and slow. I missed feisty Juanita, telling me she wasn't studden me while she held me like I was her last strong blade of river grass. I thought of missing Arlene take her first steps. I wondered if she would forget me. Nothing in prison could be worse than *missing.*

I was wrong.

eleven

OLD SPARKY

After Boss Wilson left with his saddle over his shoulder and his tail between his legs, things finally settled down. After ten months at Ramsey I, I was transferred back to the Walls Unit, Huntsville. Why? Warden Harry Emmitt "The Owl" Moore. They called him The Owl because he saw everything. That's why he had been moved to Walls—the biggest unit—some months before. He didn't miss a thing. He saw the cotton you left on your row, the shank you hid in that picture frame of your family, or that reefer tucked in a book. He had been at Ramsey a short time while I was there, and he saw I was a good worker, not a slacker. So I believe he had something to do with me going to Walls.

When I arrived, they took me straight to The Owl.

"Now Houston, you're a good man," he said. He tossed me a pouch of Red Man tobacco chew. "Here you go." He knew I liked chew and didn't get enough regular money from home put on my commissary books to buy any. "You're down here doing some serious time. You're going to need some help. I can help you. I need a man like you here, so I got a job for you. Actually, Warden McAdams can use a man like you."

C. L. "Bear Tracks" McAdams was a name I knew. They named him "Bear Tracks" because he looked like a bear—barrel chest, large head, big hands. He was over everything and everybody. To some, he was the best warden there was: family man, a strong

Christian. But to the inmates, he was known as "the executioner" because he was the man that gave the final word—"Have a seat, please"—to those poor souls who was sentenced to a date with Old Sparky, the electrocution death machine. The inmates called electrocution "riding the lighting."

I didn't know if McAdams was good or bad. Warden Moore, I knew. He saw mostly what benefited Moore. Warden Bounds, I knew. He had a heart for men who wanted to do right. McAdams—the man with the final word—wore a khaki suit with one of them string bow ties you see in Western movies. His Stetson sat on his desk, the sweat band wet all the way through to the brim like he had just come in from outdoors. I noticed things like that, that he was an outside warden, a warden checking on things for himself. He had plenty of pictures of family on the wall—a large family. He had a Bible on his desk. The cover and edges of those pages was like they'd never been turned. That meant something too.

McAdams read from my file, never once looking up. "Houston ... Let's see, ... Johnnie Ray Houston. Is that right?"

"No sir. I am Johnnie Roy. Ray is my twin brother."

"Well, pardon me. A man should get another man's name right. I'm Warden Carl Luther McAdams, Jr. I'm named after my daddy, but I'm not him. So I don't cotton to people mixing us up either." This time he was looking me right in the eye. "Looks like you gonna be with us for a while—fifty years. All these wardens—Bounds and Moore—say you're a good worker. They want to help you—I want to help you—do this time. Now here's what I need you to do for me. Go on down to see Captain Byrd. He'll get you straight on what I need." He smiled and stuck out his hand.

I looked at it. In my mind I said, *McAdams might be OK.* I grabbed his hand to shake it.

He squeezed my hand tight as he pulled me closer to him and said, "I can help you. Now, I need you to help me, OK?" This time it came out different, darker. It made my skin crawl.

A light switch flipped in my spirit. *There is two McAdams.*

"Take him to Captain Byrd," he ordered the guard. The second time he had said, "I need your help," he didn't look me in the eye. I soon found out why. My job at Walls would be almost the same as at Ramsey—almost. I was to mop floors, clean toilets, and serve men their meals—only, some of them meals would be a last supper.

Joe Byrd was the captain of death row. He sat back in his chair, his feet propped on the corner of the desk full of papers, his baggy pants partly covering his well-worn cowboy boots. "Houston, you got a set of keys that will let you in, but it won't let you out. You have to call the duty guard for that. While these boys are on recreation, you get those toilets cleaned. You'd think these poor bastards would be scared shitless by now, but I guess they ain't." He chuckled at himself. "Get it, get it? That's pretty damn good—'scared shitless.' That's a joke, son." I didn't get it.

Captain Byrd grinned as he walked me through the Wall's courtyard to the East Building where death row inmates was kept. They called it the Death House—nine cells. Before he handed me over to the guard, he turned to me and said, "Another thing: when you're serving their trays, don't get too close. Some of them are liable to grab you and shank you—take you out. They don't have anything to lose and don't mind taking down one more person with them before they go. Got it?" I nodded like I understood what he was saying. "You're headed to a dangerous place."

I looked straight ahead at the steel doors as he put in two keys. The next moment, I was in death row. Byrd walked in with me and slapped those keys extra hard against his leather belt. The sound ricocheted off every hard surface, every piece of steel and inch of cement floor and corrugated ceiling. Those keys rang like a church bell. Then, without a command, *they* appeared—eight faces moving from the back of their cells into the light at the edge of each door. There was brown, black, and white faces, all pressed against the four-inch opening between the bars, all fixed on the sound of those keys as we walked past each cell. Then, from out of one cell, someone asked, "Did he ride it like a man?"

"Yeah, he took his seat last night and rode the lightning," Captain Byrd answered back real proud. "Rode it like a man."

With that announcement, each brown, black, and white hand and face slowly disappeared back into the dark of their cells, back to whatever those poor souls did to keep their minds off the day the ringing of those keys was meant for them. Things went back to normal, but it didn't take me long to see that normal didn't mean the same here.

As Byrd led me, I pushed a mop and bucket and a cleaning cart loaded with brushes and soaps to cell eight. The walk gave me a chance to get the lay of the place. It was much the same layout as the rest of the prison units, except there was more isolation cells—four or five of them—and one room that was set apart down a dead-end hallway. I had an idea what was behind that door, but I didn't care. My job was to keep the rest of those cells clean, to feed the inmates, and to keep a watch out for any of them trying to commit suicide. If I did my job, I would stay inside and out of the reach of those field bosses and hoe squads. I could live, I thought, with death row, if it meant me staying alive to get one more day behind me. That's what I thought.

"Scrub it down good, Houston. I got it booked for this afternoon. When you finish, walk back down to the guard station. You serve them lunch at noon, so get your ass in gear, and watch your step. I've had enough bloodshed this week as it is." No sooner had he disappeared down the block and behind those double steel doors than the sound inside quickly rose to the noise of any other prison unit.

Cell eight was a mess. Bloodstains covered one corner of the floor next to the commode. But there was also splatters all over the rear wall and even the ceiling. It didn't take a genius to figure out what had happened, seeing as how everybody had their own cell. Death row had its share of suicides. Taking that scrub brush to those walls, I thought about how Momma used to sing in her low voice as she washed our clothes: *What can wash away my sins?*

Nothing but the blood of Jesus. What can make me whole again? Nothing but the blood of Jesus. Her singing played in my head as the blood on the walls slowly faded, turning my brush the color of the rusty, muddy Colorado. I thought how nothing washed clean here; stains just got passed on. I thought about how Ray had stained me. He was out there somewhere having a good time, and I was here, washing and wasting away. As my bucket water turned red from the brush, I thought about Ray's blood. A part of me wanted to see Ray's blood flow.

Maybe that Juneteenth fire had burned me after all.

I finished up and headed back toward the guard station. Within a second, all hell broke loose. A hand grabbed my mop handle, tripping me into the bars. Then another hand grabbed the lower part of that handle and pinned me at my throat.

"Johnson's got him. Get his keys," somebody yelled.

Through all the yelling, I could hear a voice from cell seven. "Johnson, let him go. Let him go, now. His keys won't help you. They're just for getting in. They won't unlock nothing. Let him loose."

"Shut up," Johnson shouted back as he pressed harder against my neck, sliding me down to the wet floor. "G-g-give me them keys," he stammered in my ear.

Cell seven shouted back, "They're going put you in the hole till it's your time to walk. And you can forget about any call from the governor. Let the boy go." Whoever was in that cell tossed Johnson a candy bar.

Johnson eased up on the mop. I slid to the floor.

"What in the Sam Hill's going on in there?" the duty guard yelled out, bringing all that commotion to a halt. "Houston, you all right? What in the hell is going on in there?"

All eyes locked in on me. I knew what happened to snitches. Glancing around, I hollered back, "Yeah, I'm all right. Slipped, that's all." There in the corner of cell six was Johnson, sitting on his bed, eating a candy bar like nothing had ever happened. He was as big as a house and couldn't have been more than my age. One moment he was hollering about keys and choking me with a mop handle, and the next moment, he's eating a candy bar.

"Houston, get on out of there and clean yourself up and get ready to feed these animals," the guard growled at me. "They always get a little crazy after they lose one. Watch yourself, like Byrd told you."

That was my first day working my inside job so I would stay out of trouble. So much for staying out of trouble.

I had learned my lesson the hard way, but I learned it: keep your distance and you won't get hurt. I did just that. For the next few months, death row was quiet. I went about my job, cleaning the cells and feeding the prisoners. Johnson, who had put that mop to my throat, was transferred to the psych unit and then to Dallas for a new trial. Turned out he didn't have the sense of a five-year-old when he had strangled some girl in Conroe. Aside from knowing Johnson's name, I didn't know the death row inmates by name, and I didn't want to. As far as I was concerned, knowing a man by name was the first step to getting close to that man—not close like getting too close to somebody who could snap your neck—but getting too close so you start caring.

But it was hard not to care when you saw a person every day, and you saw they was men just like your father, your uncle, or your brother, except they was found guilty—fairly or not, I didn't know—of doing some horrible things to people. Maybe some was innocent. Just like me.

From a distance, I did get close to a few. There was this guy who always had his nose in a book, a yellow writing pad full of writing, and lots of mail. I would hardly say nothing to him, but he always had something to say to me. "Youngblood" (that's what they liked to call me), "Knowledge is power. Knowledge is power." He said that all the time. He asked me one day, "You got any schooling before they locked you up?"

I surprised myself and did something I normally didn't do. I held a conversation with an inmate as I mopped in front of his cell. "I went up to the eleventh grade at Emile High School," I said.

He said, "Emile, Emile? Ah, yes, the French philosopher Rousseau's Emile. He believed 'you can teach a man to survive.' Did that school teach you survival?"

I didn't know Rousseau from a rat's ass, so I didn't answer him. I just kept mopping till I was away from his cell—but not from the question he planted in my head.

From a distance, I got close to another man whose every other word was, "The Bible says this, and the Bible says that." I had noticed in my short time in the belly of this beast that a lot of men got "lijun" when they got locked up. But this man's "lijun" felt different. His words grabbed like barbs on a fishing hook. They caught and drew blood. This man would sometimes preach from his cell, whether anybody was listening or not. One day while I was on his hall, he shouted to no one special, "You can't kill a man twice. Once he's dead, he's free." I found myself timing my day to be down his hall when he had his private church.

Then there was other men I saw from a distance every day who did nothing more than remind me of my father, or Precious McMarion's dad, or the McIntosh twins' daddy, or my Uncle John from McDade, or even a bit of my brother—men who reminded me of home.

Home was always on my mind, especially when visitation Sundays came around. Momma, Mozell, Immer, Juanita, or somebody visited me every week when I first came to prison. By now—a year in—the visits and money put on my commissary books slowed to a trickle. I didn't mind the money so much. But it was the slowing down of visits that made anything that reminded me of sweet home sting. I started calling those Sundays "Sad Sundays."

One visitation Sunday, Juanita showed up with Arlene. I didn't tell her I was working on death row. She came to the cubbyhole where I was waiting. A wire screen separated us. Arlene, now two, wouldn't sit still in her lap, squirming like fresh-dug worms. I spoke first. "She's getting big."

"Big and bad," Juanita said. "You ought to see her. Walking and talking up a storm, getting into everything. The other day she got into your momma's syrup jars—syrup everywhere. We had to cut some of her hair to get it all out."

"That ain't being bad. That's being a child," I said. Then Arlene looked at me with those big brown eyes, touched the screen, and said, "Dadda, Dadda."

I jumped—one of those Holy Ghost strikes of lightning that used to hit my momma in church kind of jumps—and without thinking I put my hand on the screen, pressed in close and said, "That's Dadda's little girl." That was the first time I heard her call me Dad. It was fire in my bones. And it burned like Juneteenth fire.

The guard standing near us barked at me, "Houston, you'd better—" Then he stopped right there and didn't say nothing else. Some of them guards had a heart.

I sat back in my seat, and me and Juanita talked for the rest of the hour. But I can't tell you a thing she said. My eyes was on Arlene the whole time, soaking her in, storing her up. She would be my sweetbread for the nights I was starving for home.

"Time's up," the guard hollered as he walked by us. I took the chance to touch the screen one more time. Arlene touched the same spot and said, "Dadda." Juanita told me she loved me and turned away real quick—quicker than I had ever seen her do before—without waiting for me to say the same. That night I went to sleep with the thoughts of the strangeness of Juanita's goodbye. But also resting in my bosom was Arlene's "Daddas." I carried them with me the next morning, and for many mornings after.

When about two months had passed, Captain Byrd called me into his office. "Houston, I knew the lull had to end sometime," he said. He had a bunch of papers in his hand. "Guard Reynolds is going to show you what you need to do to get Old Sparky ready."

Reynolds led me down the cellblock hall, snapping at me, "Come on, Houston! This thing is scheduled for four o'clock. People have been waiting for this one for a while. We can't keep them waiting any longer. You got to get him ready for the chair."

I fired back, "I ain't getting nobody ready for nothing. My job is to feed the prisoners, clean their toilets, and bring them food and mail. Ain't nobody said nothing about getting nobody ready for no chair."

"Look here, you dumb-ass nigger. What do you think working in death row was about—fixing a picnic? We've got a dead man walking this afternoon, and you getting him ready."

The duty guard led me down a short corridor off the main hallway, past an open door. There it was—an ordinary looking straight-backed wooden chair like you'd see in a church pulpit, except it had a bunch of wires and straps on it. You could hear a hum coming from the room next door. It was half past two.

We didn't go in. He walked me to another room further down. "Here," the guard said, handing me a pair of hair clippers. "Shave the crown of his head for the helmet. We want to make it a clean spot. Then shave his ankles and wrists."

We went to cell five. He hadn't touched any of the food I had brought him hours before: fried chicken, greens, and corn bread. The bowl of vanilla ice cream was now just a bowl of cream. The guard opened his cell, shackled his hands and feet, and we, together—the guard up front, the inmate in the middle, and me and another guard behind him—shuffled down the hall like freight train cars coupled together, trying to keep an even space between us. It was the longest forty-five feet a man will ever walk—for those who walk it a last time. Each foot down that long hall seemed like a green mile. I don't know. All I know is I didn't ever want to walk this way again. No one said nothing as we made our way to the other end of the hall where the barber's chair was. The only sounds that could be heard was the hum of those clippers against his head and the hum of whatever was behind that door next to Old Sparky. My hand shook so bad, I needed two hands to hold those clippers. The guard said, "Give me a good clean four-inch spot on the top. Then shave his wrists and ankles. I don't want to see no hair. You hear?" I did what I was told.

Afterward, the inmate rose from the chair. The guards led him by his shoulder to the hall. Captain Byrd, with a warrant in his hand, joined us in our march. He read as we walked: "It is the mandate of the court that you be put to death …" A priest then joined the parade and asked him, "Do you accept Jesus as your Lord and Savior?" The inmate never said a word.

Four more men joined in the final steps to the death chamber where Old Sparky was waiting. One, I think, was a newspaper man, one was a doctor, and as for the other two, I wasn't sure. They stood behind a rail. You could see a little bit of blue sky through wood shutters covering the tall window. The blue made me think of the blue of my momma's Sunday dress. I was trying to get my mind any place other than what was about to happen. I thought about her, as if this was me ready to die. No mother should know that weight. I wondered if maybe she felt the weight of me in prison as a son as good as dead. I wondered if this man had a momma. There was no family in the viewing room.

Captain Byrd broke through the thick silence. He asked the man, "Do you have anything to say?"

All he mumbled was, "Free." They placed cotton in his nose and then a hood over his face. Then Warden C. L. McAdams, who had slipped in while the inmate was looking out past that hood and the room we was in to another place, said those four words: "Have a seat, please."

I guided the inmate to the chair, strapped the cap, wrist, and ankle contacts on him. I was so close to his face, I know he could hear my whimpering. As I strapped the last hand contact, he squeezed my hand once, then released it as if he had left his body right then. A shiver shot through me like lightning. I managed to back up to the near wall. It held me up from collapsing to the floor, I was shaking so bad.

Captain Byrd gave the signal to the executioner. Like the grinding of the gears of a cotton gin full of rocks, green boles, and wood stems, the sound of a seizing-up filled the room. The lights flickered. The whining of the generators next door was like the crying of a wild animal caught in a trap. Smoke rose from every part of the man's body where metal touched flesh. You could see blue arcs of light dance around him. The smell was the smell of flesh cooking, not just muscle, but guts filled with bowels boiling in their own juices of a half-eaten last meal. This was the kind of smell that never leaves you. It chases you like a hound hunts a rabbit. I will never be without that smell. At four o'clock, this man's spirit burst out of his clay pot. He had his meeting with God. The doctor put that scope to his chest, nodded at the warden, wrote something down, and said, "That's it. 4:01."

Then men strolled out of the room to their ordinary suppers. Me and a guard was left alone to put this man, still warm, on a stretcher and roll out what remained of a creature when his soul leaves his body. To me, what was left was nothing more and nothing less than a rock or a tree stump in the bottoms.

That night as I lay on my bed, not even pulling Arlene's "Daddas" up from my bosom could cover up the smells and sounds of Old Sparky.

That was my first death on death row.

Then they came like a flood, three in one month. I prepared men for their ride on lightening—white men and Black men—regular men who reminded me of my father, my uncle, and pieces of my brother, except these men was found guilty of crimes. Was they guilty, or was they like me?

Executions didn't get easier for me; they got harder. With each walk down the green mile, a part of me died. So one morning six months into serving on death row, the guard poked me in the ribs with his club. "Houston, what the hell's wrong with you? Get up.

It's half past the monkey's ass. You sick or something?"

All night I had lain curled up like a baby, with a blanket over my head. I could not face another day on death row. It took a hard couple of raps with that guard's stick across my arms before I let go of the blanket. "I ain't working on death row no more," I told the guard.

He hit me again. "What did you say?"

"I ain't working on death row no more. You can beat me till you kill me, but I ain't working on death row."

"Nigger, you don't tell us what you're going to do or not do. This is the last time. Get your ass up." He hit me again, but this time I didn't even move. It was like I didn't feel it. I don't know what a nervous breakdown was supposed to feel like, but I believe I was having one.

He called over one of those lower guards as he hit me upside the head one more time. "Guard, help me take Mr. Houston, here, to the warden's office. It seems like he wants another job assignment."

They dragged me to Warden McAdam's office. "Houston, what seems to be the matter here? Captain Byrd tells me that you don't want to go to work today." The warden was calm, even caring-sounding.

"No, sir, I ain't working on death row no more. You can do what you want to do to me."

"Now, look here, Houston. You're a good worker, one of my best, but you ain't the warden here, and you don't make job assignments. Death row is one of the best assignments around here. I called myself looking out for you." Like a pot ready to boil over, McAdams was percolating.

I looked him straight in the eye. "I ain't never seen nothing like I done seen on death row, and I ain't gonna see that again. You can do what you want to do to me."

McAdams jumped out of his seat, papers flying everywhere. This was the other McAdams I always figured was hiding someplace. “I done had about enough of you, nigger. We’ll see if we can’t change your mind with a little solitary time. I told you, ‘You help me and I help you,’ but it doesn’t look like you want my help.”

He called the guard back in. “Take this nig—” He clenched his jaw, then sweetened his tone, but with hard, lumpy sugar. “Take Mr. Houston to solitary for a few weeks—no—give him a month. Let’s see if he’d like to reconsider his position.”

They threw me in a cell no bigger than a bathroom, a concrete closet barely long enough for me to lie down curled up. I had to sit catercorner to stretch my legs. At one end was a hole in the floor where you did your business. Solitary was dark all the time except when they brought me food. When they opened the slit in the door to pass me my meals, the light from the hall was so strong it felt like a punch in the face. For food, I got bread and water for three days. Then every fourth day they dished out one full meal before starting back with bread and water. It didn’t take long for me to shrivel to skin and bones.

They gave me one blanket. The concrete floor was my mattress—no pillow, no sheets, no clothes. In all that darkness and nakedness, my mind turned on me. My thoughts of the Juneteenth fire that did not burn now burned with a hatred for Ray I had not known before. It came in my sleep. I dreamed of Ray, chasing him down in a pool hall or a cathouse, locking my hands around his throat, and squeezing until I couldn’t squeeze no more. But all he would do is laugh. When I woke in the morning, I would find my hands had seized up so much that it took half a day to uncurl them enough to hold bread to my mouth. Some nights I dreamed of walking down to his house in the rainy dark and putting a shotgun to his head. Every dream was a different killing, but with the same end. I tried to not sleep so I wouldn’t hear Ray laugh.

But to be awake was worse. My waking thoughts, like hounds, chased down every good thing in my life. In the darkness of my cell, I saw, clear as day, my momma running with two sacks. The dogs always caught her. She might have made it to the house if only she had dropped one of them sacks, but she wouldn't. She would fall just shy of the door, and she would kick and kick at those dogs until she couldn't kick no more. And as she kicked, I kicked until the concrete wall was red.

In those waking hours, day-thoughts, like suck holes, spun toward my Juanita and Arlene. I screamed for them to swim, but they didn't hear me. No one heard me. They reached toward me, to grab for the long grass along the Colorado's bank, but each blade snapped, one by one until there was none left. My wife and child disappeared every time, so close to the steep water's edge.

If it wasn't dogs, or suck holes, or every kind of untrained and unnamed creature attacking what I loved, my waking thoughts cast doubts like a net over any good thing I tried to conjure up: "Your Momma can't help you," "Your wife has another lover," "You will never get out of jail."

But when I was at my lowest, I somehow found the unction to pray the habit prayer Momma taught me and Ray to say: "Give us this day our daily bread." Then I reached into my spirit and pulled out the bread from heaven I had stored away from Arlene's visits. I whispered, "Dadda" over and over until I found me some peace between my sleeping and waking thoughts.

And I remembered I had a made-up mind to do my time like a man, and that meant I wouldn't have anything more to do with cooking men to death.

twelve

SWEET IN THE MORNING

THIRTY DAYS INTO SOLITARY, INSTEAD OF A BEAM of light leaking through the slit in the door, light flooded the room as the door swung open. A voice came out of the light. "Old Houston, why are you fighting against me?" I shaded my eyes and squinted as hard as I could to make out the figure standing in the doorway. It was a man in a hat—a Stetson hat. "You ready to come out and get to work?" the figure said.

Weak from eating mostly bread and water for a month, it took me a minute to make sense of what I was seeing and hearing. My eyes burned like someone had thrown bleach in them. I knew that voice. It was McAdams. I just didn't know which McAdams—the good one with them family pictures who gave me chewing tobacco, or the bad one with a smooth Bible and solitary. So I didn't say nothing.

"Get him up. Clean him up. Get him something to eat. Bring him to my office when he's ready," McAdams ordered the other figure standing behind him.

You don't just raise up out of solitary. You have to change back into a man fit for light. I was a skeleton, so they took me to the dining room to eat my first meal after I was hosed down and given some clothes. That first meal always made you sick. You'd eat like there was no tomorrow, then you'd shit and throw up like there was no tomorrow, then throw up and shit so much that you prayed there would be no tomorrow. Your gut hurt so bad like you'd been kicked in the belly by a milk cow. My ribs ached every time I took a breath. It took a couple of days to get my system right. Usually, you couldn't stay in the building while you was recovering from solitary. You had to go out in that hot sun and work. But for some reason, they let me stay in.

Eventually, I met with McAdams. "Houston, I'm not sending you back to death row. You don't have the stomach for it, and I don't need any more drama than necessary on the Mile. These things are already a spectacle. Do you know what a spectacle is? … No, I don't suppose you do. Anyhow, I'm sending you to the dairy unit back down there at Ramsey. You and Warden Bounds are all buddy-buddy. You think you can stomach milking cows?" Before I could answer, he answered for me. "Yeah, I supposed you could."

I answered back anyhow. "Yes, sir. I could." I didn't like people answering for me like I was stupid or something. Normally, I'd give them a piece of my mind for that. But this time I didn't.

So back to Ramsey I went. The short Black Betty ride from Huntsville to Rosharon, southeast of Houston gave me time to think. As I looked out the window at row after row of bales of hay, browned to the color of wheat, dried by the blazing Texas sun, I hoped that Ramsey would wash clean my mind of what I'd seen and done at Walls, that this new dairy detail would soak up the smell of cooked human flesh like hay soaks up anything it's set in. But when we pulled up to the familiar chain-link fence, the sound of that motorized gate straining to open then clanging to a stop jolted me back to reality. Ramsey wasn't going to be any different from Walls because it didn't matter where I was. Prison was now between my ears.

Sad Sunday—visitation day—was the hardest on me no matter where I was. I understood why Juanita didn't come as much. She had her hands full with Arlene, plus she was working. But

I never knew if anybody else was coming to see me, especially Momma. I looked out the window at so many people coming in to visit their folks. Too many times, Sunday visitation would come and go without my name being called. My momma was, by now, sixty-one. She didn't have no transportation. The only time I saw her was when Mozell would bring her, and that wasn't often. So I wrote and begged, begged and wrote: "Bring Momma down to see me. Y'all done forgot about me? Bring my momma." My twin brought her once or twice, but he wouldn't come in. How could he? He just stayed in the car.

Before daybreak each day, I heard the rattle of keys hitting the pant leg of the late-shift guard as he made his way down to my wing full of 104 of the worst men in the Texas Department of Corrections to wake me to milk cows. I wasn't asleep—couldn't sleep—with all the hell that went on every night.

There was, first, the sound of inmates talking to one another in code so the guards wouldn't know what was going down after they ordered, "Lights out!" Then, slowly, all kinds of sounds replaced the light. Cots squeaked. The weak "new meat" squealed at the hands of life-timers—those serving life for murder or rape or worse. There was the sounds of violence: men stabbing men for commissary or territory, men scrambling over each other, the "hard acts"—the inmates with reputations as killers—shaking down men for cigarettes. When I went to the toilets that first night back, I walked in pools of blood. I saw a man lying there in a corner stabbed, waiting to be discovered by the morning-shift guards. Bloodshed was as sure as night followed day. Evil never slept. So I rarely slept with all that commotion going on.

Seeing so much blood, day and night, made me nervous. When I would finally close my eyes, all the meanness and the cruelty without end would play back in my mind like a movie at the Tower Theatre back home. So that guard coming to get me up before daybreak to milk cows was a rescue, an escape—more than I notioned.

"Let's go, Houston, those teats are waiting on you," the guard said, shouting his usual good morning. The cow barns was south of the main gate, inside a fenced-in area to keep the cows hemmed in until it was time to herd them in to be milked. There was ten to twenty inmates responsible for thirty, sometimes forty, cows to be milked—and only two or three guards watching over us. Most of the time, they huddled up to smoke and jaw jack about their jobs, or they took turns sneaking off behind haystacks to sleep. They might as well have not been there.

I enjoyed my walks to the barn as the night-blue sky slowly turned pink. In my "sanctified imagination"—as them old Negro preachers would say—I could see the earth turning over, sitting up, and rubbing the sleep out of her eyes. Birds would be singing—more like talking to each other, making plans for the day. The air tasted sweet. Sometimes a low-hanging fog hugged the ground and then lifted like a woman's silk slip slowly inching up the brown, bowed-legged horizon as the sun climbed the sky. The rhythm of the streams of milk hitting those metal pails and the lowing of those happy Jersey cows reminded me of church, how the rhythm of the preacher and the response of the congregation would take over: "And Gawd-duh said ..." And the people would answer back, "What'd he say?" The back and forth of the milking and mooing was music. And when you got thirsty, you couldn't help but help yourself to milk, minutes new. Nothing was finer. It was sweet in the morning.

The milking routine was this: The milk crew would shoo the first herd of cows into stalls, where we sat on wood stools ready to get after it. Each of us was responsible for four cows. As soon as one was milked and shooed away to the feed stall, another cow, udder full, took her place. I had milked cows plenty of times before, so this work was nothing compared to back home. The dairy bosses tried to test me—the new man—by giving me a Jersey called "Kick-a-Can." By the name, I knew she was going to be a handful. Right off, she tried to kick me with her right hind leg. I blocked it with my forearm. Next, she tried to kick my milk bucket, but I blocked her again. Finally, I held that kicking leg with one hand, and I milked with the other. The next time I had her, I found a green stick and popped her a good one on her leg every time she tried to kick. After the fourth or so whack with that stick, she learned her lesson and behaved.

We milked every day, twice a day, early morning and late afternoon. Between the milkings, I was out in the field with the other inmates. It was during the field work times that I would get blue. Every time they'd drive me out of that back gate, I didn't think I was going to make it back alive. You was lucky if you did. And if you did make it back to your wing, when you went to bed, you was blessed to wake up the next morning.

There was so much fighting and killing at night. The bosses and guards liked to see us fight too. It gave them some excitement so they didn't feel like they was doing time too. They agitated whenever they could till they worked up a fight between inmates, mostly new men against life-timers.

They agitated one up on me one day as we was in the field taking a water break. His name was Jimmerson. He was dark as night, short as a fire hydrant, neck thick as a tree trunk, eyes red as fire, and he had a scar down the left side of his face like he had been hit with an axe handle and his head won. I don't know what he was in for, but everybody stayed away from him.

That boss rode up on his horse to Jimmerson, pointed to me and said, "I bet you can't beat that nigger."

Jimmerson said, "I ain't seen a nigga up here I can't whup."

The boss said, "Go on out there and show us."

Jimmerson said, "I bet you a carton of cigarettes I can beat him."

The boss said, "I tell you what, Jimmerson. Go on out there and whup him, and I'll give you two cartons of cigarettes."

Whether I wanted to fight him or not, I had no choice. With my back to him and that boss, I made out like I didn't hear them. So when Jimmerson ran up on me, I planted my left foot in the ground and cocked my shoulders at my waist. I whispered, "Wait on him, wait on him, wait on him." When I felt him within an arm's reach, I swung around as hard as I could, and straightened my arm. As I lifted up off my left foot, my left fist met his face with all my weight behind it. *Ka-bam!* It sounded like the sweet part of a baseball bat hitting a ninety mile-an-hour fastball for a home run. Jimmerson lifted off the ground when his face met my fist, then landed back on his feet. His red eyes rolled back in his head, and then he closed them like he was sound asleep. He rocked back on his heels and fell one section of his body at a time. First his knees buckled, giving way to his big butt, then finally his basketball-sized head tilted back and hit the ground, bouncing twice, kicking up a cloud like a sack of flour dropped from the back of a wagon. Blood trickled down his forehead.

The inmates, guards, and bosses laughed and carried on, copying how Jimmerson had fallen like a tree and the sound he made—one big thud. I turned and walked to the water wagon, took the dipper, and scooped a drink as I dropped the brown, baseball-sized quartz rock I had hid in my hand. They never saw it. From that day on—four months back at Ramsey, almost two years in the pen, and just shy of turning twenty-one—I had a reputation: Don't mess with Houston.

I had come to the pen with a made-up mind to do my time like a man or die trying. Now I didn't have to worry so much about being a target for those hard-timers. Old Jimmerson never said another word to me.

But Warden Bounds did. As much as he liked me, he had to punish me. "Ten days in solitary for fighting. You nearly killed Jimmerson," he said calmly. He didn't seem too upset that it was Jimmerson who had got the worst of it.

I didn't know that Jimmerson had a metal plate in his head. That's why he had that scar. So when that rock in my hand hit that plate, one of them medic-trustees told me it pushed what little brains he had into the base of his spine. It took him almost ten days to wake up, and he still wasn't right—might never be.

While I was in solitary—by then I been sent to the hole maybe five times—I always came out with a lot of thinking done. In the hole, I thought about the stabbings at night. Would I be next? I thought about how weak Momma looked that last time she was here. I thought about Arlene growing up without her daddy and about Juanita without me by her side. I was never far from the fire—the burning hate for Ray—that had replaced my Juneteenth fire joy. But I also thought about the mornings at the dairy: the fog, the smell of hay, the taste of sweet milk. And I thought about leaving.

A few days out of the hole, I was back on dairy duty. The day I decided it was *the day*, nobody knew I was getting the hell out of here. You couldn't trust nobody. For a carton of cigarettes or some chocolate, somebody would snitch on you in a minute. So I went in like everything was normal that morning. The lazy, wide-as-a-house guard squatted on the same old rickety stool that squealed with every rock and sway as he nodded in and out of sleep, paying no attention to anything we did. As usual, whenever each of us finished with our first four cows, we let in four more. When we'd got through with those four, then everybody would herd out all the milked cows together. The exchange was a big old Jersey cow traffic jam. As cows was going in, and cows was going out, I crouched down low, hid behind Kick-a-Can till I had crawled close enough to the fence. Then I bolted like I was shot out of a cannon.

I climbed that fence, zigzagged like a rabbit across an open field to a line of trees, then headed north, never looking back. I ran awhile and walked awhile, ran awhile, walked awhile, all the time listening for what I knew was sure to come—a gunshot blast, barking dogs, or horse hooves, but there was nothing. So I kept running, feet springing over ditches and underbrush, logs and streams, my legs adjusting to the ground like truck wheels tied to coiled springs, covering ground as far and fast as my heart could pump and my legs could churn.

It took me a day to get as far as Sugar Land, about fifteen miles. That's where I got scared, because now I was about to lose the cover of the woods. There was in front of me farmhouses. That meant people. It came to me: the only way I was going to get away was to get out of these prison whites. I had to get some free-world clothes. Across a cornfield, I spotted a clothesline with a bunch of blue jeans and khaki shirts waving at me. I scooted low across the field, jumped a fence, snuck up behind this barn, and then I slowly peeped around the corner. I didn't see nobody. Hopefully no one saw me. About fifty yards up was that clothesline. I shot across the field, and with one hand, I grabbed a pair of pants and a shirt, clothespins and all, and ran to the side of a garage. Crouched down low, I could see between the slat boards: a car. *Shit, they're home.* And before I could snatch those pins off those clothes, a shotgun went off. *Shit.*

"Hold it. I say hold it there, by God. Don't move. Don't make me shoot you. Put your hands up."

I turned around slowly. There facing me was a tall, wiry man. Gray whiskers was stained on one side of his mouth by the tobacco he was giving a workout. He spat, then spoke, "Where you from?"

"Ramsey Unit, Rosharon," I said.

"Where you going?" he asked.

"I'm going home, uh, Bastrop," I said.

"Well, how much time you doing, boy?"

I told him, "I'm doing fifty years."

He dropped his shotgun a little. I could see his eyes better. They wasn't the eyes of a killer, but there was a spirit about them I didn't like. The farmer inched a little closer. "I understand how you feel. But, now, running off ain't going to help you none. You might get out there and beat them for two or three years or maybe four years. But sooner or later, they're going to catch you. They're going to bring you in and you'll have to start all over again. You might as well get it over with." He paused and pointed with his shotgun. "Get over to that tree." He motioned to a half-dead oak tree holding up one side of a small woodshed. He hollered out in the direction of his house, "Hey, boy."

Out of the back door of the main house ran a young boy, maybe ten or eleven years old. It must have been his son. He looked like a smaller copy of that farmer. He gave the boy his shotgun. It was almost as big as the boy. He told him, "Stand here and watch him while I go in and call the police and the warden."

I was so hungry that my stomach rumbled loud enough for both of them to stare at me. The grisly old man turned to me. "You had anything to eat?"

"No, sir. I could eat something."

That farmer snapped at the boy, "Now, you hold this right on him. If he moves, shoot him."

The boy answered him back with a high and serious voice, his eyes squinting down the barrel, his hands shaking. "Yes, sir, Paw." Sweat was pouring off his freckled face. His father went in the house. I didn't dare run.

The kid would have shot me by accident, the way he was holding that gun—the barrel slowly dropping, getting heavier by the minute. I figured I'd better ease the tension. "What's your name?" I asked him in the nicest voice I could find. Strung as tight as a screen door, he didn't say nothing at first, so I chimed in, "Now, my name is Johnnie Roy."

"I ain't supposed to be talking to you, just watching you," he said, shaking as he talked.

"I know, son. Now, I'm not going to run, but I do need to sit down or I'm gonna fall down. Then you might haul off and shoot me, so I'm going to have a seat, OK?" I slowly stuck out my arms and squatted to the ground.

"What did you do? I know you run from prison. What did you do? Why did you run?" His high, tight voice lowered as he lowered his gun down to his waist. The squint left his face.

"I didn't do nothing except have a twin brother. You got any brothers?" I asked him.

"No. I had me one, but he died. That ain't no crime, having a brother." He looked at me confused, almost sad. He said, "You see, my brother was killed—"

Before he could finish, that farmer had returned and slapped his son across the face, knocking the gun out of his hands. And right at my feet. "I told you to watch, not talk. Now get in the house, Johnny. Get. I'll take care of you later." The boy ran into the house crying. The farmer scooped up that shotgun before I could and said, "Don't try it, nigger. Run and you are dead. I get paid the same—live or dead. Now, you sit here and eat this." He handed me a loaf of bread.

I said, "Man, I don't want just bread." I thought he was going to bring me a plate of food. I knew he was going to get more than a loaf for turning me in. I heard tell that people turning in a runaway got plenty: a hundred dollars, a sack each of flour, meal, pinto beans, and meat.

"Hell, it's better than nothing," the farmer growled back.

So I ate nothing. I sat there waiting for somebody to come and get me. I could see that boy looking at me through the porch screen door. He had a look on his face I had seen a lot since I came to prison almost two years before, a look no boy should have at his age—a look of prison fear.

thirteen

WHAT A FRIEND

AFTER I SAT THERE FOR HOURS AT GUNPOINT under an old oak tree of a farmhouse somewhere between Sugar Land, Texas, and freedom—hungry, tired, and pissed off that I was caught this close to getting away—the sound of a car door slam broke the silence. That farmer, on the edge of sleep, jumped up from his chair and hollered, "Back here, Warden!"

Warden Leeford Gayther Bounds had come to get me himself, with one of those guards driving him in his big old Lincoln. Bounds spoke to the farmer like they was long lost friends. "Mr. Shaw, how y'all today?"

"Doing fine, Warden. Got another one for you," the farmer said, smiling.

The warden glanced at me with his hands on his hips, not in a mad way but with a look of disappointment, before he shook the farmer's hand. He turned to me then and said, "Houston, did you enjoy your little vacation?" I didn't say nothing, too embarrassed to say anything, seeing how Bounds had treated me better than all the other wardens, and I up and ran. He gave that farmer his reward. It was obvious they had done business before, the way they smiled and shook hands.

As the guard led me in handcuffs to the car, I smiled over at the kid, who was still staring out the screen porch door. I said to him, "You take it easy, now, Johnny. We got the same name, except I spell mine with an 'i-e' and yours is probably a 'y.' You did a good job holding that gun." With his father standing there, he didn't dare say nothing, but I could tell he wanted to. I felt sorry for the little fella. Hell, he was as much in prison as I was. Right then, I thought about Arlene. I didn't never want her to be like that little boy—caged.

As soon as we got on Highway 6, Warden Bounds, in his cool, almost glassy way, said his first real words to me. "Now Johnnie, I'm going to carry you back to my office after we get back. We're going sit down and have a talk because I know it's got to be something why you ran. You're too good a worker, and you haven't given me any trouble at all except for that run-in with Jimmerson. You one of the best working niggers I got down here on this farm."

Him calling me a nigger didn't have the same sting like it did when it came from those bosses. I didn't like the word, but for white folks in Texas, it was as natural to them as saying "Howdy" or "How y'all?" or "Sure is hot out." So, "nigger this and nigger that," it was the way they talked. Warden Bounds didn't call me "nigger" much, only when he was in the company of those other bosses so it wouldn't look like he was playing favorites.

He didn't say anything else the rest of the way. The radio played "Sugar Moon" by somebody named Bob Wills and His Texas Playboys. Then the driver switched to a church music station: *You're listening to KRCT Gospel Hour with "What a Friend We Have in Jesus." It's 7:48 p.m.* As the sun set, the low orange sky turned to night blue. The outline of downtown Houston—all lit up—looked like a million stars. All I could think about was all the living going on under those lights: people eating, drinking, dancing, singing, playing cards, and playing around—all that living being done. I came to prison a nineteen-year-old boy. In a month, I'd turn twenty-one. With all that I'd seen and done in two years, I was nowhere near a boy now. I was a man who might not ever get to do some real living again.

I thought about the words to that song playing on the radio: "What a friend we have in Jesus, all our sins and griefs to bear." Where was this God-friend they was singing about? I tried to close my eyes and get some sleep before we got back to Ramsey, but all I could conjure up was all the darkness that had been my first two years in prison. Right then—I don't know what got ahold of me, but I started to pray within myself, not believing that that prayer was going to make it out that car. But I prayed anyhow. *God, if you are God, I need this friend everybody's singing and talking about.* That was it. That was my first real prayer in prison.

The next morning, the Warden picked up in his office where he had left off in the car. "Now what I want to know is why did you run off?"

"I got tired, couldn't stand it no more—living in that wing, walking in blood on the bathroom floor in the middle of the night, trying to sleep with inmates with dirks diving over me trying to stab somebody."

He said, "Well, I believe that, but why didn't you come to me and ask me to put you someplace else. I'd have transferred you, put you in another wing."

"The same thing's happening on them other wings," I said.

"I could have put you in a cellblock," he said as he stood up and walked over to me and put his hand on my shoulder. "I tell you what I'm going to do. I'm going to have to take your good time, for now. If I don't, they'd be running away every day. So, I'm going to take all your good time and put you in solitary for three days. Can you go there and spend three days, and not go to hollering and beating on the doors?"

I said, "Yeah." And I did. Before I knew it, I heard keys rattling and felt that burst of light flood that concrete sweatbox—three days done.

"Houston!" A voice came out of the light like before. Then came that backlit face of the man in a Stetson. It was Warden Bounds. After I cleaned up and got something to eat—I wasn't sick from normal food this time—he sent for me. "Now, I'm going to put you in Hoe Squad One. You go out there and give me two good weeks of hard work. I have already told him about you. You go out there and give that boss a good effort, and I'll come and get you."

After the two weeks was up, I looked up and saw a cloud of dust coming out to our field. It was the warden's car. He pulled up to my squad and told the boss, "Send Old Houston here."

"Johnnie Roy, I told you I was coming out here," the warden said and smiled. "Well, I got something for you. You're still going to need some help to do those fifty years, so I'm giving you back all your 'two-for-one' time and I'm going to put you on a job—construction trustee." He told me that like he was proud of what he was doing. I got a feeling that his job took a lot out of him—took a little bit of the human out of him every time he had to face the animal choices he had to make—sending a man to solitary, feeding a man bread and water, every time he had to deal with men raping men. Whenever he got a chance to do good, I saw it put a smile on his face. There was rumors he drank. I understood if he did drink. Being a warden was hard. The day he made me a construction trustee made him feel good about himself, I believe.

So, he gave me a construction job. Really, it amounted to walking around the administration buildings and the yard, picking up trash. I'd run errands for them bosses. Warden Bounds also moved me out of that wing into a cell. No more walking in blood.

Things was changing. Was it that prayer I had prayed? On the first night in that cell, I tried praying again: *Lord, help me. Send me home to my family. Until then, send me a friend down here to help me. Lord, you know I ain't guilty.* I asked God to show himself. *Get me home, and I'll live for you.* As soon as I finished, something started to well up in me, bubbling like a spring of water. There was sounds coming out of me that I didn't know. Whatever was happening made me feel good like I had never felt before. Had things really started to change? Maybe, just maybe, I done met my friend.

I had that cell all to myself for only a day, and then Bennie moved in. The cellblock sergeant brought him in. "Houston, this here is Bennie Armstrong. Y'all ought to get along fine. Bennie has been here for a while, and you just got here, and ain't none of y'all going nowhere soon." Bennie threw his stuff on the top bunk, and then stuck his hand out and said, "You can call me Bennie Lee."

I stuck out my hand and looked him straight in the eyes so as not to give him any idea that I was afraid of him or that I was a punk. "Johnnie Roy Houston is my name."

"Oh, I know who you are," he said, smiling a mouth full of gold. "You the one that took out Old Jimmerson. He fell like Goliath, they tell me. Somebody had to check him."

Bennie didn't need no introduction either. I knew who he was too. He was a building tender. A building tender, mostly called "BTs," was life-timers or hard-timers who the wardens used like guards. They was given police sticks and allowed to tote dirks. These inmate-guards would control the building from the inside. So if a fight broke out, they was supposed to break it up. They'd beat up on you with those bats like those bosses, but nothing would be done to them.

Some of those building tenders was worse than the guards, like the one they called "Bay City." There was nothing he couldn't do—wouldn't do. He'd beat you or have inmates beat you to get your commissary. One time, he set an inmate on fire with lighter fluid. He also cut a man's Achilles so he couldn't run, and then had him raped. The thing was, nobody stopped Bay City—no guards, no bosses, not even the wardens. Truth is, there was a prison inside the prison—what I called the "underbelly"—run by some of those building tenders. Bay City was the unofficial warden of that underbelly. If you complained about those BTs to the guards or higher, you might find your cell unlocked when it was supposed to be locked late at night. You might not see the morning after those BTs finished with you.

"What are you in for, Houston?" Bennie asked. He wasn't a part of that underbelly.

fourteen

WRIT WRITERS

WE BOTH SAT AT ALMOST THE SAME TIME, but I waited for her to raise her head and look me in the eye before I spoke first. "Hey baby. How you doing? Where's Arlene?" I didn't give her time to answer any of those questions before I asked, "What's wrong?" I could feel it the moment she looked at me. My funny and strong "I ain't studden you" Juanita was not there.

She tried a half-assed smile and said, "I'm fine. Arlene is fine, growing like a weed. She's with Daddy."

"You ain't answered my question. What's wrong?" All that peace in my belly from the night before quickly leaked out like air from a stabbed pig's bladder. I barely had enough breath to ask again, "Something's the matter?"

She dropped her head and said, "Johnnie, me and Arlene are moving to Austin. I need to take care of her. You know how Bastrop is? I … I can't do this." She took a long deep breath, then looked up with teary eyes and said, "There ain't nobody else."

I didn't say nothing—couldn't say nothing.

"You know I love you, Johnnie Roy Houston. I got to take care of Arlene. Ain't you gonna say nothing?"

That *fire* overcame me. What I could have said I did not say. My love for her took ahold of me. I saw, for the first time, that my wife was doing time too—my time. She didn't rob nobody. She didn't have no trial. She wasn't given a number to wear. She was just guilty of loving me and having my baby. And she was carrying this like a prison number on her back. She was now like me—doing time with a made-up mind. Who was I to change that mind? I looked at her through my own tears and said, "Y'all need to get out of Bastrop. You make sure she gets a way to come down here and see me, you hear?"

"I hear you." She paused a long time, and then managed a small smile and said sweetly, "I ain't studden you. I love you."

"I love you too, Juanita Marie McMarion." I got up first, gave her one last look. We touched the screen. The guard glanced over but didn't say a word. I didn't look back—couldn't look back. I don't remember walking back to my cell. I remember lying in my bunk trying to find that place where I was the night before. But the strange fire didn't come. I cried like somebody had died, but it wasn't no "body." It was my marriage. I mourned but not without a peace—a strange peace.

Two months passed. I got the divorce papers, signed them, and sent them back. Two months later I received the official decree. On December 8, 1949, Juanita and me was divorced. She was free. A little more than two years into fifty, I still had my time to do. But she was free.

♦ ♦ ♦

For the next nineteen years—1950 to 1968—I settled in to doing that time. I had learned from picking cotton when I was a little boy, when I was looking down a long row, so long I couldn't see the end, to lower my head, bend my back, and keep my eyes on my feet and the next plant ahead. Sooner or later I would get to the end of the row. Then I'd turn around and do the same again till my sack was full and the sun was down. And that's what I did to do my time.

I did good, for the most part, with this new job at Ramsey I, going around the yard, picking up trash, doing whatever those bosses and guards needed. People who used to mess with me didn't agitate on me anymore—no fights, no solitary, no trouble. Warden Bounds also made me a building tender like Bennie, but I wasn't one those out-of-control BTs who ran the prison within the prison like Bay City. I did my work and tried to protect the new inmates, remembering that I was once one.

I now believed God was watching over me. Why? I don't know, as stubborn and hot-headed as I was in the beginning. And although the place hadn't changed, since the night of that strange visitation of peace, I had started changing. But it didn't take long before that change was tested. I was sitting in the recreation yard minding my own business when one of them hard-acts who was also a BT—he hung out with Bay City a lot—well, he just reached over my shoulder and grabbed my chew that was in my pocket. He said, "Since you a BT, you don't mind sharing, now do you?"

I started to boil. I never let somebody mess with my commissary. I grabbed his hand and loosed that pouch. Before he could reach for his dirk, I pulled him by the collar hard enough for him to choke on his tongue. I squeezed till he turned colors. But I stopped right there. We was eyeball to eyeball. I didn't say a word. I just let him go and walked away.

He wheezed out, "You better watch your back, BT. You better watch your back."

But it was over just like that. The old me would have had to draw blood for it to be over. Whoever stopped me from really hurting that BT must have watched my back too. That BT stayed clear of me. I knew who "whoever" was. I was changing. I did not boil over.

My first two years of prison was the roughest—first Ramsey I, then to Walls and death row, then back to Ramsey after I quit death row. Over the course of the next nineteen years, they moved me when and where they felt like it. And you'd better not ask why. They moved me to Ramsey II right down the road in Rosharon to Clemens in Brazoria County near Houston to Ellis, north of

Huntsville, and finally to Wynne back in Huntsville, where I was in late 1968.

Everywhere I was assigned, the units was the same because the rhythm—the beat of the beast—was the same. Every time a bell rang, you had to be where you was supposed to be, or else. Adjusting to the different wardens was the thing. They had their own way of doing things. You had to figure them out quick. There was Warden C. L. "Bear Tracks" McAdams, known to be relentless in tracking down troublemakers. He tracked down everything. Warden H. E. "The Owl" Moore saw everything. Warden L. G. Bounds was as fair as they come. Then there was Warden "Walking George" Beto, who ran the whole show now. They called him "Walking George" because he was liable to walk up on you at any time for an inspection. It didn't matter who: unit warden, guard, or inmate. I heard tell he used to be a preacher, then a teacher, and now he was a prison warden of the largest jail in the world. He ran things with an iron hand, wearing each one of the hats he'd worn before. He'd quote you a Scripture while throwing you in solitary to teach you a lesson.

But in my mind, it didn't matter who was in charge. This place was made red brick by red brick, steel bar by steel bar to change you, to break you into something else, if you let it. I came here Johnnie Roy Houston—a man, not a number—a human, not an animal. I planned to leave the same. If that meant feet first in a pine box, then that was what it was going to be. I'd as good as figured that was how it was going to be. But now, since God had got ahold of me, I figured that if I put my hand in his, I could maybe walk, not roll, out of here—and walk out of here better than when I came in.

One of the things I did to do that long row of nineteen years was to keep my head in books. I went through only the tenth grade at Emile High School. I wanted to get my GED—and more if I could. So I enrolled in the LaSalle Extension University, 417 South Dearborn Street, Chicago, Illinois. It is something how a thing can get in your brain and you remember it. I will never forget that address because every week for ten years I sent something to LaSalle Extension University, 417 South Dearborn Street, Chicago, Illinois. Nearly every red cent I had on my commissary account went to that address to pay for my books. I didn't hardly have enough money on my books to get toothpaste and a toothbrush, coffee, or chew. But I wasn't interested in those things.

When I got my books, I read and I wrote. I wrote and I read. I took tests and mailed them back to be graded. All my scores was 80s and 90s. They sent me a diploma and a letter saying that all I had to do to become a lawyer was to get my master's degree, go to Chicago, and pass the bar exam. I don't know if they was blowing smoke or not. All I know is, with my head down in them books, it helped me get down that long row of years, one year at a time.

To do my time, not only did I get ahold of books, but I got ahold of some bull. His name was "Dynamite." Dynamite was the meanest Brahma bull the devil ever made. Every Sunday in October the prison ran a rodeo. I used to drive the flatbed truck with a cage on the back to carry inmates from the nearby farm units to the rodeo arena. But I wasn't just the rodeo truck driver, I was a rodeo rider. If it had four legs, I rode it, roped it, and milked it. My favorite: bull riding.

The arena announcer would holler out my name as they strapped me on a monster with horns and tied-up testicles. "Coming out of shoot number ten is old Johnnie Roy Houston out of Bastrop doing fifty years. He's riding Ohhh–ld Dynamite." Every time that announcer said "Old," his mouth slowed down and drawled out "Old" what seemed like forever. Then when they let go of that swinging gate, the world slowed down. After a second, hell would kick in. Dynamite's first move was to kick his hind legs as high as he could. It felt like you had been rear-ended by a semitrailer. It shook you so hard, you couldn't hold your pee. Then he'd turn his body in a tight circle one way, then change directions. The jerk from the change of direction was enough to snap your neck if you didn't tuck your chin and throw out your free hand for balance. Every organ inside you went out of its normal place. The thing is, I hadn't been on but three seconds. If the bull was having a bad day, you might make it to seven. When Dynamite was having a normal day, with all his twelve hundred pounds of meanness strapped under you, you was face down in dirt and animal shit before you knew it. Then those "alongside riders" would come alongside you and protect you because Dynamite was coming back for more.

The announcer would draw out, "Oh, let's give Ohhh–ld Houston a hand. He'll get him next time." When I was out there in that arena for that short time, I didn't feel like a prisoner—a person people wanted to be protected from. I felt like a winner people cheered for. I felt like a Hollywood Western star. For four days in October, I was *Ohhh–ld Houston riding Dynamite.*

When I was a boy, the hardest part of picking those long rows of cotton was raising up to see how far I had picked, how much cotton I had missed, and how far I had to go. It was the same with doing my time. A half a dozen visitation Sundays a year, I'd look up to see what I had missed. Juanita, who had remarried, kept her promise and saw to it that Arlene came to visit me. August 16, 1964, she turned eighteen. I missed that. Except for the snips that I had witnessed through wire-mesh screens, I missed so much of her life. I prayed to God that somehow, someway, I would not miss much more of my baby becoming a woman.

Arlene wasn't all I missed. With my head down, doing that long row of years, I missed what the free world was going through: civil rights marches, Vietnam War, Malcolm killed in '65, Dr. King in April '68. My eyes were fixed on my feet, one step at a time, one day to the next.

One morning early in '68, as I was doing rounds around the administration buildings, picking up paper, deep in thought, praying, I noticed a large wad of crumpled-up, typed pages. I didn't know what made me pick it up and look at it, but I did. It had on the top: "Cause Number 4806, Application for Writ of Habeas Corpus."

I read a few lines and put it in my pocket so I could read it all later. Stopping work to read something that wasn't yours could get you demoted from a good-time "picking up paper" position to a hard-time "picking up rocks" job. How would they know I hadn't stolen it off some desk? So I put it away till later.

I had heard about inmates writing writs. I later found out that's what some of those men on death row was doing with their noses in books all the time. But I had never seen a writ, let alone known exactly what was in them. Some inmates made regular visits to what they called the "writ room." It was a big room next to the gym, a room all to itself full of typewriters, desks, and books. I didn't pay much attention to the room because I couldn't type, and I didn't know nothing about law other than what a piss-poor lawyer looked like. Inmates getting their hands ahold of law books was all new. It didn't used to be this way. Beto was afraid if inmates got a hold on the legal system from the inside, the inside might change. Inmates might take real control—not building tender control, but inmates controlling their own justice in the so-called justice system. The truth might get out—not Dr. George Beto's truth, but the truth about solitary, about bread and water, about men dying of natural causes like naturally drowning with a back full of shotgun lead, naturally dying of seizures brought on by bad building tenders swinging bats upside heads. Inmates helping inmates with the law would start a revolution. Beto wasn't about to let that happen.

But he couldn't stop it.

There was this Mexican inmate I had seen around Wynne who always had a group of inmates buzzing around him like flies because he had a reputation for knowing the law better than most lawyers that'd been to law school. His name was Freddie Cruz. He went by the name "The Counselor" and was the leader of a group of self-taught, inmate legal counselors. He and this woman, an outside legal-defense lawyer named Francis Jalet, teamed up and gave Beto holy hell. I saw her around all the time, talking to prisoners. She stirred up so much stink, Beto stopped her from visiting. She and Cruz gave Beto such a red ass with all the lawsuits they filed to give inmates access to the legal system, we got a writ room and was finally allowed to have law books in our cells. Then anybody could become a writ writer and his own legal counsel—even me.

Late that night, I read through them crumpled-up pages I found in the yard: "Now respectfully comes … petitioner by and through counsel and files this his Petition for a Writ of Habeas Corpus … for retrial." I had no idea what all that meant, but I did recognize the word *retrial*. My spirit jumped at that word. If a writ could open a door to a retrial, maybe this was why God brought that piece of balled-up paper my way, to tell me to write a writ. But even though I had my GED and those LaSalle classes, I wasn't no writ writer. I damn sure wasn't no lawyer. So how was I supposed find the words to convince the court to give me a retrial? For every excuse that came up in my head, God said (I guess it was God), "Write a writ." I'd say, "Lord, you know I can hardly read." He'd say, "Write a writ." This went on for a while till I drifted off to sleep. I woke up with a made-up mind: I'm going to write a writ.

That next day, after I came in from work, a guard hollered, "All y'all going to the writ room, let's go." So I went. I didn't know my ass from a hole in the ground there. The room was full. I stood there till a voice from behind me asked, "First time?"

I turned and said, "Yeah, and I ain't got no idea about how to type my own name let alone write something for a judge to read."

"What are you trying to do?" He was one of those writ writers I'd seen hanging out with Cruz. They was always in an area all to themselves. When they wasn't writing writs, or helping other inmates write writs, they was in solitary or on the worst work details for pissing off Beto. This particular inmate asked me again, "What are you trying to do?"

"What am I trying to do? Man, I'm trying to get up out of here," I said. "I'm trying to write a writ to get a retrial. I'm innocent of a crime that got me fifty years. What's a writ of habeas corpus anyway?"

He came back at me with a smile. "Yeah, yeah. We're all innocent in here. Look, 'habeas corpus' is Latin for 'you have the body.' A writ of habeas corpus is a petition to get the prison to bring an inmate before the court for a hearing to determine if he should be locked up. Look, my name's Campbell. I know all this is a lot. Over there's a stack of books with examples of writs. I got to finish up with a couple of guys over there. Come back tomorrow, and I'll help you get started, first thing."

I shook his hand and said, "Appreciate it, appreciate it." I jumped right in reading some of those writs. I might as well have been reading Chinese. I took a legal pad and pen and started jotting down words I didn't know and questions I had for Campbell the next day. I definitely was coming back.

The next day, Campbell wasn't there. Somebody said he got sideways with a building tender about a writ that made Warden McAdams look bad. So Campbell got solitary. But another inmate-lawyer helped me as much as he could. He said, "You've got a lot of catching up to do." What he was saying was that I was way behind on the legal talk that would get the court's attention. So I spent all my free time doing just that—catching up—reading, writing, copying from other writs, and asking questions from any writ writer around. It took me two months to write my first writ. It took one month for it to come back stamped, "Return to Sender." I had sent it to a bad address. I resent it to a good address. It was returned with a big stamp on the first page: DENIED.

I kept writing writs. Sometimes it took weeks for them to come back, sometimes months, but each time they'd come back stamped "denied." I stayed in my cell reading, writing, and rewriting. I knew my writs had no business coming back denied because I had a lot of grounds for a new trial: no witnesses were called for me, and I didn't get proper legal representation. In a word, I had been denied something called "due process" because my attorney was supposed to defend me better than he did. But he chickened out, I believed, after they threatened him. I could have done a better job representing myself even then.

With every writ and denial, I was getting smarter—sounding smarter too. I was starting to get this legal lingo down. There was a time when I was a boy, you couldn't tell me anything. When Momma saw me like that, she would say, "You smelling yourself." I was mad at the world then—mostly Ray and Bastrop. I thought I knew it all, or at least enough to get out of Bastrop and make me a better life. Now I was listening to anybody who knew more than me who was willing to help me get smart enough to get out of prison. I was changing right before my eyes, from that ignorant nineteen-year-old who nobody could tell nothing to, to a man who could read law books and write whole sentences, who could hold his temper. I was using the words *due process* and knew what they meant.

I didn't hear nothing back from some writs. There was a good chance they didn't even get mailed because Walking George was unbending on what was said in those writs about conditions in the world's largest prison system. They had prison staff reading our outgoing and incoming mail. I believe, in my heart of hearts, that some of my mail that they said they mailed, they didn't. Sometimes they wouldn't even mail letters home to family if you was discussing something the prison didn't want out. You couldn't even seal your envelope. And if your letters told of what was going on down here—the whippings, the stompings, and the kickings—that stuff was marked out, or worse, the whole letter was thrown away.

One day in early 1969, I was in the writ room looking over a writ that had been denied when I got a tap on my shoulder. "What'd they say was wrong with that one?" It was Cruz himself. You didn't see much of him: he was always in solitary for something he wrote or told that outside lawyer, Mrs. Jalet, or something he said in the newspaper. A lot of times, he was at writ hearings.

"Let me take a look at this," he said. "What's your name?"

"Johnnie Roy Houston."

While he was looking over it, we talked. He asked, "Now, what are you in for?"

"I'm doing fifty years for assault and robbery. But I didn't do it. My twin brother did. They beat a confession out of me. My piss-poor lawyer didn't call a single witness who could have told them where I was and where I wasn't the morning of that robbery. After a thirty-minute trial, that judge hit that gavel like he was swatting a fly: 'Guilty as charged.' All told, I been locked up now damn near twenty-three years." I didn't know if he wanted to hear all this, but that was my story. I asked him, "What's your story? Where you from?"

"I'm from San Antonio—the sweetest señoritas and hottest Tex-Mex food in the world. You ever been there? You like Tex-Mex, brother?" He didn't give me a chance to answer. He kept reading and talking. "Yeah, me and you could be brothers, same peas in the same messed-up pod. They convicted me of assault and robbery, too, except I didn't have no lawyer. That 'thing' I had was a court-appointed piece of shit. So I'm here doing fifty just like you," he said.

"You got any people?" I asked.

"Yeah, I got a brother somewhere. You might say we were twins because we did everything together: robbed people together, took heroin together—except I got hooked and he didn't. My mother and father split up when I was eight, so I don't know where my old man is. I been in here since I was twenty-one, but they ain't broke me yet. They get to you yet? Don't let them get your spirit. If they do, you're as dead as a man walking the green mile. They just ain't asked you to 'Have a seat, please' yet."

He kept talking and reading, but at some point, he wasn't even talking to me anymore. He was off somewhere, talking to himself. He told me in a quiet voice like he was telling me a secret, "Maybe it's bad for a prisoner to have too much spirit. Maybe too much awareness and hope pierce the heart, leaving too many sorrows. After ten years of imprisonment, I felt wasted and barren. That's when these law books saved my spirit."

I said to him, "No, they ain't got to me. But the Lord has. That's who told me to write this writ. He's going to help me get out of here."

"Well, the Lord needs a course in Jurisprudence 101. Look, I ain't got nothing against your Lord, but look right here. It's not your Lord that's gonna do this. You need to take this word out and put this word in. You are the petitioner, so put 'petitioner' everywhere you have written your name. The justice system is all about the right words and procedures and less about doing right by a man, about finding the good that is left in him before he is thrown away like basura, you know, trash."

He circled and marked and wrote over words and sentences I needed to correct. He told me I was wasting my time sending this to the lower courts because they had a "hand's off" policy when it came to prisons. They was "sympathetic to the status quo." He might as well have been talking Spanish—he did talk in Spanish, sprinkling in words from time to time so I didn't always know what language we was talking in, prison or law lingo or Spanish. "Look, you and God go and make these corrections. Put, in order, your strongest cases for a retrial, and list Beto as the 'respondent.' He's the El Jefe a Cargo—the head boss in charge—of the Texas Department of Corrections. He's got to answer you."

Cruz rattled off stuff like it was as natural as breathing to him. "Put down first that you have been illegally restrained at the Wynne Unit. Second, put down that your plea in your first trial was 'not guilty.' Third, explain how they obtained an illegal confession by beating you." He was going so fast I could hardly keep up. "Fourth, put down that in your appeal, there was no oral argument. Fifth, put down you were denied your 'Constitutional privilege against self-incrimination in violation of the Fifth and Fourteenth Amendments.' Last, put down you were denied due process under the Texas Constitution and the Fourteenth Amendment of the United States Constitution." He was big on tying your writ to the Constitution, article by article. "Your God will understand 'Constitution.' Ask Moses." He started laughing. He hardly ever laughed.

Cruz was messing with me about God. I could tell he was a believer. His spirit was too strong not to have God on his side. He said as he got up from his chair, "Bring it back in a couple of days. Then we will see about getting this to a higher court. Somos hermanos. We are brothers, amigo."

fifteen

MOMMA

After Juanita and me split, I had my writ writing, my rodeo riding, and the LaSalle Extension University, 417 South Dearborn Street, Chicago, Illinois, to help me do that long row of nineteen years, but the pickings was still hard, especially visitation days. During those years, Momma moved to Dallas to live with Mozell. She had to. Her hip gave her trouble so she could barely walk. By 1968, Momma was eighty, and "Sad Sunday" had come and gone every week for a long time without my name being called.

Then one Sunday to my surprise, they called out, "Houston, you got a visitor for station four." My heart jumped. Mozell had brought Momma. It was Christmas of '68. I was happy to see her, but it also hurt me to see her scoot with her walker. I winced with her every inch. She wore the bonnet she always wore when she went someplace special. She had on her long dress with bluebonnet flowers all over it, and she had on her apron. That's how she looked when she went to church. I asked her once, "Momma, why you got to wear an apron?" She'd smiled and said, "Well, they call it 'service' don't they? So there you go, Johnnie Roy."

Mozell stayed seated on the bench where the free-world visitors sat who were waiting their turn to go to the cubbyhole. Before Momma plunked down in the chair, she looked over her shoulder, like always at visits, like someone was watching her. She looked heavy—not fatter, but weighted down. She was dripping wet with sweat running down her face, and her bonnet brim was soaked. The armpits of her dress was dark down to her waist. I spoke first, "Merry Christmas, Momma." She looked up with teary eyes and didn't say nothing. "What's the matter. Everything all right?"

She wiped her face with the lace handkerchief she kept in her bosom and said, "Shh!" She kept looking around. There was no guard close enough to listen in, so she inched right up against the screen, leaned in, and whispered, "I am sorry. I know I promised I would get you out by now. I don't want you to get upset. I found out who did it. Your brother and Red Winston did it. Then they went to Rufus Jackson's to shoot pool and gamble. They went to bragging on what they did. Then Red Winston and Ray went to West Texas the next week."

The weight of this whole thing had plum pulled her mind down. Like the flooded Colorado, her memory done spilled over its banks. She couldn't tell where "what was" and "what is" began and ended. She had confessed this truth about Ray and Red nearly every time she had visited from day one till now.

She whispered, "I'm ashamed. They ought not to have done that to Dr. Combs. He was good to us, letting us live in his rent house for next to nothing. I didn't raise my children that way." Then Momma was about to lose it, and her voice grew louder and shakier. "Don't you worry, son. I'm gonna have something done about it if it's the last thing I do. I done lost one son. I ain't gonna lose two. Don't you give up." She repeated it and repeated it: "I'm gonna have something done about it if it's the last thing I do. Don't you give up. Don't you give up." That's how I knew her mind had done wore out, her repeating herself.

What welled up in me then was this: "If ever I get my hands on Ray, I'm gonna kill him, Momma. If I ever get my freedom, I'm gonna kill him." I thought I was past this, but I wasn't. I didn't even realize those words had seeped out loud enough for Momma to hear, that "I'm gonna kill him."

Covering her mouth with her handkerchief, Momma went to crying loud enough for the guards to hear. "Now, Johnnie, quit that talk." Those guards could tell something was boiling up in our station. It didn't take much for them to shut down a visit. That's the thing when my mother came to visit me. I was glad to see her; it made my heart happy. But I hated to see her this way. It stirred up something in me I didn't think was still in me—the will to kill my brother.

"All right, let's bring it to a close," the guard called out as he strolled by, hitting the wire screen with his stick.

She touched that screen with her hand, and I touched her hand with mine when that guard wasn't looking. "Johnnie Roy," she said, "don't you worry none. Your momma is going take care of this. I'm going to get you out." She took a long pause, gathered herself, and said, "Merry Christmas, baby. I put some money on your books. It ain't much. I love you, Johnnie Roy." She turned and looked at me just before she pushed that walker, grunting with each inch. I didn't know when I'd see her again.

I didn't eat much in the mess hall that evening. Normally, Sunday's food was better than them other days. There'd be chicken, potatoes with gravy that didn't taste like they made it from sawdust, and dessert that was something that looked like cake with a thin coating on it they called icing. It was better than nothing. But I wasn't studden eating. I went back to my cell and sat on the edge of my bed and went over and over in my mind the look on my momma's face—the worry that hung on her like a saddle, her teary "I'm gonna have something done about it if it's the last thing I do," and her repeating herself. Her "don't give up" was ringing in my spirit. I stared into my hands until the lights went out. I don't remember going to sleep. I don't think I ever really did. I laid my head on my mattress and drifted off to a place I did not know and had a strange half-dream.

It was raining the kind of rain they call a frog choker—rain coming down like a cow peeing on a pole bridge. There was this house—not the house we rented from Dr. Combs but worse—a sharpshooter, a cotton picker's house, long and narrow with front and back porches and screen doors full of holes. Between the front door and the back was one room that was really three: living room, kitchen, and bedroom. It could hardly be called a house, more like a chicken coop or a barn fit for animals. Rusty nails barely held termite-eaten boards together. Rain dripped through holes in the corrugated roof.

There was people sitting in the yard and on the porch, drinking and carrying on in the downpour. Their faces was blurry, their skin lighter than most of the people I knew. They was speaking in a language all unto itself. I couldn't make out a word. I walked around and between them. They paid no attention to me like they didn't even see me. Before I got to the rickety front steps, I heard my momma scream, "Help me, Jesus! Help me, Lord!" I heard the dull thud sound that an axe makes against a hollow tree. "Lord Jee …" The hollering stopped.

I ran as fast as I could up the porch stairs, but the more I ran, the more stairs there was. I managed to grab hold of the screen door and pull myself off the stairs and into the house. As I stumbled in, I saw the backside of a man whose figure looked familiar, but whose face was turned toward the night and pouring rain. I couldn't make him out. I fell next to my mother who was lying on the floor lifeless, her head cracked like a melon, her blouse ripped at the neck. The handkerchief she hid in her bosom, the place where she kept her money—all the money she had—lay in her blood. The money was gone. She was gone. *I cried out, "Momma, Momma, Momma …"*

"Momma!" I woke screaming so loud that the inmates on the block took it to mean something else was going down, like I was getting stabbed or worse. "Somebody's getting theirs," an inmate hollered out of the dark. A guard hollered back, "Pipe down or I'll come in there and crack some heads." An inmate hollered back, "That's what they doing, laying pipe down." But it wasn't none of that. I sat up on my bed, wet with sweat from head to toe like I had been hosed. In those wet clothes, eyes wide open, I curled up with my knees to my chest until morning trying to figure out what this dream meant—that house, the people, my momma in a pool of blood.

That was my Christmas week in 1968.

From that night on, all I knew was that none of the letters I got from my sister said anything about my mother. When my forty-first birthday came and went—Saturday, March 1, 1969—and the birthday card from Mo didn't say nothing about Momma, I knew something was wrong. It took me a month and a half to get up enough courage to ask somebody. I asked to see the chaplain.

His office was right down the hall from the warden's. I had seen him before in the mess hall from a distance. Except for that white collar some priests wear, he looked like any other guard—cowboy hat, boots, and a gun. I had never talked to him before. I needed to today. He spoke soft and even. "Well, what do you want to talk to me about today, Mr. Houston? What seems to be the problem?"

I told him the dream I'd had after my momma's last visit and that I hadn't heard from Momma at all since then. "That ain't like my momma." I wiped my eyes, but I couldn't wipe fast enough before the dam broke. I broke down. Where I come from and where I was now, you don't let people see you cry, but I couldn't hold it. "Something done happen to her. I know it."

He said, "Well, you have any relatives I can call? I'll be glad to for you, Johnnie."

I told him, "Yeah, my sister in Dallas—Mozell—Mozell Hudson. My momma is living with her." I gave him the number.

The chaplain said, "Well, I'll sure call her, and I'll get in touch with you and let you know something. It's going to be OK, Johnnie. Don't you worry any."

I said OK, but it wasn't OK. I could feel it. I'd had that feeling before, when my father walked out on us. Daddy said it was going to be OK, but it wasn't. I didn't see much of him and things got harder for us. When they convicted me in a thirty-minute trial, Momma said it was going to be OK, that she'd get me out, but it wasn't OK. I was still in here. Ray was the only one OK. So when people tell me "OK," that means to me "OK, here it comes." It was two whole weeks before they called me in, and it wasn't the chaplain who called. It was the warden.

"Come on in here, Johnnie Roy, and take a seat." He wouldn't look me in the eyes at first. His eyes locked in on something outside that big window that overlooked the main yard. He mumbled, "They never tell you that when you take this job running a prison, you become a prisoner yourself—thankless." Then he turned and looked at me straight on. "Now I don't want you to get out of control. I need you to promise not to break down. You are a grown man and a strong man—one of the strongest we got down here. I got some bad news for you. The chaplain called up to Dallas and talked to your sister—I think her name is Mozell. Well, she told him that your momma died April 17 ..." He went quiet, turning back to the window before going on to say what need be said. "And they have already had the service back in Bastrop."

A groan came out of me like the sound of a cow when they knock them in the head with a sledgehammer to slaughter. "My momma dead? What you mean they had the service? She's buried?"

The warden walked around his desk and sat on the corner, with his eyes level to mine. "Now look here Johnnie Roy, it wasn't right what they did. They should have written you and told you, or called me. I would have seen to it that you got a funeral reprieve to go to the service. I got a letter here. I want to read it to you." He went on and read the letter about how my momma took sick and passed and they shipped her body back to Bastrop and buried her. He never gave me the letter to carry back to my cell. He laid it back down on his desk.

I don't know whether he was telling me all that was in that letter, or if there was anything on that paper at all. I got to thinking he should have given me the letter so I could put it in my pocket and carry it to my cell and read it for myself. I still don't know what was in that letter.

All I could do is sink my head into my shoulders and hold it with both hands so I wouldn't fall headfirst to the floor. The warden put his hand on my shoulder. "I tell you what I'm gonna do. You took this like a man. I want you to go to your cell. You don't have to go to work. I'm gonna call the hospital and tell them to check on you every hour. If they see any signs of a nervous breakdown, I'm going to tell the hospital steward to put you in the hospital. You don't have to worry about going to work until I come to you and you tell me you're ready to go to work."

Two guards walked me back to my cell. I could hear one of them sniffling. That's the only thing I remember about that walk back, not the chatter of inmates, not the rattle of keys or the grind of gears opening and shutting the doors. I was a dead man walking.

For weeks, I did nothing—just lay in my cell trying to eat, but couldn't. Then late one night, I couldn't help it. I broke down and went to screaming and hollering and crying. The hospital steward had to carry me to the infirmary. They kept me in there for about three weeks, giving me medicine and watching over me until I settled down enough to go back. And when I did, I still didn't have to go to work. They kept me in for another two weeks.

I finally went on back to building tender duty. During my walk around the yard, picking up trash, I went over my momma in my mind. I could see her in her starched dress with the tiny blue flowers and with her bonnet and apron. I could feel her hand rub my head in a gentle circle as she whispered my name and held me in her bosom. With every circle of her hand around my nappy head, she spoke softer and sweeter.

I had spent twenty-three years locked up. The hardest thing wasn't the solitary. It wasn't all the bloodshed. It wasn't even death row. It was April 17, 1969—the day my momma died and I didn't get a chance to say goodbye. The one thing that had kept my hope alive of getting out of prison was the hope of being with her without bars between us. That was gone. Sitting on my make-shift table of books and bed slats was the last writ returned denied. I took those papers that Cruz had marked up himself and started to tear up each page, one by one.

sixteen

BACK IN BASTROP

I STARTED TEARING UP THOSE PAGES, and then I heard these words: "I'm gonna have something done about it if it is the last thing I do. Don't give up." The voice was as loud as if someone was in that cell with me, but there wasn't nobody. "I'm gonna have something done if it is the last thing I do. Don't give up." I heard it again, but this time, something was added: "Don't give up, *baby*." It was Momma.

I collapsed on the floor in the middle of those torn papers, spread-eagled, face down. Only those papers was between me and the cold concrete. No part of me touched the floor.

One more time, the voice spoke, "Don't give up, baby."

"Yes, ma'am."

I picked myself up, gathered all those torn papers and matched them together the best I could right there on the floor. I walked around them and prayed the rest of the night. When morning came, I borrowed some tape from the writ room.

I spent all my recreation and mealtime making those changes and looking up words and procedures so when I saw Cruz again, I could understand more about "hands off," and "nolo contendere" this and "evidentiary hearing" that, and constitutional amendments. Two weeks later when I met him again, he looked over what I had done and said, "Looks better, mi amigo. Let's send it to the Fifth Circuit of Appeals and see what happens." He sent me over to some of them writ writers to clean up a few other things.

When we finally finished this writ, addressed a big envelope, and left the flap unsealed like we had to do, I said a prayer and put it in the afternoon mail cart. That was the last time I saw Cruz. They separated out a bunch of the writ writers and made them their own squad—the Eight-Hoe Squad. It was a way to keep them from taking over the prison, from giving men who had no hope some reason to get up in the morning.

I checked the mail every day like the Fifth Circuit of Appeals was going to get to it right away, like it would appear the next day. But days turned into weeks, weeks into months. It took two months. Then one day, the mail trustee rolled by and called out my name, "Houston, you got a big fat envelope here." I took it and sat on the edge of my bed and looked at it for a minute. Finally, I said a prayer, took a deep breath, and opened it.

DENIED was stamped big and bold across the top of the first page, like the others. I didn't read any further. I threw that envelope and the rest of those papers as far as I could, but it was like they was made of lead, landing right at my feet. Ready to curse, I fixed my mouth to, but didn't—couldn't. Instead, I kicked the little desk I had rigged up with books and bed slats. Like the day I got the news my mother died, a dark cloud settled over me. All the hope I had put in that writ sank like leaves caught in the swirl of the River. I thought, Whatever is against me in this life is too strong.

Then I heard these words in my spirit: *God will never put more on you than you can bear.* I had heard my momma say that before when she put out plates for supper and we didn't have a crumb of food in the house. Then one of those women that she worked for stopped by with leftovers from one of her parties. Momma thanked her and then said, "God will never put more on you than you can bear. He is never late—never." I heard those words this day, but it wasn't Momma talking. It was God. *Johnnie, trust me. I'll never put more on you than you can bear.*

The old me would have said, "I ain't studden you, God." But the new me said, "OK." That was it, one word—"OK"—no speeches to God, no long prayers. I had never spoke one word that made me feel as much at peace as that "OK"—a word that once meant nothing to me now had this strange power over the word *denied*. I found the spirit to reset my rigged-up table of books and bed slats, like Momma had set that dinner table with faith. I picked up those papers and read them and looked them over for mistakes, but I couldn't find any. So I sent those papers to some of the inmate-lawyers in the Eight-Hoe Squad. After a few days, they sent back my writ with all the i's dotted and the t's crossed including something that was missing: an "Affidavit of Pauperis" saying I didn't have the money to pay for the whole proceeding. They had me sign it in front of a witness, who had to sign it too. The whole thing was notarized. This was all new to me. The last thing we did differently was to send this writ to the original lower court, the Twenty-First Judicial District Court in Bastrop County, where this whole nightmare began.

This time, I didn't run to the mail cart everyday like a kid expecting a gift under the Christmas tree. I settled into the routine of doing the long row of hard time the easiest way I knew how: head down, one step at a time, nose clear of trouble. I did my job, stayed away from bad building tenders, and hid out in my cell and talked to God. The only thing I expected was that it would take months for this one to come back.

It was on a Wednesday almost a year after Momma had passed—April 1, 1970—when a guard came to my cell and ordered me, "Houston, get your things. You're taking a little trip."

"Taking a little trip? Where I'm going?" I thought it was some sort of joke, seeing how it was April Fool's Day. I was in no mood for a joke. "Where y'all taking me?" I asked him again.

The guard said, "Get your shit. You can leave them books. We ain't got all day." He took me down to the bullpen where they normally processed inmates for release to the free world. There was two men there waiting for me. One of the men asked me, "Are you Johnnie Roy Houston?"

I said, "Yeah, I'm Johnnie Roy Houston. Who y'all?"

The same man who asked me my name did most of the talking. "I'm Sheriff Jimmy Nutt, Bastrop County. This here is my deputy, Weldon Dixon." The sheriff knew all about my family. He asked, "Your momma is Ella Houston. Your daddy is John, right?"

"Yeah, that's right. Where we supposed to be going?"

The one who called himself Jimmy Nutt said, "You're going home to Bastrop for a writ hearing to get you a retrial. Let me say right here, if I'd been sheriff then, you never would have gone through what has happened to you."

I thought they was going to have to catch me from falling. I leaned against the wall, then straightened up, thinking this might still be some kind of April Fool's joke. I wasn't going to let them see me break down. "If this here is some sort of joke, I'm here to tell you it ain't funny," I told them.

"No, sir. This is no joke. I have a bench warrant signed by Judge C. B. Maynard to have you in Bastrop by April tenth to prepare for your hearing. You have a court-appointed attorney that will meet with you there. Let's get a move on."

He showed me that warrant. It wasn't no joke. All I could say was, "Thank ya. Thank ya, Lord." I put my hands in back of me so they could handcuff me. After twenty-three years of jail time, I was headed home. *Thank ya, Lords* bubbled up in my spirit as we walked to their car.

No sooner had we got on the highway than that deputy pulled over. Sheriff Nutt said to me, "You going back for a hearing to get you a new trial. I'm pretty sure you know that you're subject to be freed." Then he turned to Dixon and said, "I don't see any reason to handcuff him. Do you, as long as he's been down here? No, I don't see him trying to run." So they took the handcuffs off, and we was back on Interstate Highway 45. A few more miles down the road, they decided to pull over again to get something to eat at one of those new restaurants that you could drive up to and order or go inside. It was supposed to be fast food. That's what the sign said. I had been in the pen so long, a lot of things was new. We went inside, sat down, and they started ordering their food. When it came my turn, Nutt said, "Come on and order what you want."

"I, uh, I don't want anything. Thank you." I said that because I thought I had to pay for it.

Sheriff Nutt could see that I was hungry. He said to me, "I know you got to be ready for some good food. Come on and order what you want. We're going to pay for it."

I said, "Well then, give me a hamburger."

He said, "Oh, no. I don't want you to order 'a' hamburger. You order yourself two, with the works. I can imagine the kinds of food you've been eating down there."

Grinning from ear to ear, I said, "You don't even want to know." The waiter handed me a menu, and with eyes bigger than my stomach, I ordered "a cheeseburger—no two—fries, a strawberry shake."

When I finished eating, Sheriff Nutt said, "Order you another one to go." I told him no, but he wouldn't let it go. He said, "You sure? The State of Texas is paying for it." Since he put it that way, I ordered a to-go bag.

Not much more was said as we got in the squad car and sped over the speed limit toward Bastrop, the highway stripes flashing by like bullets. A while later, Sheriff Nutt finally broke the silence. Once he did, it was like he couldn't keep quiet. "Mr. Houston, we knew your family. I'm sorry for your mother's death. Damn shame you couldn't come to the funeral. You got a sister that lived off Main Street, Leola Hunter?" The sheriff kept rattling off names. "You got another sister, Mozell, and a brother in Corpus—Immer, right?"

"That's right." After a few more questions, the sheriff finally quieted down. For the rest of the trip, I looked out the window and drifted into to a half-sleep. Half my mind was locked into the rhythm of Wynne, what I'd be doing now. The other half of my mind was already home. But I wouldn't be coming home to a wife. Juanita had moved to Austin and gotten remarried to a fella named Sneed. We promised "till death do us part." But we didn't figure in prison when we made that promise. I was determined to see my baby Arlene while I was there though, not so much a baby, now a twenty-three-year-old grown woman.

It took three hours and thirty minutes to get to Bastrop. The sun was on the other side of those tall pines. As we crossed the Colorado bridge into downtown, I hardly recognized the place. There was a new bridge. People was walking around under streetlights—all shades of people: white, black, brown. It was not Saturday.

They carried me on down to the jail and locked me up. Sheriff asked me if I was hungry. I told them, "Yeah, I ate that to-go bag on the way."

"You want me to call your family and have them bring you anything?"

"Yeah. Tell them to bring me something to eat, sheets, and some clothes, too," I said. Still in my Huntsville whites, I didn't want them to see me as 109051. I was Johnnie Roy Houston before I left for prison. I was coming home Johnnie Roy Houston. Thirty minutes later, I looked out the back window of the jail cell, the same cell I exchanged with Ray a lifetime before, and I saw my sister Mozell toting bags.

"Welcome home, Johnnie Roy," she whispered in my ear as we hugged. "The sheriff called me yesterday and told me you was coming home." That's all she said. I wanted to ask her why she didn't tell me about Momma. I wanted to ask her why they stopped writing and visiting. I wanted to know why nothing was done when everybody knew the truth. The one thing I wasn't going to ask was, "Where is Ray?" But I didn't ask any of those things. I hadn't been home in twenty-three years. I hugged her back. There'd be time later for questions.

"What y'all got in the bags?" In one was home cooking: a big old peach cobbler, steaks, pork chops, cornbread, mustard greens, pinto greens. In the other bag was towels and sheets to put on my mattress. Before she left, she hugged me again and said, "Oh, yeah, I almost forgot the lettuce." She smiled and slipped me a twenty-dollar bill. My mother used to call unexpected fun money "lettuce" because she would say, "It's green like salad lettuce, and salad goes good with everything."

With a full belly and, for the first time in a long time, a full spirit, I slept that night. But I didn't go to bed right away. It was too quiet. There wasn't any of the noise I had gotten used to—the yells of the weak and the threats of building tenders tending business. This night, only the snoring of the other jailbirds and the Bastrop night noise broke the quiet—car honks and train horn blasts from the M-K-T. Eventually, all the night sounds faded into the chirping of crickets. A bit of moonlight cast a shadow on the wall. I could hear myself think: What if this hearing is like my first trial? What if nobody believes me now like no one did when I was nineteen? But what if, this time, justice shows up, and God does too? Maybe I'll walk out of here a free man. Maybe I'll …

I "maybe'd" myself to sleep with the hope that all this would soon be over. That was my first night home.

Sunlight poured through that same window the next morning, tapping me in the face to say, "Get up. You gonna sleep all day?" It had been a long time since the sun woke me up kindly. In prison, you got up before the sun. You came in from the field before the sun set. Between the rising and the setting, the summer sun beat down on you like a sledgehammer. The sun wasn't a friend of mine. To have the sun be so kind as to wake me up put me off balance for the first couple of days. I had no hoe squads, no bosses, no building tenders to bother me, and I had all the food I wanted to eat. It was heaven on earth, if there could be such a place in jail.

A few days later, the deputy came and took me downstairs. "Houston, you got a visitor."

Waiting for me was a tall, thin Mexican man wearing a double-breasted suit that fit him like it was made for somebody bigger—shoulders sagging, pants legs lapping over his shoes. He stuck out his hand. "Mr. Houston, my name is Philip Juarez. I'm your court-appointed attorney. I'll be representing you in your writ hearing." It surprised me how he sounded. He didn't sound Mexican. He sounded like an educated white man. All the Mexicans I knew had little or no education. They came from Mexico to live on the same side of the tracks as Bastrop colored people with one thing in mind—work to send money back home. Schooling was something of a sacrifice. They quit if they had to, like me and Ray. Those Mexicans sounded like where they came from, but not this Juarez fellow. I had a different feeling about him than the shit-for-brains lawyer I had at my first trial. He sounded like he knew what he was doing and that he cared about my case.

"Mr. Houston—may I call you Johnnie? We are scheduled for a hearing on May fourth, so we have some time to go over what is going to happen. You've got a good chance of getting out, but it won't be a cakewalk. Judge Maynard won't be easy to convince to grant you a new trial. Trust me, Bastrop doesn't want to reopen this can of worms. Kershaw, the DA, is a hard-ass too. He's going to be rough on the witnesses we're going to call: your wife—sorry, ex-wife—your sister and brother—"

I interrupted—more like erupted. "My brother?" A fire burned in me now, not like the fire I use to hold in my hand without hurt, harm, or danger, not like the fire that came down into my spirit in my prison cell. The flash made Juarez step back. "He ain't gonna get up there and tell the truth after all this time," I yelled at him. "He didn't say nothing when he came out of the same cell they threw me in them years ago. He didn't say nothing about Momma dying."

"Well, we've got to hope that he will say something that's going to convince the judge that you had that confession beat out of you and that you didn't get a fair trial because neither you, your brother, nor your sister were called to testify," Juarez said.

I thought, Juarez don't know Ray a minute. I was born with him. A snake don't change his crawl. But I had learned to cool my temper some. It didn't do no good to yell at my lawyer. "Nobody was called—people who could have told where I was that day: Mrs. Rosanky, my mother-in-law, my wife. They all could have vouched for me," I said.

"Well, some of the people we need to talk to on both sides are dead, so that will be their attack, but we're going to do the best with what we have, señor." He shook my hand again and told me he would see me in a few days. "Now you stay safe. If you are a praying man, pray."

During the time before the hearing, the sheriff made me trustee. The deputies had me cooking, cleaning up around the jail, serving all the rest of the prisoners their food, even going out to the sheriff's house and cutting his yard, culling cattle, picking vegetables, and washing his truck and cars. You name it, I did it. I even went fishing with him, and they took me to the rodeo. It was like I was already out of prison. Every now and then, they slipped me money when I did work around their houses.

Before we went to court, they drove me to Austin to this polygraph place. My lawyer thought it would be good to bring as much ammunition to the fight as we could. This older man at the polygraph place spoke to me like he knew me. "Mr. Houston, it's been a while. I remember this case. How'd they send you to prison?"

"Railroaded him," the sheriff mumbled.

The polygraph man said, "Well, I figured that. Come back here and let me show you what I got." They went behind this fella's desk to a file drawer, where he opened a file. "They took fingerprints off the car that was at the scene where they found the victim—Combs. See here? They got some fingerprints, but they didn't match Mr.

Houston's. How did they ever get a conviction?" Nutt didn't say a word as he looked over at me, knowing I was hearing the whole conversation. The polygraph man turned and looked at me too. "There's no value doing a polygraph on you. I will if you want to, Mr. Houston, but I know how the first one came out. You passed. I still got it." Sure enough, he went back to the storage and got it. "Here you go. Clean as a whistle."

Nutt shook his head and said, "Look, it won't hurt. We drove all this way, let's get'er done. You OK with that, Johnnie?"

"Sure. It's gonna show the same, that I told the truth that I didn't do it."

The polygraph man took me in the back, hooked me to the machine, and asked me the same questions as before: "Is your name Johnnie Roy Houston? Are you from Bastrop?" They asked those obvious questions to get what they called a baseline. Then they asked the important one. "Did you rob Dr. H. B. Combs?" Ten minutes later we came out.

"Well, how did he do?" the sheriff asked.

"He passed it just like the first one—just like it," the polygraph man said as he gave Nutt the role of paper with the squiggly lines.

Those squiggly lines didn't matter before. I wondered whether they would make a difference now. But I wasn't gonna start doubting God, not this time. I spent the next few days before my hearing trying to keep my mind stayed on Jesus. That last night, I prayed one prayer until I fell asleep: "If you're willing, Lord, open up this jail this week, break these chains like you did for Paul and Silas so that I do not spend another day in jail. I promise to serve you for whatever is left of my life."

◆ ◆ ◆

Monday morning, May 4, 1970. It took twenty-three years, seven months and twenty-one days for this day to come—the day I was back in a courtroom Bastrop to right this wrong—back in the same court that had taken half my life. I was a nineteen-year-old boy when I went in. Now I was there as a forty-two-year-old man, but not really. With all that my eyes had seen and hands had done, those twenty-three years changed me. I strapped men in a chair to be cooked. I saw a man get his head blown off, his body toted around on a water wagon all day. I had a ten-year-old boy hold a shotgun on me. I almost beat a man's brains out to save my own head. I saw a dog tear a man apart. I can't sleep without hearing men beg for their lives and manhood. No, I wasn't forty-two. I felt the ghost of an old man walking in me.

My attorney, Juarez, met me in a side room at eight o'clock. "Johnnie, you ready? I'm gonna call your brother, your sister, and your former wife to the stand. I've talked to them and told them to tell the truth. I know you don't trust what your brother is going to say, but with all the world watching, I believe he's going to step up. Now, the DA is going to try to confuse you when you get up on that stand, try to trip you up with your own words and what you remember. You tell the truth. We got truth on our side. Got any questions?"

When Juarez mentioned Ray and the truth, I didn't hear a thing he said after that. My mind went to that place—that dark place where I wanted to do something bad to him for what he had done to me and for never admitting it. What made that dark place worse was that it wasn't a pure place. Mixed in was this: he was still my blood brother from my Momma. The mention of Ray was a tug-of-war.

Juarez broke through. He asked me again, "Mr. Houston—Johnnie—Got any questions?"

I answered back, "Are we gonna be done today? Will I go home today? They gonna take into account my lie detector test?" I asked.

Juarez said, "Judge Maynard is probably going to stretch it to two, maybe three days. The thing I don't know is what Kershaw, the DA, is going to do with his ace witness, Leslie Williams. You remember him? He was the district attorney who prosecuted you at your first trial. He went on to be the district judge back then, and his word is going to carry a lot of weight with Maynard. The 'good old boys' club is going to be against us. They're going to stick together.

"So to answer you, it's gonna take a couple of days to rule on this hearing. And I did learn that they're not going accept the lie detector test because they say it's not reliable since it has been so long since the offense. But if they deny your writ, we're going appeal right away. I expect you won't be going anywhere for at least a couple of weeks, maybe a month. But right now, we're going to focus on telling the truth on that stand." He smiled a big smile, and shook my hand, holding it tight. "My mother died a month ago. If she were here, she'd be saying rosaries for us. But where she is now, amigo, her prayers won't have as far to go. You just focus on the truth."

seventeen

TO THE STAND

"ALL RISE. THE TWENTY-FIRST JUDICIAL DISTRICT COURT is now in session. The Honorable Judge C. B. Maynard, presiding." As we rose, the bailiff barked out, "Writ of Habeas Corpus, Number 4717, Johnnie Roy Houston, petitioner versus Dr. George Beto, Director, Texas Department of Corrections." We was in the new courthouse. To get there, they took me in handcuffs—even though Sheriff Nutt didn't want to—through the hallway that connected what was left of the old courthouse and jail to the new building. We had to pass by the "hanging ring"—the ring they hung Tobe Cook from—still mounted on the wall. My fear was this: new courthouse, same justice. I prayed that this was not true as I sat there with Juarez to my left, my brother, sister, and my ex-wife sitting on the bench behind us. On the other side of the room was James B. Kershaw, the DA. He looked like a mean cuss—coal-black eyes, a jaw that stuck out past what it should, a nose like a blue jay's beak.

Juarez called my brother first. "What happened to you on June 19, 1946?"

Ray answered, "Well, I heard the laws was looking for one of the Houston twins, so I turned myself in." He spoke without looking my way. "An hour later, they brought Roy into my cell and let me out. We didn't speak."

"Did your brother have any marks on him?" Juarez asked,

walking over and sitting on the corner of the desk where I was sitting.

"No, he didn't," Ray answered.

"When you saw him next, what did he look like?" Juarez asked.

Ray looked down at the floor as he spoke. "I tried to see him the next day, but they—Norman Owens—wouldn't let me. I came back four or five days later, and they finally let me see him. He had bruises on the side of his face, a cut under his eye, and a bump on the back of his head. I wanted to ask him what had happen to him, but Owens was right there, so I figured it wasn't none of my business," he mumbled.

Juarez pressed in on him. "Speak up, Ray. Did you ask your brother what happened to him?"

Ray spoke up, "No, I didn't ask him right there because I figured it was none of my business with Owens standing there, you know. A couple of days later, I went to see him again, but they wouldn't let me. So I went around back to the parking lot below Roy's cell window where he could see me. I asked him what happened to him and did he get into a fight up there? Roy told me, 'They whipped me and beat me, and they called Dr. Bryson to fix me up.'"

Juarez moved back to his side of the desk. "One last question. Did you testify at your brother's trial?"

Ray said, "No I didn't. They didn't call me."

Juarez said, "No further questions. Your witness, Counselor."

Kershaw got up and moved toward Ray. "Mr. Houston—may I call you Ray?" Ray shook his head yes. "Ray, you said you saw your brother four or five days later. Which was it: four or five?"

Ray hesitated. "Uh, four or five. I'm guessing, you know."

Kershaw jumped right in, "Yes, you aren't sure, are you? You are guessing. And, of course, Dr. Bryson is dead, is he not? Let's move on. Who hired your brother's attorney?"

Ray started to fidget in his seat. "My mother hired him. She didn't know him. I don't know how he came about. All I know was that he was from Waco, and she got in touch with him about his fee."

"You were at the trial? Were there witnesses called?" Kershaw turned up the heat. "I mean you were there the whole time?"

Ray hesitated, taking longer to answer with each question. "Uh, in my mind there was no witnesses called. The DA was the only one asking questions, as far as I could remember."

"In other words, the trial was held without witnesses?" Kershaw closed in on Ray even tighter. "Did you speak to Roy's attorney?"

Ray scratched his head. "Well, I tried to speak to him to tell him that I had got some threatening notes while I was in the jail cell. Owens had them. I thought Roy's lawyer should have mentioned it to help my brother, but I didn't get to speak to Roy's lawyer."

"*You* got threatening notes?" Kershaw smiled. "I believe that's all."

That was the first I had heard he got threats. I was the one in jail. Juarez tried to fix it the best he could. He approached Ray. "Ray, how do you know the man that your brother is accused of robbing and beating?"

"I knew him personally. I was working for him at the time."

"Did you see him in court that day? Did he testify?" Juarez asked.

Ray hesitated again. "No, he did not."

"As far as to who testified and who did not, would you say that whatever the record shows to be true is true?" Juarez asked.

"That's right, I would," Ray said.

As far as I was concerned, Ray didn't help me at all. He wasn't sure of much, and Kershaw jumped all over him. The next witness Juarez called was my sister Mozell, who was now a Hudson. She had been an Arnold but divorced him. She was nervous on the stand. Her hands shook so bad she had to hold them in her lap. Juarez asked her a simple question to calm her nerves. "When did you see Ray the morning of June 19, 1946?"

"You mean 'Roy,'" she corrected him. She looked at me and said, "I didn't see Roy. I tried to see him, but I couldn't."

I couldn't believe what I'd just heard. My own lawyer got confused with me and Ray's names. Now imagine how that came off to the judge. I began to wonder at that point if this lawyer was any better than the one I'd had at my first trial. It upset Mozell too. She was on the verge of breaking down when Juarez asked her to tell what happened that morning.

Mozell looked up above the heads of the people in the audience as if she was watching June 19 projected on the back wall. She spoke slowly and softly. "I didn't see Roy that day. I tried. They—I believe it was Norman Owens—came to our house early that morning. We was living in one of Dr. Combs's rent houses. They said they was looking for my brothers, that one of them had knocked Dr. Combs in the head that morning and robbed him. My mother told him, 'I don't believe nary one of my twins done it because Dr. Combs helped raised my boys.' Ray went on down to the jailhouse, and they arrested him. Then I heard they had Johnnie Roy. I went on down there, but they wouldn't let me see him. I went around back and talked to him from the parking lot below his window, but I couldn't see him from there. Then I went back home and told my mother, and we started crying."

Mozell looked at me when she said that and then broke down and started crying. Her body was heaving up and down like she was being swallowed up and she was trying to grab some air. It took ten minutes or so before she got under control. During that time, nobody said nothing, not the judge, not Juarez. Twenty-three years of broken heart was on the stand. Nobody dared call for an objection.

Finally Juarez saw an opening to ask the question he should have asked from the get-go. "Mrs. Hudson, when did you see him, Roy, and what did you see?"

Mozell said, "I think I saw him three or four days later. He had bruises and cuts on his face and head. I saw him in his cell, as close as I am to you. He was beat up."

Again, Juarez asked about Dr. Combs. "Mozell, did you see Dr. Combs give his testimony?"

"We was there, and he didn't testify while we was there," she answered back.

Juarez said, "That is all."

The DA didn't even ask Mozell any questions. He was smart. She didn't say anything that wasn't said by Ray. He wouldn't have gained anything by attacking a crying woman. Neither he nor Juarez called any more witnesses that day.

I wasn't sure why Juarez asked if Dr. Combs had testified. I didn't ask him. He knew the records would show that he did or didn't. Maybe he was banking on those records doing the talking in the hearing for all them people that testified at the first trial and now was dead. I don't know. I wasn't no expert, but I did know a little more by now about the law, lawyers, and the courts from working with Fred Cruz and them inmate-lawyers. I went back to my cell, not feeling good about it. What I felt in my bones after day one was this: I may not be going home.

It took two days to get back to court because the prosecution needed time to bring in their star witness, retired Judge Leslie C. Williams, the DA who had sent me to prison back in '46. But before he got up, it was my turn to take the stand. I wasn't allowed to take the stand at my first trial. Now it was my time to speak for myself. I was surprised how scared I was.

This is how my lawyer started: "Are you basing your writ on two, actually, three primary contentions? First, the confession allegedly used in the trial against you in regards to a crime that occurred was not a voluntary confession. In order to attack that contention first, Mr. Houston, let me direct your attention to, on or about, June 19, 1946. I imagine that was a very outstanding date in your mind, isn't that true, sir?"

"Yes, sir." I had so much to say, I didn't expect that that was all I had to say after the speech from Juarez. He was more nervous than me.

"What were you doing in Bastrop?" he asked me.

"I was in Bastrop for Juneteenth, to be with my wife who went ahead of me to visit her mother and daddy. We had come from Corpus Christi where I worked."

"Could you speak up?" Juarez asked.

I tried to speak up, but I couldn't breathe. All them people there looking at me, the only one I wanted there—my mother—not there, the DA ready to tear into me, and my lawyer had confused my name—it was all too much. All the sound I could squeeze out, I pushed out. I tried to speak louder. "Yes, sir. I had come to town for June nineteenth to celebrate with my family and in-laws."

Juarez asked, "Did you have money with you? And please speak up so we can hear your answer. Did you have a few dollars in your pocket?" Juarez was trying to ease my nerves by walking up to the witness stand as he asked his questions.

"Yes, sir. I had just got my check from Osage Motor Company where I was working for my brother, Immer. I had about twenty, twenty-five dollars left because I spent some of it to get some groceries for my wife to get ready for Juneteenth. When I got back home to my in-laws, I found out that the law was looking for me. So I went out looking for them."

That DA had heard enough. "Your honor, I believe that all this is immaterial."

My lawyer jumped right in. "Yeah, I think it is, but we've got to consider the witness." Juarez then turned to me. "I want to know about that arrest. Now, just answer my questions because I'm going to move a little bit faster. We want to give you a chance to say everything, but this is not your trial on the merits. In other words, we are not retrying your case, and we have other things in this case to handle. Now, just tell me what happened next."

I sat up. I wasn't shy now. My heart pumped like it was trying to jump out of my chest. "I went to my father's house to see if he had seen Ray. That's when those deputies arrested me and took me to jail."

Juarez gave me a smile with his back to the DA so he couldn't see it. "Did they have you sign a confession?"

"They didn't *have* me sign a confession. They made me sign one. Sheriff Cartwright and them, Owens and Justice, came into my cell. They took off their guns and came in on me with black-jacks, and started kicking me and stomping me until I was almost unconscious."

"Was that the only time you were put upon … uh … they beat you?" Juarez asked.

"No, sir, it's not. After I came to, I was at the water basin washing the blood from my head and face when they came in and told me to come on out. They carried me downstairs to a little room that is the sheriff's office. The DA came in with some papers and laid them in front of me, handed me a pen, and said, 'Sign your name at the bottom of this.' Well, I picked it up and read it. The DA said, 'I told you to sign it, not read it.' That's when Norman Owens took a running start and hit me upside the head and knocked me from my chair."

"Was Mr. Williams there when Owens hit you?" Juarez asked.

"Yes, sir. Him, Norman Owens, M. A. Justice, and Dude Milton—they was all there. Owens took out his pistol and drew the hammer back and said, 'If you don't sign it, we're going to kill you.' That's when I signed that confession. I was scared they was gonna do what they said they was gonna do."

My lawyer, sounding more confident, asked me, "Did you have to have a doctor because of the injuries you received?"

"Yes, sir. It took a couple of days before Dr. Bryson came up."

Juarez came back quick, "Now, let's talk about your lawyer and what the records show. You contend that you had inadequate counsel? You had alibis where you were that day of the robbery. You were with your mother-in-law. And you did tell your attorney about your confession and beatings. If the records showed that he presented your alibi and injuries to the jury, then that's what the records show. Right?"

"That's right," I answered.

"Thank you. Your witness, Counselor."

Kershaw attacked me right away. "Johnnie Roy, you were at your trial, I hope. So you can tell me if Dr. Combs was there?"

Juarez jumped right in. "Your Honor, Mr. Houston has already said that what the records show, the records show. He may or may not recall everything."

Kershaw didn't hesitate. "Well, he definitely recalled everything else. I don't see why—"

Juarez snapped back, "I am saying whatever the records show is what is there. I'm going to object to that because of its relevancy. I see no relevancy whatsoever."

Kershaw answered, "The relevancy is this, Mr. Juarez. The records may say one thing, that Dr. Combs testified. But your witnesses say that they didn't see him testify. They may have been at a prehearing. That's my point." Kershaw turned to me and asked, "Mr. Houston are you telling me that no one testified?"

I answered him back, "No one testified as I recall, but I don't know what the records show." Juarez had warned me Kershaw would try to confuse me, and he was doing a good job of it. I know the judge must have had plenty of doubts about what I remembered about who testified when. To my recollection, Combs testified at the grand jury hearing. They didn't call me to the stand at the trial because they had their confession. Today, I was hoping the judge would see: a confession with blood on it ain't no confession at all.

Kershaw continued his attack. "Now with regard to the people who you allege beat you, where is Sheriff Cartwright?"

"I don't know," I said. "I been gone twenty-three years."

Kershaw drilled me. "He's dead. You know that. Where is Norman Owens? Where is Dr. Combs? Where is Mr. M. A. Justice? Where is Dr. J. Gordon Bryson?"

"I don't know," I said.

Kershaw didn't let up. "Where is your attorney from back then?

He is dead. They all are dead. I really don't have any other questions." Kershaw sat down like a man who had played a winning domino hand. He slapped his hands on the desk.

The judge said I could step down. I didn't have to step down. I was as good as down and dead. I don't know why my lawyer didn't object. I was being badgered. I had been gone so long. I didn't know what had happened to them all. Of course, they was dead. And dead people can't be questioned. Did the truth and my chance of getting out of prison get buried with all those dead witnesses? My last chance was my wife.

Juarez called Juanita to the stand. He wanted people to know that I was a good provider. "Now Mrs. Sneed, you were married to Johnnie Roy Houston. Did he have money the day y'all came to Bastrop on June eighteenth? Did he have a job?"

She answered, "Johnnie had, I think, about twenty to twenty-five dollars. It's been so long. He was to get paid from his job at Osage Motor Company. So he may have had more that weekend."

Juarez asked, "Did he have enough money in his pocket to support you? Did you ever go hungry?"

"No sir. He worked and took good care of me," she said.

Before Juarez could fire off another question, Kershaw jumped in. "Your Honor, I object to this line of questioning about an alibi. We are not trying this case based on alibi for Mr. Houston. We are here to question the validity of a confession and the adequacy of Mr. Houston's counsel."

Juarez turned to the judge. "Your Honor, I will be more to the point and be a better steward of the court's time." Then Juarez turned and walked toward Juanita and asked, "Mrs. Sneed, when did you see Johnnie after his arrest, and how was he?"

She answered, "Well, when I saw him about a week after his arrest, he had cuts over his eye and bruises on his face."

"Your witness, Counselor."

Kershaw went right after Juanita. "Mrs. Sneed, were you allowed to see Johnnie? If so, what was his condition?"

"The day I went to see him, Mr. Owens let me go up. When I got up there, I asked him what was the matter with his face, but he didn't say anything," she said in a shrinking voice.

"Well, I believe that is all I have." Kershaw sounded like he had won that one too. I didn't know what else Juarez had in his bag of tricks. All I knew was that I felt like we was headed backward, not forward. He had to have something else up his sleeve.

Now, it was Kershaw's turn to present his case. He had only one witness—the man who sent me to prison—District Attorney Leslie D. Williams—now retired Judge Leslie D. Williams.

Kershaw spoke with a syrupy respect, like Williams was still a judge. "For the record, you are now our retired district judge of the Twenty-First District, and prior to that you were the district attorney who prosecuted Mr. Houston? So, you are the gentlemen who the petitioner, Johnnie Roy Houston, has previously identified as the district attorney who took a statement from him on or about June 19, 1946?"

"Yes, I was the district attorney for the Twenty-First District for eighteen years." Judge Williams sat on the edge of his seat like he was nervous. I don't know why. These was his friends, his court, his town.

Kershaw asked him point-blank, "How would you sum up Mr. Houston's trial?"

William did not hesitate in his comeback. "It was a simple case of a colored boy attacking a white doctor here in Bastrop, and that was about it."

Then Kershaw started, again, down the road of the dead. "At that time, Ed Cartwright was the sheriff, and he is deceased now? Right?"

"Yes, sir," Williams replied.

"And his deputies—Norman Owens, and M. A. Justice, the city marshal—they are now deceased? Right?" Kershaw asked. "Dr. Combs, the victim of the assault and robbery, he, too, is deceased?

"Yes, sir," Williams replied.

Kershaw continued, "And Dr. J. Gordon Bryson, who the petitioner has spoken of in his testimony as the doctor who attended the alleged wounds of Mr. Houston, he, too, is dead?"

"So I understand," Williams answered.

"Judge, when you first saw Mr. Houston in the DA or sheriff's office to take his confession, did you observe any cuts or bruises about his face or person?" Kershaw asked.

"No, sir. There were none, or I wouldn't have taken his confession," Williams said.

On a roll, Kershaw then fired off a bunch of questions to Williams attacking my confession. "Did you type out this confession? Did you tell him not to read it but to sign it?"

"No, sir," Williams answered.

"At any time did any deputy or person threaten to kill him?" Kershaw asked.

"No, sir. If they had, I wouldn't have taken the statement. I know a statement's not good if taken under those circumstances."

With every "No, sir," it was like I was punched all over again, whipped with the butt of a gun, slapped with the back of a hand. This man had sworn on a Bible to tell the whole truth. I tried to stare him straight in the eye when he was up there, but he wouldn't look at me. I didn't know why. If he wasn't afraid of God, why would he be scared to look me in the face?

Kershaw continued with Williams. "From your experience, do you think that Walden, who was the lawyer of his choosing, adequately represented the defendant?"

"I believe that he did," Williams answered.

Williams thought Walden was adequate, but I bet he wouldn't trust his life and freedom on "adequate."

Kershaw smiled and winked at Juarez, then walked back to his seat. "I pass the witness."

Juarez approached the retired judge and turned up the volume. "From what you told us, it was a simple case of a colored boy attacking a white doctor here in Bastrop. In other words, it was the word of a white respected citizen verses the word of a Negro?"

Williams hesitated, then spoke. "Well, that's the way it turned out from the state's viewpoint."

Juarez said, "Now, regarding your opinion of Mr. Houston's lawyer's competence, if he had a witness that would give Mr. Houston an alibi and didn't present him, would you say he was competent?" Juarez was trying to nail Williams down on his opinion whether my attorney represented me right, but this old judge was a sly fox.

Williams answered, "It's not my opinion. I'm telling what I saw in court. I tried cases for a long time, and I never did see an incompetent attorney in court. I understand he was making a living practicing law in Austin. He had a license from the State Bar of Texas, so naturally you could presume that he was adequate," Williams said.

Juarez came back, "But it leaves room for a lot of inadequate representation, doesn't it, Judge Williams?"

"That may be true, but I don't know such a thing. Presenting a witness depends on the circumstances, and I didn't know all the circumstances," Williams answered.

Nailing down this judge was like trying to swat a bee, but Juarez kept trying to get him to admit that Walden was incompetent. He let it rest for a moment and shifted to the confession. "If the attorney had an opportunity to present an alibi to support the defendant's claim that his confession was beat out of him in your presence, what would you say of that attorney?"

"I can't speak of Walden's competence, but all I know is that the defendant was not beaten before I saw him or right after I saw him. It didn't happen."

Juarez wouldn't let the confession go. "What would you say if I told you that we could not produce that confession today?"

Williams answered, "It could be true. It could be in the Statement of Facts, but I didn't keep confessions that I presented before the court, not one. As a usual practice, the sheriff kept them because they had a sort of a file. Now, I wouldn't swear to it, but I do know they asked for them when the case was over. I didn't touch the confession anymore." Judge Williams was getting hot under the collar. "It's my idea the confession was introduced."

Juarez pressed him more. "Judge, what I am driving at is the adequacy of counsel."

"All right, you're asking me questions about him that I don't know, and I can't answer, and I will not answer because I don't know anything except what the man did in the court where I was district attorney and he was on the other side. He was adequate." Williams was boiling now.

Juarez took a long pause, and then walked toward his seat. "Well, Judge, I'm going to move right on, and believe it or not, I'm done. Thank you."

Then Kershaw strutted like a rooster up toward the witness bench. "Judge Williams, did Dr. Combs testify at the trial?"

Williams answered, "I believe he did. I'm not sure he did. I think the record will show whether he did or not."

Kershaw didn't hesitate. "The record shows that he did."

Judge Maynard, who was as quiet as a mouse the whole hearing, was ready to end the day. "Counselor, any other witnesses?"

Kershaw couldn't help but take his last shot. "No, sir. They're all dead."

It seemed like it was over as quickly as it begun. My defense counselor turned to me and stuck out his hand as they was getting ready to take me back to my cell. "Johnnie, we did our best. It will be about a month before we know something. Look, I don't want you to get discouraged."

"What do we do next?" I asked.

"We wait. We pray," Juarez answered.

They let me hug my sister before they took me out. Her eyes was full. Mine was, too, but I didn't drop a tear. I ain't really cried since my mother died. It's like I was emptied that day, so no matter what happened to me, there wasn't enough tears left for crying. As we headed back to my cell, we passed the hangman's ring again. Seeing it didn't do anything to me. I was numb. I had learned one thing since I stepped foot in prison: to get through a day sometimes you had to go numb. If you don't feel, you can't hurt. They can't get to you.

Sheriff Nutt met me at my cell door. He could tell I knew how things looked. He put his hand on my shoulder. "You keep your head up, Johnnie. God's gonna make this right. We're going to make this right. This ain't what Bastrop is now. It used to be something I wasn't proud of. This never would have happened if I was sheriff back then."

I said nothing, shook his hand, and gave him a nod. When that cell door clanged shut, though, it hit me—you won't be going home. As I lay in my bed, I thought about all that was said and not said those three past days. My lawyer did the best he could, I guess. One thing he did do was sum it all up, in my own words, as he questioned Judge Williams: "This is really about a young Negro boy who people believed robbed and beat the town's prized white citizen." It was my word against his. Today was no different: a convicted Black man's word against the former white DA, now a retired district judge—the prized symbol of southern justice. I was in the place that my father had been when he apologized to that white man who shortchanged him. My father said back then, "I know my place, but ..." What happened this day was Bastrop—an old Bastrop that refused to die—saying to me, "Know your place."

I already knew what the court was going to say about my writ. It was only a matter of time.

eighteen

TWICE DENIED

WHILE I WAITED FOR THE TWENTY-FIRST District Court's decision, I went about my days as a trustee. They let me do odd jobs around the jail and help out with cooking meals and cleaning up the jailhouse. I went to the sheriff's house and barbecued for them. My family visited me as much as they wanted and brought all kinds of food. My half sisters from my daddy's first marriage, Leola and Sallie, were regulars. Mo came from Dallas as often as she could. I was still in jail, but it wasn't the jail I knew from Walls, Clemens, Ramsey, Ellis, and Wynne.

During my time on bench warrant in Bastrop, I got acquainted with L. A. Jarosek. He was a local cattle rancher cut right out of the "Wild, Wild, West."

Sheriff Nutt drove me out to Jarosek's spread outside of town off State Highway 304. "Johnnie, we're going out to meet L. A.—L. A. Jarosek. He can help you. He knows a lot of people, plus he's got work. Now, I need to tell you he's a character, but he is as good as they come," Nutt said and then grinned from ear to ear like a schoolgirl trying to hold onto some gossip, but not too tight.

I said, "OK, that's fine. Anybody that can help me is OK by me." But the way Nutt set him up, I was beginning to wonder. We drove through a big cattle gate into Jarosek's ranch. He had some nice Herefords, Angus, and Holsteins, with a few calves grazing in the front of his house. When I stepped out, a big old dog came out of nowhere and charged at the car, sending me headfirst into Sheriff Nutt's lap. Nutt busted out laughing. "Go on out there. That dog ain't gonna bite you. Go ahead and knock on his door."

I told him, "I ain't come all the way from Huntsville with Old Rattler snapping at my heels to come back home and get bit by his cousin. No, you go knock. You the sheriff."

Nutt said, "I don't see L. A.'s car. Well, maybe he's home, and his wife has his truck." So Sheriff Nutt lay on his horn, not once, not twice, but three long blasts. Immediately, every cow that rancher owned strolled toward the car from every direction. I mean they surrounded that squad car, one bull directly in front of the hood ornament staring us down.

A Jersey stuck his head in the back window. Nutt hollered, "Shush, heeyah! Git, git on out of here, now git." We managed to get that cow out of the window, but the rest of them wasn't budging, rocking the car with their wide bodies. It took me a minute to figure it out. They wanted something to eat. I bet Jarosek fed his cows from the back of a truck, tooting on his horn to call them. They heard our horn and came a-strolling, looking for dinner.

Soon enough, they figured out there wasn't going to be none, so one by one, they moseyed like a Sunday stroll back to what they was doing before, but that bull was none too happy. He gave a snort, then turned and let loose a grassy pile, ambling on his not-so-merry way, tail swishing, wishing to leave all he could behind, leaving no doubts, signifying his discontent. Me and the sheriff looked at each other and laughed and laughed so hard we cried.

Then from the cattle gate road, a truck came hauling ass, kicking up a cloud of dust. It came to a stop, skidding and throwing up rocks everywhere. Out jumped this barrel-chested man, mouth going ninety-to-nothing the minute his foot hit the ground. "What in the Sam Hill, cotton picking, blue blazes is going on? How did all my cows get up here?" He was fit to be tied till he realized it was the sheriff. Then he broke out in a language I knew and hollered his cheerful greeting as he walked to the car, "Ahoj Nazdar! Ahoj Nazdar! Jak se máš? Jak se máš?" Then that mean-as-hell dog ran to him and rolled over belly-side up for a boot rub. "Y'all can get out. He ain't gonna bite. Sorry I'm late. I had some things to tend to in town." No sooner had we stepped out than that dog ran to us, too, for a belly rub. Jarosek stuck out his hand to me. "Jak se máš?"

Well, now I was doing fine, so I answered him back, "Ahoj Nazdar! Jak se máš?" He jumped a little to hear me come back at him with Czech. But this whole area had been full of Czechs since I was a little boy. They came over here from somewhere over there and took to this part of Texas. We had some who was neighbors, and they taught me and my twin to speak a little Czech.

Sheriff Nutt jumped right in. "L. A., this here is Johnnie Roy Houston. Johnnie, this here's L. A. Jarosek."

Turning to the sheriff laughing, Jarosek said, "Johnnie, good to meet you. Now, tell me, are you a hard working nig—"—he caught himself—"colored? I don't mean no harm what comes out of my mouth." Then he put his hands on my shoulder. "I mean can you herd cattle, because I can use some help around here."

I said, "If it's got four legs, I can herd it and ride it. If it's got four wheels, I can drive it." I shook his hand real hard and stared him in the eyes.

Jarosek said, "Well, we'll see, won't we. Get on 'round back. My Mex—uh, my man will show you what I need done. Me and the sheriff are gonna have a few cold ones."

I set out to work hard that day like I ain't never worked before, moving cattle from one pasture to another, and finally to pens so they could be loaded on trailers to be taken to auction in San Antonio.

At the end of the day, L. A. walked up to me and threw me a beer. "Sheriff, you didn't tell me he could work like this—like damn near four men. Johnnie, I like you." That began a friendship that made me feel good about myself and Bastrop. There was nothing L. A. wouldn't do for me—I mean nothing—whether I asked him to or not. One night a woman showed up at my cell. I knew who sent her.

While I was in Bastrop waiting to hear about my writ, there was other signs that there was hope for me. I had served almost twenty-four years. During that time, I had worked hard and kept out of trouble except for my escape and that fight with that old-timer Jimmerson. So I had thirty-eight years of commutation time. We called it "good time." For every month I was there in prison, I got twenty days credited to me along with time served. So I was up for parole, but I needed some help.

Sheriff Nutt came up to the jail one morning. "Johnnie, I told you that we're going to try to make this thing right. You're going to need some recommendations to the parole board if this writ doesn't come through." He showed me a letter and read a part of it to me:

> To the Texas Board of Pardons & Parole: This letter is to you on behalf of Inmate no. 109051, John Roy Houston. John came to Bastrop from the Wynne farm on a writ attempting to get a new trial. His case is now being reviewed by the court. We, the undersigned people, have come to know John quite well in the past few months, and wish to express our desire to see John make parole and give him a chance to prove that he can make it on the outside. Your consideration in this matter will be most appreciated by the following men: …

Sheriff said, "What do you think about that? Look here. It's signed by these deputies, chiefs-of-police from Taylor and Elgin, and justices-of-the-peace and constables from around here. I got more of these letters too." He was excited, like they was writing those letters to free his son.

"I appreciate all you doing, Sheriff." I tried to put on a smile, but inside I was blue. He knew it. Me and him both knew that the court was gonna come back with bad news. But I was happy to know that maybe Bastrop was changing. When I was growing up, the law was nothing but trouble for me and people like me. They treated us how they pleased, always reminding you that you had a "place" and you'd better not step outside it, or else. And now the law was writing letters for me? Maybe Bastrop was changing—maybe?

But it hadn't changed completely. Sheriff Nutt came to my cell a month after the writ hearing and handed me a letter from Juarez and a copy of the Bastrop court's verdict dated June 8, 1970: DENIED.

My lawyer wasted little time in filing an appeal. And it took the Court of Criminal Appeals four months to get around to me. Then on October 16, 1970, they used that word I had become used to when it came to the courts: *denied*.

They both thought the farmer-turned-lawyer, Harold Walden, who my momma gave her hard-earned money to represent me, did an adequate job even though he didn't call a single witness. I learned later that he was suspended for not filing divorce papers for a lady in Waco. She wound up marrying again while she was still married. I wish I could have gotten to her first to tell her that Walden wasn't worth the paper that gave him the right to call himself a lawyer.

The appeals court agreed with Judge Maynard that there was no evidence to show that the confession had been beaten out of me. Never mind my black and blue face. Never mind that the deputy testified at my grand jury hearing that he slapped me when he took me out to the scene of the crime to match my footprints. The Criminal Court report read, "He (the deputy) slapped him, but he didn't strike him." How can you slap a person but not strike him? They said none of my rights was denied, but last I checked, the rights in the Constitution belonged to me too.

So with one word they made official what I knew was coming: *denied*. There's some words no matter how many times you hear them, they never lose their sting. I used to toss buckets of burning coal-oil rag balls in the air and never get burned, but some words burned deep every time they touched me: any words against my mother, the word *nigger*, and the word *denied*.

Sheriff Nutt said, "I'm sorry about this, Johnnie. But you got to get your stuff together. We got to hit the road first thing in the morning. I know you are disappointed, but don't give up."

He did his best to lift me up, but I was mad. Not so much at the court, my lawyer, Bastrop, or any of them. I was mad at me. I thought I was a new person, that I had completely trusted God, that I wasn't the old Johnnie who was mad at the world—but I found out I hadn't totally changed. I wondered again where this God was who was supposed to be my friend.

The night before my return to prison, I tried to fight sleep because I knew where sleep would take me after a rough day. For some time, I had been having this dream, not every night, but nights that followed really bad days.

I would get up from my bed, put on my shoes, and reach behind the door for my shotgun. I'd load it and put some shells in my pocket. I would walk down a moonlit street, wet from a short, heavy rain, and walk by my mother. She was in her blue-flowered, print dress, her handkerchief in her right hand, her hat cocked the way she always wore it. She would be waving her hands and trying to say something to me, but I couldn't hear her. I would walk to a house I did not know, but I knew who was in there. The unlocked porch door creaked as I went straight to a rear bedroom. Beer cans was everywhere. I would raise my gun waist high, pull back the safety. The click was loud enough to wake a man lying there in shallow sleep. Then he'd sit up in the bed and say, "Roy? What is you doing, Roy? *Quit fooling a—*" I always woke up at the same point.

Monday noon, November 9, 1970, we rolled into the Wynne Unit. Hoe squads was kicking up clouds of dust as usual. The men was singing: *Well, Old Rattler, Old Rattler was the sergeant's dog.*

Being away seven months and five days hadn't changed a thing. The rhythm of prison flooded over me like the Colorado.

Warden C. L. "Bear Tracks" McAdams greeted me like he'd missed me. "Welcome back, Old Houston. You get settled in. You've got an appointment with Legal. Go on down to see Greenwood."

"Now what they want with me? I ain't been here long enough to be in any—"

The warden interrupted. "You're not in any trouble. I imagine they want to talk to you about something legal. Just go see him, all right?"

I did. The "Greenwood" he told me to go see was Roy Greenwood. He was one of those new staff lawyers that the federal courts forced Chief Warden George Beto to provide inmates. Those staffers was young and fresh out of law school. This was practice for them. But Greenwood was different. He was young, but he seemed to give a damn, and he was smart too. He said to me, "Johnnie, I am sorry about your writ, but we're not done. You have thirty-eight years, six months, and eight days credited to you, so you are due to get out of here November 25, 1977. But we're going to try to get that cut. You spent seven months on bench warrant down there in Bastrop on your writ, so you are due one hundred forty-six days. But Beto is not giving you that time. So we're going to submit another writ to get those days. Every day counts, right?" Greenwood said.

"Every minute should count, if you ask me. They ought to give me my good time while I was in Bastrop. They made me a trustee down there. They even took me to the rodeo, but I was still in jail," I told him.

"Yeah, but you know you can't tell what the court will do. We got a similar case out of Fort Worth that landed on our side. They gave this fellow James Black his commutation time for his bench warrant time," Greenwood said as he handed me some papers. "We'll have to see. Sign here for this writ and here for the 'Forma Pauperis' saying you can't pay for this, and then we are on our way. Be safe. This might take a while because it has to go to Bastrop first, then Austin. I suspect Maynard will deny it, and the court of appeals will uphold the lower court. If that is the case, we'll take it to a federal judge. Remember, this is Texas."

"It ain't like I ain't heard 'denied' before," I told him. "Do what you got to do to get me out of here."

Weeks turned into months. There was nothing from this writ. During that time, I heard from Sheriff Nutt. He was good on his word to work on the parole board. He wrote me to tell me that he had more letters, and he wrote one himself to vouch for me. He told them that I had a job lined up with L. A., so there was hope. It made the time pass faster. I got up each morning with two things on my mind—stay out of trouble and stay alive. People was still dying around me. Building tenders was still running things when the lights went out. But I hadn't given up on God. My job was to wait.

Nine months passed after Greenwood filed Writ # 4772: *Johnnie R. Houston vs. Dr. George Beto, Director, Texas Department of Corrections* to try and get my bench warrant time credited to me as commutation time. The Monday mail was late. Usually by noon, if the mail trustee hadn't called your name, then it would be tomorrow—the world's worst word when your world is prison. All you had was tomorrows. "Today" was where hope lived if you had been in here any length of time. You hoped "today" would be the day that something happened to get you out of here. But around three o'clock, I heard my named called, and a large envelope landed on my chest as I lay on my bunk. It was addressed from Roy Greenwood. My hands was shaking. I nicked my thumb on the metal tab as I pulled out a copy of the Findings of Fact and Conclusion from the Twenty-First District Court.

Greenwood had a note clipped to it: "Johnnie, as you can see, Judge Maynard was true to himself. He ruled that Huntsville was right to deny you that good time. They said that the difference between the James Black case and your case was you already had a credit of thirty-eight years. That's the law, but that law needs to change. The court of appeals is going to go along with Judge

Maynard, but as I told you before, we are going take this to a federal judge. Don't give up. It's time for you to get out of here. I will get back in touch with you."

I didn't even read the whole thing. Ready to blow, I threw the envelope against the wall. But I didn't curse. Something came over me instead. I heard these words, "God ain't never late. What God has for you is for you." It wasn't God I heard. It was my mother's voice, as clear as if she was in the cell with me.

I went over to that envelope and tacked it on the wall. I said to myself, loud enough that the whole cellblock could hear me, "God ain't never late." I went to bed with those words on my lips—no dreams that night—just those words: "He ain't never late."

♦ ♦ ♦

The old year passed into a new year with no word from Greenwood. I did hear from Sheriff Nutt a few times, but as winter turned into spring, and I turned forty-four, I was certain that no news was not good news. Except for my birthday, spring was never a joy for me as it is for most people who look forward to short rains and cool days and Easter eggs. Spring, for me, meant another summer was on the way: egg-frying heat, hoe squads from sunup to sundown, and steamy nights. The night-heat would hang in our cellblock until almost morning. To get four hours of real sleep was a blessing. Most times, I would lie in bed staring at the ceiling till my eyes gave up and closed. If I slept at all, it was only long enough for the always-waiting dream:

I would get up from my bed, put on my shoes. I'd reach behind the door for my shotgun, walk to a house I did not know and make my way to a back bedroom. I would pull back the safety. The click was loud enough to wake a man in a shallow sleep. Then he would sit up and say, "Roy, what you doing? Roy. *Quit fooling a—*"

The morning bell rang. Another day gone—9,490 days gone.

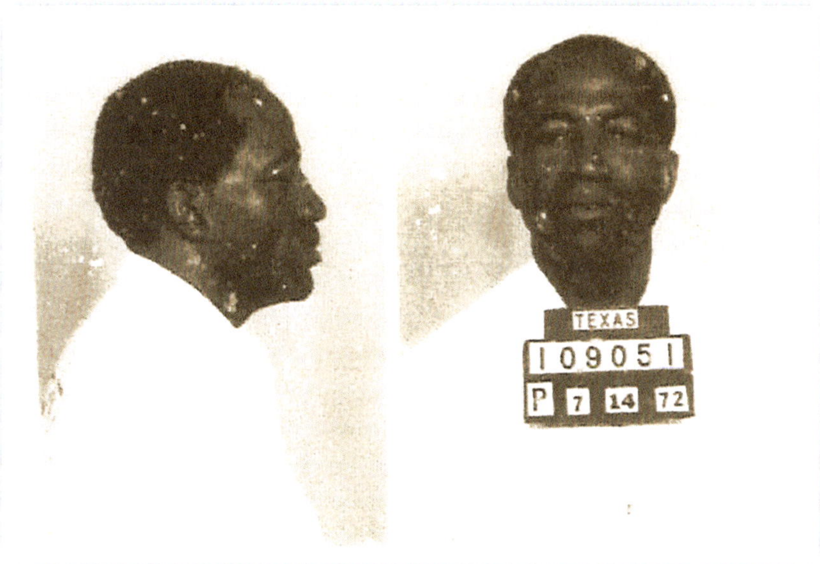

Johnnie Roy Houston wears #109051 for the last time, July, 14, 1972.

nineteen

TIME

"HOUSTON, THE WARDEN WANTS TO SEE YOU," the guard hollered from the hall. But when he escorted me from my cell, he led me down to the office next to the warden's office. When I went in, there was two men in suits, each one a carbon copy of the other except one was taller and older. They each had gray hair at their temples, wire-rimmed glasses, and the same dark pinstripe suits. These were lawyers. I had seen enough of them to know a lawyer when I saw one. They must all get their clothes from the same store: striped suit, white shirt, red tie. The taller, older one turned to me and said, "Mr. Houston, my name is Horace Shelton. This is my son, Polk." They both stuck out their hands.

"OK. What y'all want with me?" I didn't mean to be mean, but I had so many people stick out their hands to me who, in the end, didn't do any good to change my condition. So I wasn't one way or the other when someone stuck out their hand to shake. I figured they was with the parole board to tell me I was going to be here a bit longer.

"Mr. Houston, are you ready to get out of here?" the son said, smiling and sticking out his hand again for me to shake.

"What kind of question is that? I been ready to get out of here since the day I got here. What y'all talking about?" I asked.

"Your writ to get your bench warrant time credited as commutation time has been granted by Federal Judge Dorwin Suttle. Now, you're going to have to go to Austin to the Court of Criminal

Appeals, but there is a good chance you won't have to come back here. You'll have to do parole, but at least you won't be locked up. We will see you tomorrow," Horace said.

"Well, I guess I'll see you tomorrow then." That's all I could say. We shook hands. As I was taken back to my cell, I thought, Handshakes and tomorrows—only time will tell if they mean any good.

Nine o'clock the next morning, Friday, July 14, 1972, the same two men showed up to take me to Austin. It wasn't a trial like the first one—no jury, just a judge. It took less time even than that blink-and-you'd-miss-it first trial in Bastrop. The judge asked me, "What does it feel like to be a free man? You do want to go home, don't you?"

And you know I told him, "Yeah, I sure do!" He pounded his gavel (not a hammer, a gavel). The judge said, "You are released." He rubbed his brow. "How did you do twenty-six years down there? I can't believe it. You must have a strong constitution." That's when the judge stood up and shook my hand and patted me on the back. "Good luck."

When I heard those words, "You are released," my body went numb like my body had gone numb when I heard, the words "Guilty, fifty years." I couldn't move. When I used to haul a day's picking to the cotton gin, that full sack pressed hard on me so much so that when I dropped that load, it took a while for my body to get used to normal standing. Feeling normal would start with my legs straightening. The ache like fire would fade, and then my back would grow, bone on top of bone, till I was tall as I once was—normal. Finally, my shoulders and head would sit right so that if I wanted to, I could look up at a star or a hawk crossing the sky. When the judge said, "Released," slowly the weight of twenty-six years dropped like a load of cotton, and my spirit stood up straight. I began to feel normal again. I could look up. The words "Thank you, thank you, thank you, Lord!" welled up and spilled out.

Poke Shelton put his hand on my shoulder to steady me before I rocked over. "You are a free man," he said.

The only thing that came out of my mouth was, "Thank you, Lord."

The judge told me that the lawyers would be taking me to the clerk's office to sign some papers. He said, "You won't have to go back to Huntsville."

Horace Shelton whispered, "I have something else for you to sign. I have a check for twenty-six thousand dollars—a thousand dollars for each year you were in jail. Now, I am not at liberty to disclose where this money came from. If I were representing you, I could probably get you more, but it might take a year in court, maybe two years or longer. The decision is up to you."

I said, "I did twenty-six years down there. I'm done. Twenty-six thousand dollars is more money than I have ever seen in my life. I'll take it."

So they took me to the clerk's office. We waited there about ten to twenty minutes to sign some papers. Then one of those lawyers reached inside his pinstriped suit and handed me a check. There was my life in dollars and cents. As I figured it, twenty-six thousand dollars broken down for each day I spent in prison amounted to $2.74 a day. That would barely buy me a full meal now at that diner where I had to go around back on Colored Saturday to be served.

I was not sure where the money came from. It may have been guilt money from somebody or somebodies in Bastrop who wanted to right a wrong, to get it off their chests, to buy forgiveness. The lawyers wouldn't tell me where the money came from. It didn't matter. There wasn't enough money in the world to make up for seeing what I saw and what I did in prison. How can you put a price on not going to your mother's funeral? What mattered to me was I was a free man and I didn't have to be rolled out feet first. I did the time. But it wasn't none of my doing. God did this. When I went into prison, nobody could tell me nothing. I wasn't thinking about God. But now I was different. Somebody might say to me that God was late, that I did all that time for nothing. I had a made-up mind on this: God felt it took twenty-six years to change me.

As we walked to the car, all I could think about was what Momma told me the last time I saw her: "Don't give up." She was right when she said, "I'm gonna make this right if it's the last thing I do." The last thing she really did was to remind me not to give up on God 'cause God's never late. Now it was time for me to make up whatever time I had left.

Those lawyers took me downtown to a bank. I had never seen buildings that big close up—nothing but glass and moving stairs. I had never been on an escalator. "Go ahead, Mr. Houston, step on it. It will find your feet, and you stand there and let it do the work. Put your hands on the rail and hang on," Horace Shelton said.

I grinned all the way up to the second-floor lobby of Republic Bank. I never saw so many people in suits and people behind desks doing business. Here I was in my prison dungarees. I knew I stood out, but I didn't much care. In a couple of minutes, I was going to have more money in my pocket than I ever had in life. Then I could buy me whatever I wanted to wear. Nobody would know I was convict number 109051. I would be Johnnie Roy Houston, that's all.

Attorney Shelton, the son, led me to the shortest teller line and asked me, "Johnnie, how would you like it?"

I laughed. "How would I like it? I'd like it *all* if it's fine with y'all."

He laughed back. "No, no, Mr. Houston. What denominations would you like your money—you know, tens, twenties, hundreds?"

"You've got a lot of money here," the older Shelton said. "I suggest you get mostly hundreds."

"Hundreds will be fine. Maybe some twenties, tens, fives, and ones," I said.

The younger Shelton spent about five minutes in front of the teller window. The teller, this tiny, blue-haired woman with winged-rim glasses, looked over at me, then whispered to Mr. Shelton so I couldn't hear, but I did. "You sure you don't want any higher denominations, perhaps some thousand-dollar bills?" He didn't say anything to her, so she counted out twenty-six thousand dollars in stacks of hundreds, and put it all in a cloth zipper bag. She handed it to Poke and gave me a look like something illegal was going on. I smiled back at her as he handed me the bag.

"There you go, Mr. Johnnie Roy Houston. Where are you headed?" Horace asked.

"I'm fixing to go to the bus station to catch whatever is going to Dallas. I got a sister there—Mozell Hudson."

Horace jumped right in. "Mr. Houston, that is too much cash to be riding the bus alone. I tell you what. I have to be in Dallas Monday on a case. I don't see a reason why we can't take you and stay over."

"I thank you. That'll be fine. But before that, can I buy me some clothes? I'm ready to get out of these prison whites."

"Sure thing." We went to a JCPenny, and I got a medium-blue plaid shirt and blue pants and shoes. I left number 109051 in the dressing room. I walked out of that store wearing new clothes, tags and all.

Then we climbed in their Cadillac and drove I-35 north to Dallas. We hardly got down the road before they pulled out cigars and lit them up, laughing and talking like they was celebrating their freedom. One of them asked me, "Mr. Houston, I know you seen some pretty terrible things, but what is the funniest thing you saw in prison?"

I thought for a minute, then smiled. "Well, I hate to say it, but the funniest thing I saw was in the same place I saw the worst thing. My first job was working on death row. I had to get inmates ready to ride the lightning. After they had been fed their last meal and moved to their isolation cell, shaved, and given their last rights from a preacher, they got to have their last remarks. Now if it was me, I would be begging for my life. But this particular boy, when they asked him if he had any last words, he held his head up and said real proud, 'Yeah. I got something to say.' They told him to go ahead and say it. He looked all around, took a long pause, and hollered out, 'Let her rip! Let her rip!'" I thought Poke was going to lose control of the car, he was laughing so hard.

Horace turned to me. "Let me ask you something else. Why aren't you going home—Bastrop? It's been a while."

The whole mood in the car changed with that question. I told him, "It's hard to call Bastrop home now. I can't go down Main Street or anywhere else I used to hang out without feeling something bad following me—like June 19, 1946, was a ghost. I can't walk by that courthouse and not feel those licks across my head for reading a confession I wouldn't sign. Everywhere I'd turn, I'd see my mother coming around the corner wearing that dress with small blue flowers, wearing that hat with that net covering her face. I would hear those townsmen, with hanging on their mind, banging at the locked back door of the jailhouse hollering, 'You a dead nigger!' Those words is locked in my head. No sir, I wouldn't be free if I went back to Bastrop. It's not home no more."

We drove for about an hour, then pulled over to get something to eat. I tried to pay for the bill, but they wouldn't let me. "No, no, Mr. Houston, your money is not good here," Horace Shelton told me.

I said, "No, no, Mr. Shelton, if you don't mind, I got to pay for this. It's been a long time since I been able to buy somebody a meal. The state has been paying for my meals half my life." So he let me pay, and then we got back on the road to Dallas. I bet I didn't close my mouth from Austin to Dallas. I was steady talking and smiling, grinning and bobbing my head to all the things they was telling me about a world all new to me: shopping malls and something called "Pong" where you play ping-pong on a TV. That was the best ride I ever had. Yeah, that was the best ride I ever had.

Before I knew it, the Dallas skyline with even more glass and steel buildings than I seen in Austin filled the windshield, and highways stretched six lanes wide in every direction. I had been through Dallas before, when I was a boy headed to northwest Texas to pick cotton. None of this was there then. This was a whole new world. Then one of those lawyers asked me, "Now, who are you going to be staying with, again?"

"With my sister, Mozell," I told him, my face pressed against the window. "She stays in West Dallas off of Furey Street."

"Well, if you know the way, we'll take you there," Polk said.

I told him I knew the way. I had called her from the restaurant to say that I was coming, so she had given me directions. In twenty minutes, we was there. "Well, here you go, Mr. Houston." They each shook my hands and gave me their cards. The son said, "If ever you needed anything call us. Good luck to you. Keep your head up." Their Caddy sped off in a cloud of blue smoke.

So there I was—home. I stood there for a minute and soaked it all in. The night before, I had been a prisoner of the state. I had been that for more days than I had been anything else. Tonight, I would sleep in a bed that didn't have bars around it.

I was more scared than happy.

twenty

HOME

THERE WAS A CHURCH ACROSS FROM WHERE my sister lived. When that church bell rang, I jumped—jumped like it was time to go to chow, jumped like it was time to go to the fields, jumped like it was time for lights-out. In prison, the bells was the real bosses—they rang, you jumped. In the free world, they was still my bosses because the bells—any bell tied to a schedule—was now inside me. So even when that church bell wasn't ringing, a bell in my head was telling me I had to be somewhere, to do something. When Mozell would see me jump for no reason, she would tell me, "Johnnie, you ain't there no more. You are here, and you don't have to be anywhere or do anything you don't want to."

I would come back to her with "Just because you're out of prison don't mean prison is out of you."

Then there was the nights. When I would cut the lights off and go to bed, there was a strange darkness. Not all darkness is the same. In prison, when it was lights-out, the lights was never completely out. They'd dim them enough to try to keep track of the night going-ons—shankings, punkings, killings. That was the dim darkness. So when I cut the lights off in my sister's house, it was too dark and quiet. Like owls and bats hiding in the woods waiting for sundown so they could fly and feed, prison-night creatures would come out in my head, only louder, closer, and more real. I could reach out and touch that man rolling up on me, running for his life from building tenders. In those free-world night visions, he was always caught and stabbed. When I'd wake up in the morning, my sheet and t-shirt would be wringing wet. I would rise up, not remembering if I had closed my eyes at all. The first thing on my mind was to count off another day served, only to sit on the side of the bed, head in hand, and realize I didn't have to count days anymore. Try telling my bones that. I was doing the hardest time now, trying to get prison out of my marrow.

The first and hardest thing came two days after coming home. Ray was to show up at Mozell's. She was worried. "Now Roy, your brother is supposed to come over here. Don't do nothing crazy. You just got out. I just got you back. I don't know what I'd do if you went away again. So you don't need to go asking him a lot of questions, getting worked up, and doing something crazy."

"Mo, you don't have a right to tell me not to ask questions. I want to know some things—like why didn't y'all help Momma get me out. She knew it wasn't none of me. Then y'all didn't tell me she died. I had to have the warden call. I didn't get a chance to say goodbye before y'all put her in the ground. If I'd known my momma died, the warden would've let me come to the funeral."

My heart pumped like an old diesel engine that had been run too long with low oil. I was ready to throw a rod. That's no exaggeration. I was about to blow a valve for real. The prison doctor had told me I had a bad heart when I fainted once in the field for no reason, that one of my heart muscles was weak. The stress of prison life had worn on me. I lived too long with no joy to grease my living. I looked at Mo and said to her face, "Mo, I got the right to ask any damn questions I need to." Then I started coughing.

She said, "Now, Roy, you need to calm down. See, that's what I'm talking about. You're making yourself sick."

"I ain't making myself sick. Y'all made me sick." I had to take my seat at the kitchen table. My chest was tightening up. "Tell you what, if I had my gun, I would blow his head off."

"Stop it. Stop that talk." Mozell bent over at the waist like she'd been sucker punched in the gut. She balled up her fist and slammed it on the table, sending the sugar bowl and sugar flying all over the place. She lifted up, pointing her finger in my face. "We tried to help get you out, but we didn't have any money to get a real lawyer. We sold your grandmother's house to get you your first lawyer. All he did was take that money. We knew it was going to be tough to get at the truth because Ray and them took off for West Texas till things cooled down."

She paused to grab a broom to clean up the mess, then turned to me and said, "Momma loved both you and Ray no matter what. You know that. No matter what we could have done, as I saw it, Momma was going to lose one of her boys. It broke her heart. It wasn't no stroke that killed her like the doctor said. It was having to choose sons. What's killed her was a broken heart. I wanted to call you—tried to call you—but they wouldn't let me. We were scared. We didn't know what trouble might get stirred if you came to the funeral. We didn't want that cloud over Momma's home-going. You know Momma didn't like trouble between you two. We was wrong. I was wrong. I should have been stronger, but I wasn't. This has been hard on me too. I lost both my brothers from all this. Now, I got you back, and I don't want to lose y'all again."

Mo spilled over like a dam break. "You went to the pen, and Ray took off with Red Winston. When he got back, Ray went from one get-over scheme to another. He got worse when you went to jail. He'd show up every now and then, but you couldn't count on him, especially when Momma died. You the only one who could ever talk sense into him for a minute, and he's in a bunch of trouble now. I know you lost those years in the pen. But you done done that time. Don't do no more. I don't want to lose—"

Before she could finish, there was a knock at the door. "Mozell! Mo, what y'all doing?" It was Ray. He crawled in like a snake, like it was just another "Ray" day. I looked straight ahead. He walked right by me and straight to the icebox looking for a beer. Since we was old enough even to think about drinking, he'd always had a beer in his hand or was looking for one. "Mo, you got any beer?" he yelled with his head in the fridge. He could tell something was up—Mozell, wiping her face, and me not saying a word, trying to catch my breath. He hollered out, "We need to be celebrating. My twin brother is home. And I hear he got a bunch of money too."

He finally came out of that icebox. I glared at him and said, "Ray, ain't none of your business about my money."

Wearing a shit-eating grin, he stuck his hand out for me to shake. "Roy, now don't get your drawers all up in a knot. I'm just messing with you. You ain't gonna shake my hand?"

I grabbed his hand hard and pulled him to me till we was face-to-face. "I been locked up for twenty-six years, and all you got to say is something about my money. Ray, you better get out of here before something happens."

Still holding hands, he pulled back just as hard. "Now, I know you don't want to wrestle me. You couldn't whup me when we was boys, and you can't whup me now."

I jumped up from that table, knocking over my chair. I was ready to smash what was left of that sugar bowl upside his head when Mozell jumped in. "Y'all stop it. Stop now!" She stepped in between us. "Ray, you need to go on home. Now."

He slid back from me with his hands in the air saying, "What I do? You know how we play. You always taking up for him, like he's all goodie-two-shoes. Y'all don't know." Ray crawled out the door the same way he crawled in, with that look like he had gotten away with something—the same look he had on his face that day at the jailhouse when we exchanged places. I didn't say a word to him as he left, but he had a last word for me. "Roy, how about a little lettuce?"

It took everything I had not to run after him and knock him upside the head. He knew that would gig me—"lettuce." He knew that would send me right back in my mind to Momma when she used to slip me, and not him, some fun money. I hadn't been out of prison a week. No "How you doing, Roy?" No "I'm sorry, Roy." No, he was about the money. June 19, 1946, was about money.

"Sit down, Roy." Mozell said, trying to calm me down. "Don't let him get to you. You know how he is. I know you don't know this, but your brother has money problems. The IRS found out he hadn't been paying taxes on his plumbing business. He hadn't been paying his workers right, either. I think they turned him in. The IRS says they gonna take his house and his business. They might throw him in jail."

"That's where his ass belongs."

"Don't say that!" Mozell snapped back. "You know what Momma used to say to you when she would wake you up in the middle of the night to go get Ray off the streets before the laws got him. 'No Houston belongs in jail. You are your brother's keeper. Y'all got the same blood in you.' I heard her tell you that on them nights when you didn't want to get up and go find him, but you did. That was what Momma wanted, and you did it because you loved her. You did what she said when it came to Ray. You went and found him and brung him home. Right now, you need to ask yourself what Momma would want you to do."

I didn't say a word. I knew what Momma would say: "Ray is your brother." So I did, later, give him money from my twenty-six thousand to keep him out of jail. It was supposed to be a loan. He never paid a cent back.

That was my first run-in with Ray.

The days that lay ahead was now about one thing: doing parole—making my meeting, staying clear of the law, and paying my probation fees. Money wasn't an issue at first, seeing as how I had that guilt money. But it went quick. I helped Mo out. I helped out other family who asked for help—a hundred here, a hundred there. I spent money on things I had never had: new cars, new clothes, and new friends. It didn't take long for the money to leak out like a handful of water, more wasted on the ground than went into my mouth. Having never had nothing, you don't know how to handle hanging on to something. Soon, most of the money was gone.

While I was trying to rebuild a new life in Dallas, my "always baby"—Arlene, now a full woman—was building her own life in Austin. She had gotten heavily involved with the Jehovah's Witnesses. She probably was introduced to them by Juanita who, I believe, got involved when she married Loyal Sneed. Now I was "Baptist born, Baptist bred, and Baptist dead," so me and Arlene didn't see eye to eye on this. But I didn't make this Jehovah's Witness thing a big deal. I had been locked away for so long. I wasn't there for her back then. Who was I to try to run her life now? She got married December 28, 1974. I couldn't square it with my probation officer to leave the city, so I couldn't attend her wedding. We talked on the phone when we could, but we both understood without saying it: Rome wasn't built in a day. I couldn't undo twenty-six years of absence in a day, either. Right now, my focus was keeping my head down and doing the long hard row of probation, step by step, day by day, to stay clear of the law.

It was not possible.

One day, I was driving to meet my probation officer when I heard sirens behind me. I looked in the rearview mirror, and there was the law on my tail. I pulled over. My heart raced ninety-to-nothing. The sound of that siren sent me back to June 19, 1946, when Norman Owens, Dude Milton, and Ed Cartwright pulled up on me with sirens and changed my life. I could see them as clear as if it was yesterday—guns drawn and billy clubs raised. Sweat poured off my forehead when that policeman walked up to the car, with one hand at his gun side and one hand holding a ticket booklet. He tapped on the window and said, "Boy, what you think y'all doing?"

That tap on the window snapped me back from Juneteenth '46. It was a Dallas motorcycle cop not a Bastrop deputy. "Is something wrong, Officer?"

"You're going down a one-way street the wrong way. Driver's license and registration, please."

"Officer, I didn't know this was a one-way." I handed him my license and registration. "I guess I had my mind on something else. These here downtown Dallas streets get me confused. I been locked up for twenty-six years. They didn't have all these streets back then."

When I told him twenty-six years, that policeman stopped writing and looked over his sunglasses. "Is that right? You wait right here." He walked back to his motorcycle and started talking on his radio. I guess he was giving somebody my name. A couple of minutes later, he walked back to the car, pencil and pad in his left hand, his right hand resting on his gun side.

All kinds of things went through my head when I saw that gun—those deputies beating that confession out of me with the butt of a gun. I flashed back to the little boy holding that gun on me when I was caught escaping—a gun almost bigger than he was—with the words of his father ringing in my ear: "If he moves, shoot him." All those thoughts sprung in my head when I saw that policeman's gun. I didn't know what he was going to do.

He put one hand on the door, and he reached the other hand in the car. "Here is your license, Mr. Houston. I'm going to let you go with a warning. You've got to be careful down here. This here is Akard Street. Turn around and head north. You'll be able to turn right at the next street." He cracked a tiny smile, his mouth giving a toothpick a workout. Under his breath, I heard him say, "I'll be damn, twenty-six years." Then he smiled and said, "Now, y'all drive safe, you hear?"

"Uh, yes, sir. I will." He sped off. I had to sit there for a minute to get myself together. My legs felt like Jell-O.

Any run-in with the law put me in a bad place. I had many anxious days in the free world. When those dark days would come on me like a cloud, everything reminded me of prison—a bell's ring, a slammed door, a car backfiring, the jingle of keys, the smell of certain raw meat cooking, or the mention of my brother's name. When I would lay my head down at night in the dark-dark, after a rough day, I would be afraid to go to sleep because sleep would take me to that dream:

I would get up from my bed, put on my shoes. I would reach behind the door for my shotgun. I would walk down a street, past my mother who was trying to speak to me, but I couldn't hear her. I'd walk to a house I did not know. The door would be open. I would walk to the back room. Only a slit of light from the full moon would light the way to the edge of the bed where a face was barely visible. I would raise my gun, pull back the safety latch. The click would cause a stir. Then the figure in the bed spoke, "Roy? What you doing, Roy? *Quit fooling a—"*

On Friday, December 12, 1975, I got an early Christmas gift—a letter from Governor Mark White—a full pardon and restoration of my citizenship. I did my time. I did my parole. In the eyes of the state, I had paid my debt to society. In my spirit, I was still paying.

But day after day, night after night, the more days and nights I put between prison and the present, the easier it got to do freedom. Now I was able move about without asking for permission from a parole officer. So on May 31, 1984, I was able to go to the funeral service for my brother Immer in Corpus Christi. I looked up to him. He got out of Bastrop before Bastrop got him.

It had been more than ten years since I been behind bars. I was free. But I had come to realize that prison is more than a place. People cage you. The hope that Ray would someday tell me he was sorry stood between me and being "free like a bird" free.

One of the reasons I was able to do the hard row of doing freedom was Mary. I was working for Ken's Plumbing. I used to see her every morning at the bus stop that was right across from Ken's. I would get to the shop about seven o'clock. There she'd be, all dressed up with a white blouse and black skirt, her hair done up in a bun, her chocolate-brown face dusted with a dab of cinnamon rouge. I imagined, as I drank my coffee and peeked out a window, that she was a sweetheart. After a month of watching and imagining, I made up my mind to talk to her. So one morning I was waiting for her at the bus stop. I walked up to her and said, "How you doing? My name is Johnnie Roy Houston." I was nervous as a cat on a porch full of rocking chairs—as the old folks used to say—fidgeting and swaying. She looked straight ahead like she didn't hear me, so I asked her again, but this time louder. "How you doing? My name is Johnnie Roy Houston. What is your name?"

"Mary Azard," she huffed back, with a frown that slowly spread to a small, ruby-red smile.

I said, "I been watching you from over at that plumbing company over there where I work." I had to hurry up because the bus was at the corner. "Where do you work?"

She shifted her shopping bag from one shoulder to another to get her money as the bus pulled up. "I work at the Fairmont Hotel."

I yelled over the screech and belch of the bus as it pulled up and the doors opened, "Do you mind if I call on you?" The people getting on the bus—mostly colored folks who worked downtown as cleaning and cafeteria help—they heard me, and it made her frown even more. She stepped back to let some people go ahead of her, so I saw it as my chance to ask her again. "I said, Ms. Azard, can I call on you?" By now, people's noses was pressed against the window trying to get in her business. I didn't have much time, so I kept the questions coming. "Can we go to lunch? Do they have a cafeteria where you work? Can we go out?" She still didn't say a word. Then I got out my wallet and gave her a twenty.

Then the quiet mouse spoke. "What's this for?"

I said, "You don't mind if I buy you lunch today? How do you get to work?"

"I ain't got but one way," she snapped, scrambling for her bus fare. "The bus. What way did you think?"

"Well, I'm your bus from now on. I will pick you up every morning and take you home. What time you get off?"

"Between four-thirty and five o'clock." She smiled as she stepped onto the bus. I could hear some of the people on the bus who had their noses in her business tease her, "All right, now."

Before the bus driver closed the door, I called out, "My car will be at the Fairmont waiting for you." I could see her slump down in her seat as some of them passengers teased her even more. As the bus drove off in a cloud of exhaust, I coughed and smiled all the way back to Ken's. Ken didn't get much work out of me that day. My mind was stayed on Mary with the cinnamon cheeks. My eyes was on the clock all day.

At half past four, I was parked out back at the Fairmont Hotel employee entrance, 1717 North Akard. The day-shift employees started pouring out. Mary came out a few minutes later. I stood by my car with the trunk popped so she could see me. "Ms. Azard, how was your day?" I asked as I handed her a beer with a straw in it and ran around and opened the door for her like one of those chauffeurs. She was grinning from ear to ear. It was a normal "hot as hell July in Texas" day, so I figured she could use a cold one. I didn't know if she drank or not, but I took a chance to make it clear I was her knight in shining armor. I was here to take care of her.

Her supervisor was with her. "Oh, I sure wish I had someone to give me a beer." So I gave her one, too, and offered to take her home. On that "hot as hell July in Texas" day, me and Mary Azard and her supervisor loaded up in my Buick. With the windows up, the AC blowing, the radio blasting Stevie Wonder's "Signed, Sealed, I'm Yours," we rolled down North Akard headed to sunny South Dallas. With Mary sitting between me and her supervisor, we sang and popped another beer or two. It came to me as I drove, I had not thought about prison all day. It might have been one of the best days I'd seen since I had been free. We got to know each other quick. I saw her almost every day. Mary was a lot younger than me—thirty-eight—and she had two kids, but none of that mattered. She helped me feel free. I planned right then to ask her to marry me. Mary Azard would sit between me and twenty-six years of hard time.

I took to her girls like they was mine. I fed them, clothed them, took them places. When they had candy to sell for their school, I would buy the whole box so they could resell the candy and make more money. I took Mary to work and picked her up every day, and I helped her with rent and bills. Then finally I told her one day, "Pack up you and the girl's stuff. Y'all moving with me after we get married." She said yes. I packed my things from Mozell's. The next Friday—September 5, 1986—we was married in the house on Grovewood where we set up a home, a lot like the home my Momma made where I lived in Bastrop. We may have rented the house, but we owned the love that made it a home—where everybody had a load to carry, where nothing was thrown away, especially the people under that roof—no matter what you had done. And we kept our house open to neighbors. That was our home on 5316 Grovewood Street.

♦ ♦ ♦

As it turned out, Grovewood was also where Johnnie Ray Houston decided he wanted to live. He got a Section 8 house right down the street from us. Just when the days I thought of prison had grown fewer and fewer, he showed up down the street as my neighbor—a constant reminder. It was hardest at night when I went to bed, long after Mary had kissed me goodnight. I would drift, not to sleep-sleep, but to that dream. Now that Ray lived right down the street from me, the dream wasn't some story that haunted me. The house in the dream was his house. Each night of this visitation, more details that was once fuzzy, was now clearer, more certain:

I would get up from my bed, put on my shoes. I would reach behind the door for my shotgun. I would walk to a pale-green house, six doors down on the left. It had a porch window that let you look inside the living room, where a large, framed mirror hung over a couch. I would walk in—the screen door always unlocked—pass the living room, and head on to the back room. I would pull back the safety latch. The click was loud enough to wake up Ray. "Roy?

What you doing, Roy? Quit fooling a—" *Boom*. I would wake up at that spot.

As long as Ray lived on Grovewood, Ray lived in my head. As much as I thought I was a changed man, that I had forgiven him, the very sight of him stirred up a storm. I was as tight as a hair-trigger pistol around him, ready to fire at the drop of a hat. It didn't take much to cock my trigger.

But money got short with more mouths to feed, so as much as I hated to, I took a part-time job working for Ray, digging sewage line for a house in North Dallas. "Ray, I'll help you with that line for ten dollars an hour, but you got to pay me every Friday. I got bills to pay, so come Friday, I got to have my money," I told him.

"Roy, you know me," Ray chirped back.

Well, come Friday in the cold rain, Ray's son, Junior, handed me an envelope, first thing. Junior and his daddy was more twins than me and Ray. They walked the same, grinned the same, and schemed the same, always trying to get over on people. As he walked off to the ditch where Ray was trying to connect the pipe I had laid all week, I opened the envelope and counted what was in it. Because Ray was trying to hide money from the IRS, he paid all his help in cash. It was full of tens and ones, and the envelope was fat. There was twenty tens and the rest in ones—three hundred dollars all total. I knew I had worked fifty hours that week, probably more. I should have gotten five hundred dollars. But before I could holler at Junior that he had shorted me, he jumped in the hole with Ray. I could hear them laughing. That lit my fuse. I hollered, "Ray, you owe me two hundred dollars. I want my money!" By the time I made it to the hole, they had stopped laughing and was gluing and fitting like they didn't hear me. As I looked down on them, the steam of my breath came gushing out my nose and mouth against the freezing cold air like smoke from a fire-breathing dragon. I screamed, "Ray, y'all know y'all hear me. Y'all know y'all owe me two hundred dollars. I want my money, and I want it now!"

Ray came back, “Now, Roy, keep your shirt on. I ain’t stopping work to get out of this hole to get you your money. You come back Monday, I’ll have your money, and it ain’t two hundred dollars. It’s one hundred dollars I owe you.” He turned to Junior and started laughing and working again like I wasn’t even there.

I didn’t say another word. I stomped back to my Buick and reached under the front seat for my snub nose .38. I could barely hold it in my hands because I was so mad and cold from the icy, drizzling rain. I straddled over that ditch looking down on Roy and Junior and pulled back the hammer. That click got their attention. “Ray, I’m gonna say it once, then I’m going to start shooting right here in this hole till I’m out of bullets. I want my money. I want all of it, now!” I had the shakes so bad that gun nearly slipped out my hands.

“Now, Roy, quit playing. Put that gun down, now. You ain’t gonna shoot nobody,” Ray hollered back.

I raised that gun, pointed it right at Ray, and fired a shot above his head. That’s all it took. He saw in my eyes that I meant business, that it wasn’t about two hundred dollars. It was about twenty-six years.

Ray couldn’t get the words out quick enough. “Junior, go and get your uncle two hundred dollars.” Junior flew out of that hole, ran to his truck, and came back with the money. Ray hollered out of that hole. “You satisfied, Roy? You got what you want. You crazy, you know that? You need to see somebody about your temper. Damn, man. I was going to give you your money.” He laughed and said, “I was just messing with you.”

If there was a thing Ray would say that got under my skin the most, it was “I was just messing with you.” It was never about “just messing with you.” It meant he had found a sore spot to jab me to see me hurt. I went back to my car and sat there for an hour to cool off and warm up—not because of the cold, wet rain, but because I had it in me to kill my brother. I was gonna shoot him and his son because I wanted to get even, to make up for the life he took from me. I had pointed that gun at him and tried to pull the trigger a second time, but it wouldn't fire. It was like another finger was in that trigger guard so it would not go all the way back. I believe God had his hand on the trigger.

With Mary in my life, though, that "night dream" urge didn't come as often as it had before. Whenever I was mad enough to walk down to Ray's house and shoot him, she would talk it out of me. "Roy, don't do that. They gonna put you back in jail, and then what're we gonna do? You done spent enough time in jail because of him. Don't let him take another day from you. Put the gun down." So I would, if for no other reason than I had to be here to provide for Mary and the girls.

I had to make the most of my job at Ken's Plumbing. I worked for him for three years, crawling under houses, digging ditches, and gluing pipe, until one day I hit a bump: my head hit a nail. I was under a house, raised up, and hit a nail. I got stuck, had to be rescued, and went to the hospital. It was God telling me it was time to move on.

My next job was at the Continental bus station. You name it, I did it: loading and unloading luggage, cleaning up the station bathrooms, even selling tickets. Again, I knew how to work. That lesson my Momma taught me about doing a job nobody wants to do and doing it better than it has ever been done paid off at the bus station. I was sweeping one day in the lobby when my broom caught a white envelope that moved like it was full of something out of the ordinary. I had a mind what it was, the way it moved. I pushed it down the hall to the bathroom. There, I took the envelope inside, went into a stall, and opened it. Lord a mercy! There was tens, twenties, and hundreds—all total, five hundred dollars. No names, no notes, no questions. It was mine to keep. I took it and hid it in the spare tire of my car. I called Mary with news. "Look what the Lord done done!"

I worked at the bus station as long as I could. Still, my heart wasn't up to it. Those days in dark and damp solitary, those years of watching my life through jail bars weakened my heart. After I had episodes of fainting because of a low heart rate, the doctors told me I would always need to carry glycerin pills in my pocket. In 1988, I had to go on disability.

With three mouths to feed and only a disability check coming in, I fell on rough times again. I was in a rock-and-a-hard place. I had been there before: in a courtroom, in a cotton field fighting for my life, in a cell full of writs with the word *denied* stamped on them. I had promised God, "If you will get me out of jail, I will serve you." But I didn't keep my promise to serve him like I should have when I got out. I didn't talk to God like I used to. I didn't go to church like I knew I should. But now, I needed him again. Would he hear me now? I got on my knees, in the dark because I couldn't pay the light bill: "Lord, you did not bring me this far to leave me." We had heard there was a church in the north end of Dallas that had a benevolence ministry to help people out with utilities. So we decided to go there—Munger Avenue Baptist Church—one of the oldest black churches in Dallas.

Mary, me, and the girls showed up for the eleven o'clock service and was shown to our seats, the first row, just as we was. We didn't have any "church clothes." I wore some old work pants and shirt. They was clean, but I was ashamed that I didn't have anything better. Mary was in a dress she hardly wore because it was out-of-date, according to her. The girls was in their school uniforms. That's the best we had. All I heard growing up about coming to church was "Come as you are." That's what we did, but it didn't make me feel any better about our situation.

But then the choir sang one of my favorites that Momma use to tear up on the piano with: "This Little Light of Mine." Something hit me. My leg jumped like I was hit by a bolt of lightning. It was a Holy Ghost strike—that same Spirit that shot through me in that prison cell so many years before. It was early in the service, but the way I was feeling, there wasn't no way I was going to get through it without shouting and jumping all over the place. Then this little preacher got up. He was short and stocky with thick-rimmed glasses that slid down his nose every other minute. He talked so fast—almost stuttering—his mouth barely stayed ahead of his thoughts, it seemed. I didn't follow all he was saying, but what I did understand put gasoline on my fire. The more he preached, the more I got a feeling I knew this preacher. I leaned over to Mary and said, "I think I know him. I *know* I know him from somewhere." Mary patted me on the hand. She could tell I was ready to explode, I was so full. The more he preached, the hotter it got.

The preacher pushed his glasses up on his nose, tipped up on his toes, pointed his finger like he was talking to just me. "I know you think that God has, uh, forgotten about you, that he has given everybody else the blessings—the good jobs, the good houses—but don't you worry none. God has not forgotten you."

I tried to keep my peace, but I couldn't hold it in. I erupted like a volcano. "Thank ya. Thank ya, Lord!" God was talking to me.

That preacher whipped it up even more. "God's got a hill country for you. Stand up and tell your neighbor, 'I got a hill country. If you're my enemy, you got to go.'"

I couldn't keep my seat. I took my cane and stood up. "I got a hill country. Satan, you got to go! Thank ya, Jesus. Thank ya, Lord. Thank ya." I started coughing. Mary had to stand next to me and put her hand on my shoulder to get me to sit down. Ushers came with water and fans.

I wasn't the only one on my feet. Other people was standing and shouting. They shouted, "Preach it. You better watch it, Barry Jackson."

It took me a minute to calm down. I was simmering over like a full pot on a hot stove that's been there too long. Again, somebody in the congregation said, "You better watch it, Barry Jackson." Then it hit me. I know where I knew this preacher. He was Rufus Jackson's boy—Rufus Jackson, the man that had owned the juke joint back home that had everything you needed to have a good time. This was Mr. Jackson's son. It'd been forty-something years before, but I remembered him when he was a boy at his daddy's place. He and his daddy used to get in some doozy arguments that made me sick to my stomach to watch—the way he would dip in the cash register and then cuss his daddy out. That stutter I heard this morning was the same one that I'd heard at Rufus Jackson's. He and his daddy was always going at each other. But now he was a preacher—Oh my God—and I wound up in Rufus Jackson's son's church. That sent a shake through me. But what really mattered that morning was that God spoke to me. I turned to Mary. "We going to get up and unite with this church."

She smiled and said, "OK."

When they "opened up the doors of the church," as they called it, we came down and sat in the chairs the deacons were standing behind.

I said to the church, "My name is Johnnie Roy Houston, and this is my family. We want to unite with this church. God has been good to me. I spent twenty-six years in prison for a crime I didn't do. Wasn't nobody but God that got me through that. I promised him I would serve him the rest of my life if he got me out. It's time to keep that promise. Me and my family have fallen on tough times, but if God don't do another thing for me, he has done enough. We don't have much. I got a heart condition and can't work, but whatever we can do to serve God here, we're here to do it. God's got a hill country for me."

Before I knew it, I boiled over again. "Thank you. Thank you, Jesus. Thank you, Lord." I felt so good that day. I asked the usher if I could have a tape of that sermon. She gave me two. Thank God, because I wore out the first one listening to it every day. Because I needed to hear—every day—God was still with me.

twenty-one

GROVEWOOD

THINGS GOT BETTER ONCE WE GOT BACK in the church. They helped us get caught up on our utilities and rent so we didn't have to leave 5316 Grovewood. It was south of Fair Park in sunny South Dallas. People used to ask me why I stayed in that neighborhood considering all the not-so-sunny things that went on there. I got a bullet in my chest as proof how unsunny things could get.

One night, not long after we first moved to the neighborhood, I came home late from work. Mary and the girls was at her mother's. I noticed the front door was cracked open. I peeked in and saw two men. So I tiptoed back to my car and got my .38. No sooner had I made it to the porch than they opened fire. I got off six shots into the living room. When my last shot ricocheted off something, I heard a grunt. Then those two men rushed past me, knocking me to the ground. There was a trail of blood from the doorway into the yard. I must have winged one of them, but not before they winged me.

There was blood on my shirt right above my left rib cage. There wasn't much pain. But when the police and EMS showed up within minutes, they wanted to take me to the hospital. I wouldn't go, so they dressed the wound. The next morning, police returned to ask me more questions. They didn't like the look of the wound and made me go to the hospital. They x-rayed me and found a slug stuck between two upper ribs. The doctor said, "Mr. Houston, where the slug is, you're not in any danger. We'd do more harm if we tried to get it out. But it's up to you."

I told him, "Well, if it's all right with you, we'll leave it be."

So, every day in the mirror I am reminded by that bullet that Grovewood can be an unsunny neighborhood at times. Nearly every night, there was sirens going off and police cars zooming down the street. This neighborhood was "the hood." It could chew up and spit out weak people hooked by the pull of the street life. There was a time when street life was a little drinking, smoking, and shooting dice. Now, Satan had upped his game with crack and weed. Crack houses was everywhere there was vacant houses, connected like a string of trot lines full of people hooked by the "highlife."

One of those caught was Patricia, a friend of Mary. She was young—too young to be out there, especially with a son. His name was Tobias, but we called him "Boodlum." I'm not sure why we called him that. It didn't mean anything. It just fit him. He was four or five when we took him in, off and on, when Pat was on a roller-coaster ride—sober one week, strung out the next. Two or three times, she was picked up by the police for one thing or another, so we paid out of our pocket to get her out. We prayed that the streets wouldn't take Pat under and take Boodlum with her. Finally, she dropped him off for good, knowing that it was going to be a while before she could get herself together. We took Tobias in, Mary and me. She raised him like we knew something about raising boys different from raising her two daughters. It was mostly Mary. She did a good job with him. The streets didn't win. It took four years, but Patricia finally got it together and reunited with Tobias for good. No boy should be separated from his mother—I know.

That was what I liked about Grovewood—the sunny side: people not giving up on people, neighbors sharing what they had with each other. While the mean streets of South Dallas could be as mean as the Colorado River, Grovewood Street was a little island for many. We had neighbors and friends who surrounded us like family: Mr. Moses and Eddie May Johnson and C. J., their son; Cicero, who cut our yard for free; Sister Maddie Davis, who worked in the church kitchen. And then there was Wild Bill. He was the assistant fire chief of Station 44 on Frank Street, right off Grovewood. I'll never forget the first time I met him. He came along with the EMS one day when I was having trouble with my heart. If I got the least bit excited and my chest started to tighten up, Mary would call EMS. That day, he jumped out of the back of that ambulance and rushed into the house with "guns a-blazing"—his mouth, that is. "Howdy, Mr. Houston. You're in good hands because old Wild Bill is here."

"Well, I don't know if I want my heart to be in the hands of somebody named Wild Bill," I told him. He laughed, and I did, too, but not so much. I hated hospitals and anything to do with anybody who wanted to take me there.

Wild Bill could tell I didn't want to go. "Now, you take it easy. Let's see what we got here." He took my blood pressure, listened to my heart, gave me some oxygen, and put two glycerin pills under my tongue. "You're gonna be fine. Try not to get excited, and take your medicine at the right time. But someday you're going to have to have a pacemaker," Wild Bill said.

I told him as he was finishing up, "Well, when that time comes, I'll do that, but not today. Why they call you Wild Bill, anyway?"

He laughed as he rolled that oxygen tank out the door. "You sure you want to know?"

"No, I might be better off if I didn't, thank you very much," I told him. From that day on, me and Wild Bill was friends. He would stop by on his big red firetruck to check on me and bring me some Williams Chicken—short-thighs mostly—and a Big Red soda. Sometimes he would bring a couple more guys from the fire station with him to keep me company. It was a part of their Neighbors-First Program.

On Grovewood Street, it wasn't nothing for neighbors to get together for a special reason or no reason—like we did in Bastrop.

All I needed was to stoke up the barbecue pit and put up a domino table, and let the smoke do the inviting. Neighborhood get-togethers was a time to forget the past, but with Ray in the neighborhood, reminders of bread and water, hoe squads, and bloody water wagons was always a few houses down.

One afternoon when the neighborhood regulars was out in my front yard enjoying the cooler-than-normal summer air with some bid whist and barbecue, a sudden cloudburst dumped sheets of rain down on us, sending everybody running to their porches. As quickly as the rain came, it stopped. We went back to cards, cooking, and some cold ones. But without warning, something came over me. A foul, familiar thought reared its ugly head. Maybe it was the few beers that had loosened me up. I got up from the card table without saying a word, and I walked toward Ray's house, but not before I went into my house and picked up my protection that I hid behind the front door. I tucked it under a towel and held it to my side, away from my neighbor's nosy eyes. "Hey, Johnnie, where you going?" Cicero asked, but I didn't pay them no attention. I cuffed my hand to hide the black tip that stuck out from underneath the towel, and headed down toward Ray's. The wet street was shiny under a full moon out at the same time as the setting sun. As I marched, my mind shuffled snapshots of my past like a deck of cards: I saw Momma waking me up in the middle of the night to go and find Ray and bring him home before the law found him and locked him up. I saw that prison boss ride his horse up on the back of my sack for fun. I could see Old Sparky's blue arcs. By the time I got to Ray's, I was full, cocked, and loaded.

Through the large, front window, I could see him and his wife, Dorothy, sitting on their couch drinking beers. I slipped past the window to the side of the house. The next thing they knew, all hell broke loose. *Boom! Boom!* I heard Ray scream to his wife, "Hit the floor. Hit the floor!" *Boom, Boom!* You could hear it clear down one end of Grovewood to the other. *Boom, Boom!* The echo shook the window. Ray hollered again, "Hit the floor!"

I stepped in full view of the window.

Ray hollered, "Roy! Roy! You don't have to do this. You don't have to do this!" This was the second time I saw fear—real fear—on my twin brother's face. The first time was when I held that .38 on him until he coughed up the money he owed me.

I raised my arms and hollered back, "How you like that, Ray?" Then I dropped the towel and showed it to him: the long black pipe I had used to bang the aluminum siding on the side of his house. You should have seen his face. He looked like he had shit a brick with his name written on it.

Ray screamed at me. "Goddamn it, Roy. Goddamn you. You scared us half to death!"

I whooped and hollered as I stepped off the porch. Not looking back, I said as I headed back to my house, "I'm just messing with you, Ray, just messing with you." I laughed all the way home. My neighbors was laughing too. Some nights I lie in bed and giggle myself to sleep, thinking about that summer evening when I put the fear of God in my twin brother.

It was good to have neighbors on Grovewood who was like family, especially on dark days like the day Mozell died, July 9, 1999. They helped me get through her passing. It hit me hard—almost as hard as Momma's death. She was so much like Momma in the way she walked, talked, and helped raise me and Ray. We was a handful. Mozell would cook for us one minute and get a switch and tear our hinds up the next, but not before me and Ray would give her a run for her money. It was kind of fun watching her be momma. I wished she'd had better luck with the men in her life. Her first husband, Mr. George Arnold, drank anything in a bottle that didn't have a picture of a skull and crossbones and the word *poison* written on it. I will never forget how Momma picked up a brick and hit him in stride one day as he—drunk as a skunk—tried to run after he'd cussed out Mo. Momma got him good. Mo married him anyway, but they divorced. She then married Mr. Hudson and moved to Dallas, where I met him when I stayed with her after I got out. I didn't like him much. He raised his hand on her—but only once after I'd come to stay.

When Mo died, there was as much time passed since I'd been out of prison as time I'd been in prison. I had fewer bad days when the dark cloud of prison covered me, shutting me down, when I would sit on my couch and cry over the smallest thing. But because Ray lived down the street, I could never escape the cloud completely. It was better for me not to think about him, something that was hard to do when my neighbors was constantly telling me the goings-on down at his house.

After his wife Dorothy Joyce died, Ray found himself a new version of his old Get Over Gang. I called them the "Nutty Buddy Gang"—the neighborhood people caught up in the street life—the crack, pot, pills, and sex girls. You could see it in their eyes—as nutty as a fruit cake. They was liable to do anything to get what they needed to get off. Roy would have parties at his house, beer flowing like it did when he was down at Rufus Jackson's. Back then, it wasn't nothing for him to holler out, "Drinks on the house!" when he had a little money in his pocket. I'd be there ordering me some food, but when drinks was on the house, it was time to get out the house because nothing good was about to happen. Now, I heard it was flowing good down at Ray's. He had girls coming in and out. Booze and sex pills without prescriptions was everywhere. Home health care people who was supposed to be taking care of him was in cahoots with him, supplying him with what he needed. I saw it. I used to walk down there to talk to him, to get Ray to stop all this hell-raising. No matter what he had done to me, he was still my brother. I could hear Momma tell me, "Go down there and see about your brother." Sometimes he would listen, come home with me, get a bath and a good meal, get cleaned up and dried out for a few days. But it wouldn't last. He'd be back down the street with his Nutty Buddies in a few days.

Then one day, I got a call from one of the neighbors. "They done took your brother to the hospital."

Me and Mary got down to Baylor Hospital as soon as we could. They had him all hooked up to monitors and IVs. I leaned in close to him so he could hear. "Ray, this is Roy. How you doing? You take it easy."

He opened his eyes and whispered, "Roy, get me a beer." He laughed as much as he could with all that stuff attached to him. "I'm just messing with you. It ain't nothing wrong with me. Get me out of here. I'm not kidding."

I told him, "Now, you know I ain't going to get you no beer. Man, you almost blew out your heart with all that stuff you been messing with. You need to be here to get right." He drifted back to sleep.

The nurse pulled me aside. "He is going to be here awhile, Mr. Houston. You're his brother, right? We need to get his heart stabilized. He mixed pills and alcohol that he had no business mixing. This is serious, but he's not taking it seriously. He keeps harassing the nurses. Has he always been this flirty? You need to talk to him. This is nothing to play with. He had a heart attack. He could have died. And he needs to stop messing with the nurses while they're trying to care for him. Tell him that for me."

I told her, "I'm sorry, ma'am. That's my brother. He's hardheaded. That's the way he is. But I'll talk to him. Thank you." As she left the room, I couldn't help but think that this is what he deserved. But my next thought was *Lord, don't let him die*. For the longest time, that was how my mind worked—a tug-of-war over Ray, pulling and tugging in opposite directions. One moment I was hating him; the next moment, I was loving him.

They say you should forgive and forget. I never understand how you can forget something or someone that has hurt you. Like a scar from a stove burn, you see the scar every day. You're healed, all right, but that scar is there to say to you, "Remember when you got too close to the stove?" You don't ever really get close to a stove again without flinching a little because it's in you—the memories your mind keeps long after your body has healed up. You don't forget.

I asked the Lord to forgive me for what I had thought about what Ray deserved. I leaned into Ray and whispered, "Look here, Ray, I'm gonna go and let you get some rest, but you need to leave them nurses alone and let them do their job. You're sick, real sick, and you ain't going get no better unless you behave. Now, you don't want me to come up here and kick your ass like I used to when we was boys?"

That opened his eyes. He whispered. "Nigga, you wish you could kick my ass—never did, never will. You know you couldn't fight worth a …" Right in the middle of what he was saying, he dozed off. So me and Mary tiptoed out the room.

Ray was there for three weeks, and I was there every day. Then one night, the phone rang. It must have been past eleven o'clock. "Mr. Houston, this is Baylor Hospital, Nurse Williams. Your brother has taken a turn for the worse. He is asking for you. I think you need to come down here as soon as you can."

"Ma'am, I don't have a car, so I'm going to have to get somebody to bring us up there. Can you put him on the phone?" She said she couldn't and that we needed to get there as soon as possible. So my neighbor, Mrs. Eddie Mae, drove me and Mary as fast as she could. All the while she was speeding to Baylor, my mind was speeding faster. I prayed, *Lord, don't let my brother die. Immer is gone. Mozell's gone. My mother and father are gone. Don't let Ray die too.* When I got to the hospital, the nurse met me in the waiting room. "I'm sorry, Mr. Houston. We did the best we could, but your brother is gone."

"Ray? Dead?" I cried his name—didn't call it, I cried it—toward his room like that nurse was lying, like he could still hear me. Mary grabbed my arm to keep me from pushing past the nurse. Mary said, "Now, Johnnie, calm down. It's going to be OK. Ray is in a better place." I sat in a chair in the lobby to catch my breath and slow my heart down. I don't know why people say "in a better place" like they know where a person ends up, like they God. I know they trying to make people feel better about their loss, but it didn't help me none. My momma used to tell me, "Sometimes the most you can say is nothing."

Once Mary settled me down, I asked the nurse, "Can I see him, talk to him?" She said yes. They had removed tubes from his arm and the oxygen mask from his nose. His eyes was not quite shut, his lips chapped from all the dry air in the room. I got close as I could to him. "Ray … Ray …" That's all I could say at first. Looking into the face of my dead twin was like looking at my own dead self. What do you say to your dead self? Finally, I spoke to him. "What did you want to tell me, Ray? I'm here." As I stared into his cold face, my sorrow slipped into anger. I wanted Ray to talk to me. I wanted him to tell me why he let me go to jail, that it was him and Red Winston, mostly Red, who robbed Dr. Combs. I wanted to believe that that is what he wanted to tell me before he died. But whatever it was he wanted to say crossed over with him. Ray trumped me again, left me hanging like he did so many times.

But as quick as I slipped into anger, sorrow overtook me again. I leaned over him. Tears rolled down my face onto his. I thought about how we fought for each other at school, how we hunted with each other to bring food home, how we swam the Colorado together. "My brother is dead, my twin's dead," I kept repeating. I leaned into his lifeless body and said, "I love you, Ray. I forgive you." I closed his eyes. Mary and the nurse took me by the arm and led me back into the hallway.

As they drove me home, I fought that tug-of-war in my head again. I hated him for what he took from me. I loved him for what he would always be—my twin brother. Part of me died the day Ray died, April 12, 2007. As I lay in my bed, I asked God to help me forgive Ray and to show me why he left me here. I cried myself to sleep.

I was missing Ray something terrible—until I got a call the next morning. "Uh, Mr. Houston, this here is Lincoln-Lamar Funeral Home. We've got a body from Baylor Hospital listed as a Johnnie Ray Houston. We was getting ready to prepare the plot for him.

You've been paying for two plots, almost paid in full. Which one do you want him in, plot one or two?"

I snapped back, "What do you mean which plot? He doesn't belong in nary one. I been paying on one for me and one for my wife."

"Well, this man came in a couple months ago and put a new name on the plot assignment card—'Johnnie Ray Houston'—then signed the change 'Johnnie Roy Houston.' We—the secretary—didn't catch it, so we assumed it was authorized by you," he said.

"I be damned. That Ray," I said, covering the receiver. "I be goddamned." I then moved my hand and spoke to the man on the phone. "You assumed wrong. That ain't his plot. I paid for that, been paying for it for years, for me and my wife. I don't care where you bury him, but he ain't paid a nickel for that plot."

"I'm sorry, Mr. Houston, I'm looking at the signature right here: 'Johnnie Roy Houston.' But now that I look at it, it could be 'Ray' or 'Roy,' the way he signed it. We are sorry. It was our mistake."

"Damn right, it's your mistake." I was so mad that I slammed the phone down so hard I nearly broke the glass coffee-table top. Mary asked me what was wrong. "That Ray tried to get in that plot at Lincoln that I done almost paid for us. And here I was feeling sorry for him." I was so upset I had to take a glycerin pill—two.

Mary tried to calm me down. "Now, Johnnie, don't get yourself all sick. They straightened it all out, right? So let it go. We don't need two funerals."

A week after he died, they had a wake and funeral. I spoke at the wake. "Most of y'all know me. I'm Ray's twin brother, Johnnie Roy Houston. We swam the Colorado River together. We hunted together. We worked side by side to help our mother make ends meet. We didn't always see eye to eye. But my mother told me, 'Twin don't always mean y'all the same, but there ain't nothing that should ever come between y'all because the same blood runs through both of y'all. Y'all still—will always be—brothers just the same. Don't let nothing separate you.'" My eyes started to fill up.

"Death ain't gonna separate us. Ray just gone home first. That is a switch—because when we was growing up, I always beat him home, and many a night, Momma used to make me go back out and bring him home." I started to break down. "I ain't got to do that now, Momma. He's home first now. He's just home first." That's all the talking I could do, so I started to sing: "This little light of mine, I'm gonna let it shine, let it shine, let it shine, let it shine." Then I took my seat.

They had the funeral the next day. It was short. There was no graveside burial. I think they was still trying to get up enough money to put him in the ground. I didn't have any to give. All I know is on Monday, Lincoln Memorial Cemetery called me to say they was going to lay him to rest that morning. Two deacons from Munger Avenue Baptist Church took me there. We didn't even have enough pallbearers to get him from the hearse to the hole. We had to asked some of the diggers to help us. One of the deacons said a prayer as they lowered him in the ground. I cried one last time.

There ain't been a day I haven't thought about Ray—good and bad. When he died, I hurt more than I thought I would. But Mary was my salve. Like she always did before, when I was thinking about doing something to Ray, to walk down to his house in the middle of the night and empty my shotgun in him, she would talk me down off that ledge. Now, she was talking me down from another ledge—giving up. With so many of my family gone home: Momma, Daddy, Immer, Mo, and now Ray, I wanted to go home too. Not that I would put a gun to myself, but there's all kinds of ways to give up and take yourself out: stop taking your medicine, not going to the doctor, not going the hospital when you should, or stop wanting to live and let nature take its course. But Mary would sit on that couch with me and say to me, "Johnnie, you got a lot to live for—me. Ain't I enough?" She was enough. Mary was my salve, I tell you.

♦ ♦ ♦

Living without Ray was a longer row than I imagined, but I managed to make the turn thanks to Mary. I began to notice, every now and then when she got up from the couch, she would grab her stomach and make a face like she was hurting. Her stomach looked larger than it was supposed to. Finally, I asked her, "Baby, you all right?"

She would say, "I'm fine, woman issues." But she wasn't fine, so I made her go to the doctor. She would come back with prescriptions for pills and say, "My liver's acting up. The doctors say that these pills should do the trick." But they didn't do the trick. She had to go the hospital several times to have them drain fluid off her stomach. She would always come back saying it was nothing, but it was something. And being the Mary she was, she didn't let on how sick she really was so I wouldn't worry and get sick myself. Saturday, May 16, 2013, she went to the hospital, and she never came home. Her liver failed.

I nearly went crazy with sadness. My best friend, my sounding board, my eyes—my own eyes was going dim, so she would read the mail to me—was gone. She was my prayer partner, the best cook next to my mother, my lover—all gone. Her daughters handled the arrangements. I was no good to make any decision except one—the color of her burial dress. Her favorite color was powder blue. It was the color she was wearing when we got married. She wore that blue at her oldest daughter's wedding. She would wear blue the last time I would see her on this side. Her lace dress was blue-as-the-sky blue. So was the casket. Her makeup was rosy like she liked it, a touch of cinnamon on the cheeks, a touch of red on the lips.

I couldn't speak at the service. I was too full. Like my mother said, "Sometimes no words says more." Other people said plenty. They more or less said the same thing, ignoring the requests to keep remarks to two minutes:

"Mary had a heart bigger than her body."

"Wasn't anything she wouldn't do for you, like what she did for Patricia and her son, Boodlum."

"Mary took people in and cared for them as if they were her own. And in a way, they were—hers—because her heart couldn't say no to somebody in need."

Even Wild Bill from Fire Station 44 came and spoke. I know the people was asking, "Who was this white man in uniform?" He started out talking to the people and then turned directly to me. "Mrs. Mary was a fine woman, Johnnie. We loved her, and we love you. We know you will miss her. If you need anything, you call Station 44, and we will be right there with horns a-blowing. They don't call me 'Wild Bill' for nothing." He made us laugh when many wanted to cry.

I held up as good as I could until I got to the gravesite. As the preacher was saying his final benediction, I couldn't hold myself. I stood up. "Let me go. Let me go! Mary! I want to be with my wife. Let me go. Mary! Mary!" I believe that if they would have let me go, they would have had to pull me out of that hole. That's how much I loved Mary.

I finally calmed down after we left Lincoln Memorial. People was already at the house for the repast—some I knew, some I didn't. I had an uneasy feeling about some people who was there who was up to no good. They was going in the back of the house, trying to take some of Mary's things, like her jewelry, furs, and stuff. So I let loose. "Y'all need to put that stuff back. She ain't been in the grave an hour, and y'all already hauling her stuff away, stuff I got her, those rings and furs. Put it back or else." I reached under my recliner chair and pulled out my pistol. "Now I mean business. Put her stuff back, I tell you." I might have had only one good eye, but I meant to shoot somebody that day if I needed to. Mrs. Eddie Mae and some of my good neighbors calmed me down and took the gun away.

After that, people started to clear out one by one till there I was—the sun setting on Grovewood—in that house by myself. I made my way to the back room, but I couldn't sleep in that bed without my Mary. So I made my way back to my recliner chair and sat in a house gone near-dark. I called out in tears, "Mary, Mary, Mary, Mary ..." until, I guess, I fell asleep. I woke up the next morning in that same chair dressed in my funeral clothes.

Not all Juneteenth nights was clear summer nights. There were those times when storm clouds covered the moon's glow. It was in those darkest nights that the orange tails of those fireballs shined the brightest. Some of the darkest times of my life was on the other side of prison. Mary was my bright, shining light, my love—my fire that did not burn. Now, somehow, I had to go on.

EPILOGUE

I Dream of Fire

It's late February 2016, and winter has not put up much of a fight with early spring. As Texas winters go, it's been a weak one except for the rains that came out of the ordinary. The television news said those rains caused the nasty Colorado River to crest over her banks and wash away some homes that never should have been built in that bottomland of Bastrop, the place where I was born.

My eyes, too, are weak, catching only bursts of light here and there, and dim images. These eyes used to keep watch over my brother Ray when we were young. They saw him walk free while I was sent to the pen for a crime he did. In twenty-six years down there, these eyes saw men ride lightning and boys beg for their manhood.

My legs that used to never fail me in races across that Colorado are hardly able to get me to my wheelchair. I have a pacemaker in my chest to regulate this old heart, weak from months of solitary confinement. Hands that once threw Juneteenth fireballs in the sky are worn and stiff from leading hoe squad after hoe squad—sunup to sundown—down long rows of hard time.

As I sit in a nursing home in Austin, Texas, I'm doing this last stretch of time with weak eyes, legs, and heart, but my mind is good—a made-up mind made right by God. Come March 1, I will be eighty-eight. I thank God every day for the work he done in me in every one of them years. I'm not what I used to be—stubborn and angry. Now I'm not mad at nobody—not even Ray—for the hand I got dealt. I'm at peace with the world.

I may not be able to toss the fire with my hands anymore, but I can *dream-throw* that fire made of memories, like the time me and my twin started our daddy's old tractor—I can dream it like it's yesterday, see it as clear as orange-red flames against night-blue sky.

It was one of those Bastrop spring days, when March winds bring heavy rains, when the Colorado was too swift and full to swim. The woods was too wet to go hunting. The rains, it seemed, was hell bent at every turn, of spoiling any chance for some fun the week me and Ray turned twelve. We was bored. I don't know who had the idea first, but we walked down to my father's house. He wasn't there, but his tractors was. I said, "Let's drive one."

John Houston had two tractors—a John Deere and a Farmall. With them, he could haul, clear, and bale anything. He loved that old Farmall. It was red with front wheels close together. It had a crank starter and a battery starter. The keys was in the Farmall. Ray ran in front and gave the handle a hard crank as I turned the ignition. It coughed blue smoke, and then, *vroom*, it took off.

Ray tried to get on, but he was thrown to the ground. I managed to hang on as it plowed over the road and across several ditches. I pushed every button I could find to stop it, but it kept going. Ray was running behind me hollering, "Put your foot on the brakes." But my feet couldn't reach the brakes as I hung onto that steering wheel for dear life. That tractor finally slowed down enough for a neighbor who saw the whole thing to jump on and kill it.

When my daddy got home, he nearly killed us with a hickory switch. With every lash of that switch on our butts, he said, "Y'all could have killed y'all selves."

A couple of days later, once we could walk right, my daddy put us back on that tractor and took us to a job he had. He was humming and grinning with that hand-carved corncob pipe full of Prince Albert tobacco dancing in the corner of his mouth. He blew smoke like an idle steam train ready to roll out the station. The sweet smell of tobacco circled around us like a morning fog. We smelled like our daddy.

He didn't say a word as we bumped along the road like nothing had happened two days before. He had told me once, "Son, you better learn how to forgive and forget some things, or you won't make it through this life." *That's what that ride was about that day—forgiveness.* Days like today, I dream of John "Tude" Houston—the tame one—quiet, at peace with himself, who smells of Prince Albert and the smoke of that Farmall tractor.

But every now and then, my mind, like a roulette wheel, lands on dark memories. I think about my momma's funeral that I was kept from going to. There are things I wanted to say to her on this side. I think about the cruelty of some folks who can kill a person—shoot off his head—then drink a cool drink of water next to that body and ride off like it's just another day's work. I think about my town that saw the truth and was blind to it, and sent a man to prison for most his life. I think about that same town that gave that same man more money than he ever held in his hands—guilt money—but money, nonetheless. I think about the value of a man's life, how it can be worthless one moment in the eyes of some, and worth at least pennies, the next, in the eyes of others. I try not to dwell too long on memories that is dark like that.

In my *dream-throwing,* I dream of Juanita and Mary—wives who loved me on either side of prison. Juanita, fun and feisty, loved me before prison when all we had was nothing but hope ahead and a baby—my pot of gold at the end of twin rainbows. She was willing to climb tomorrows with me, but we barely got a foot up out of Bastrop. She didn't deserve to do my hard time. I never held our breakup against her. How could I? She was *studden* me. She loved me despite me and gave me my Arlene.

On the other side of prison was Mary, who loved me when all I had was a row of bitter yesterdays—9,490 to be exact. I dragged into our marriage a ball and chain of numbers and dates: *06-19-1946—TDC109051—Writ-of-Habeas-Corpus2999—Parole722674—Original Cause3834—21st Judicial Court-12-1-75—Pardon number75-6582* … I've heard tell of grown circus elephants who are chained down by weak cords tied to posts because they were taught as calves they couldn't break free. Like those elephants, I couldn't completely break free from the cord-training they fixed in my head when I was a nineteen-year-old boy in a prison made for grown men. Mary deserved more, yet she told me many times, "You are enough, Johnnie Roy Houston. You're enough for me."

I *dream-cast* about the faces I want to see for the first time. I want to see my sister Bernice. She died before me and my twin was born. My mother would take us by her grave. Momma wouldn't say a word as she stood over the headstone while we picked the weeds around it. We would ask questions about Bernice—How she died? What was she like? What did she look like? Momma would stand there till the water welled up in her eyes and rolled down her face. "Let's go, boys. I'll tell you about her someday." That day never came. I want to see my sister Bernice.

I dream of my brother Immer, my north star. If I ever had a chance to escape Bastrop, it was gonna be through him—my guiding light. He got out. So could I. He started him a good business, made something out of himself. I can see him in my dreams, sitting behind the desk of the Osage Motor Company, Corpus Christi, Texas, running it like he owned it, giving orders and taking names. He'd tell me, with his legs propped up on the corner of that desk and a cigar hanging from his mouth, "Johnnie Roy, simonize those cars till you can see yourself. You do a job that nobody wants better than it has ever been done, and you will never be without work." I know where he got that saying from—my mother. I would snap back like I was in the military, my chest sticking out, almost popping the buttons on my shirt. "Yes, sir, will do." I was so proud of him. In my dreams, I tell him. But I think he knew.

I smile whenever I dream about my sister Mozell, how she was like a momma when our mother was spread too thin, helping raise me and my twin. She was everything that was good about Momma.

And there is not a day that goes by that I don't think—dream—about Ella Houston, my momma. She had all them children, so finding time when me and her was alone together was heaven. Ray would be gone getting into trouble with Red Winston and the Get Over Gang somewhere. Mozell would be out courting. Daddy would be out drinking. It would be me and Momma. She'd be at the kitchen sink washing dishes or pretending to, her back to me as I sat at the table, listening to her talk about nothing or everything. Once she said to me in a voice that was full of tears, "Roy, don't ever leave your family. No matter how hard it gets, y'all have to stick together. Y'all is all you have." She wouldn't turn around for me to see her crying. I guess she got full, as the old folks would say when all the bad stuff in your life gives you a visitation. She got full of losing a child, the road Ray was on, the ruination of a good man—my father—and the constant struggle to keep a roof over our heads. It just filled up her dam to overflowing. That day the dam broke. It made me cry to feel her cry.

Sometimes me and her would sit on the porch. She would let me have the last of the Neapolitan ice cream—the strawberry part. As I sat on the top step at her feet and she sat in her rocker, keeping time with the cicadas, she would rub my head with those lye-bleached hands and say real slow, "Roy." And I'd say, "Momma." And she'd say, "Roy." And I'd say, "Momma." We would go on like this for what seemed like hours. I dream of Momma's hand gently rubbing my head, and I will remember her last words to me at her last prison visit before she died: "I'm gonna get you out if it is the last thing I do. Don't give up." She kept her promise. The last thing she did, that last word, "Don't give up," gave me the hope to not quit.

Finally, there ain't a day goes by, that I don't dream about my twin, our best times together before we dropped out of school.

After that he changed, I think, because of the crowd he was running with. But when it was just him and me, it was good, especially when we went hunting.

So much of our food came out of the woods. We was serious about the hours we spent hunting. But it was as much fun as you could have without drinking and carousing around. We'd set out before daybreak sometimes, fog lifting like a stage curtain on robins and squirrels, rabbits and raccoons playing the parts of feisty robins, squirrels, rabbits, and raccoons—serious about their next meal—as serious about eating as me and Ray. Most times, all we had was our rubber shooters and a pocket full of rocks. We'd sneak up in range of those robins—the hardest to kill. You had one shot. If you missed, they was gone for good. We would flank them. I was the better shot, so I shot first, then Ray would pop them from their blind side. He didn't like it much that I was a better shot, but he liked the results—a bag full of birds by the end of the day. When we walked home, me and him talked and talked. Ray would say, "Man, I can't wait till momma fry these up, and brown up some onion gravy. I'm gonna tear up that big one I shot."

I'd bark back, "You didn't kill him. I did and you know it."

He'd come back, "I ain't studden you, Roy."

And I'd come back, "I ain't studden you, Ray."

We'd go on like this till we was in sight of home, knowing Momma would be happy that her twins had crossed a two-sided town divided by tracks, home, safe. The only other thing you could hear as we walked and talked through those bottomland woods was the chatter of robins, doves, and blackbirds who was happy we was done for the day. I dream of those times with Ray—my twin—in the woods down in the bottoms.

People who know my story ask me how I could forgive Ray. The only thing I tell them is this: I love Ray. He is my brother. Like my momma told me, "He gonna always be your brother because y'all always have the same blood. He is in you and you is in him." So I figure holding ought against him would be holding ought against myself. To hate him is to hate myself. And what good can come from that? It wasn't easy, forgiving him. I didn't come by this overnight. It took time.

When I think about the Juneteenth fireballs I played with when I was a boy, I don't remember ever getting burned. Somehow, I had all the time I needed. As I see it, God gives you the time you need to forgive. He's never late. His love is a forgiving fire.

◆ ◆ ◆

Today is March 1, 2016. I am eighty-eight years old. Friends show up with chocolate cake and strawberry ice cream. They bring me fried pork skins to snack on later, but I can't wait till later. They roll me outside—bag in hand—to get some sun. It feels good to have that warmth on my face and to breathe in un-air-conditioned air. The birds are in full voice. I say to my friend as he pushes me down the uneven walkway from shade to sun, then from sun back into shade, "You hear that dove? No, it's a robin. If I had my rubber shooter, I'd get him." I can't see my writer and friend, but I hear him smile and dream my dreams with me.

"You know what today means?" I ask him. "Ray is eighty-eight too. I miss him. Can't wait to see him again."

My friend pushes me to the end of the street, and then we head back, chatting up a storm. "Did I ever tell you how me and my brother used to throw fire in the sky?"

A Foreshadowing

—a final word from the author, Olin Fregia

An orange, pink sunset washes over the nursing home patio garden. A robin delights in a birdbath all to himself. A wind chime picks a distant, familiar song.

I bring his birthday cake close so he can blow out a single

candle flame fighting a sudden breeze to stay alive one more moment. "Make a wish, Mr. Houston," I say to him.

He closes his eyes and tilts his head as if to see clearer what plays before him. From all our talks, I am certain what he sees …

♦ ♦ ♦

I wish blessings for all the people who will gather at the Juneteenth table where the nineteenth has no end. I see Momma there, so is Ray, Tude, Mozell, Immer, Juanita, Mary, Arlene, Tobias, Tobe Cook …

♦ ♦ ♦

On December 23, 2017, Johnnie Roy Houston slipped off peacefully in his sleep to the bright side of a bottomland where strange fire burns, to forever be with the Lord at the table.

Johnnie Roy Houston, Dec. 24, 2016, sports his favorite cap.

ACKNOWLEDGMENTS

Special thanks to Dr. Reg Grant, Department Chair and Senior Professor of Media Arts and Worship, Dallas Theological Seminary, for first encouraging me to bring this story to the marketplace, to write with strong verbs and stronger character.

Thank you, Kelli Sallman, editor extraordinaire, for guiding me through the joys and pains of cutting for the sake of good story.

ABOUT THE AUTHOR

OLIN FREGIA, TH.M., is a seminary-trained (Dallas Theological Seminary) ordained minister, blogger, and speaker. A former television reporter, advertising agency copywriter and video producer, he has served as a church communications specialist, commercial on-air and voice-over talent, and college chaplain. He currently lives in East Texas.